COLLINS

BIRD SONGS & CALLS

GEOFF SAMPLE

Collins

This edition published in 2010 by Collins, an imprint of HarperCollins

HarperCollins Publishers
77-85 Fulham Palace Road
London W6 8JB

Collins is a registered trademark of HarperCollins Publishers Ltd.

First published in 2010

15 14 13 12 11 10
10 9 8 7 6 5 4 3 2 1

A catalogue record for this book is available from the British Library.

ISBN: 978-0-00-733976-1

Collins uses papers that are natural, renewable and recyclable products made from wood grown in sustainable forests. The manufacturing processes conform to the environmental regulations of the country of origin.

Design: Steve Boggs
Cover design: Kate Gaughran
Layout: Susie Bell
Proofreader: Janet McCann
Indexer: Ben Murphy

Printed in China by Jeming Srl.

Audio recordings are all by the author except for:
Raven & Peregrine encounter – Simon Elliott; Chough – Roger Boughton; Long-tailed Duck, White-fronted Goose, Spotted Redshank, Green Sandpiper – Heather and Charlie Myers
Photo credits: all photos are by the author, except for Fulmar and Corncrake, courtesy of Roger Boughton

CONTENTS

PREFACE

Christmas 1995 for my family was marked by my absence. Not a complete absence – just disappearing for long periods into my work-room, trying to pull together the audio and text of my first book, the *Collins Guide to Bird Songs and Calls*. It must have been a stormy period out and about, but I wasn't really aware of it much, other than that there was a spate of power cuts; and that's a serious problem when you're in computer time and trying to make a deadline. It was also still the early days of digital audio and most systems had their temperamental sides: mine's little quirk was to miss out the odd file on playback, when it felt like it.

I'm back here again, a hermit in my studio-office, Christmas has gone and the second edition is shaping up. It's still a surprisingly intense process trying to finish things off, but so much has changed. The audio editing and archiving systems we have now are an exquisite luxury compared to those early frustrations.

But then one can look back to the days of reel-to-reels and razor-blade editing and imagine how those in the field of wildlife recording and study would have drooled at the capabilities of modern audio. You still need a good mic and good fieldcraft (most of the time!). But relatively cheap recorders with a far wider dynamic range than tape (so a lower noise floor), inexpensive media, transfer and duplication of digital recordings with no loss of quality, non-destructive editing and subtle equalisation processors have all contributed to improve the potential for great-quality audio from the natural world, at a modest cost.

But possibly the most significant factor for those of us interested in the subject matter is in the storage and archiving of recordings: a computer and hard-disk system offers almost instant access for listening to and comparing sounds. In the past we might have had to change reels or cassettes and done some nifty fast-forwarding and tape manoeuvres; now it's easy to set up playlists to follow a theme or investigate an idea – quickly and with no degradation of the original recording. This is so important with sounds, since it's particularly hard to retain an accurate impression of a sound in the mind for any length of time. How Ludwig Koch would have enjoyed the benefits of IT.

Having spent 20 years out there making recordings, it's a real pleasure, and an exploration in the full sense, to spend time reviewing (by ear) the fruits of that work. Put together 30-odd different recordings of Skylark calls, from different times and different places, and you really come to recognise the voice of 'Skylark'. All of which has resulted in me starting this second edition pretty much from scratch; the text has been rewritten and most of the audio is new – just a few recordings from the first edition have made it through.

With the extra 14 years of fieldwork and the associated benefits of study from my recording library, you might think it would be so much easier now to compile this second edition, but this hasn't been the case. Trying to distil it all into a balanced and accessible work has proved rather hard going and has involved some difficult decisions over which recordings to use. This is particularly true of the habitat sequences where I've tried to maintain a natural continuity and yet cover a whole range of species in a short time. One thing I've learnt – selecting wildlife recordings is an incredibly time-consuming process.

The first edition was surprisingly well received, considering my relative inexperience of the subject. There were a few reviewers who felt the need to point this out and I suppose I stepped on a few toes, because I'm not really a birder and wasn't much aware of the delicate political sensibilities of birding society. But wait a minute: recording and investigating birdsong has been the major part of my life for the last 20 years – surely I must be some kind of a birder. I am genuinely fascinated and absorbed in this subject, but I tend to work away at it by myself, so maybe I should apologise if I sometimes appear out of touch or disregarding of the wider birdwatching community.

This is not really a book about finding rare birds; it's more concerned with taking notice of events that so often pass us by, or the existence of which we are unaware. I hope it helps in bringing some of the scarcer bird species to your attention, but I hope more that it brings the natural world closer to your heart. An awareness of bird sounds sharpens one's experience of any outdoor space. I walk out to the shops down the back lane: the whole ambience is alive with Starling song and chatter. A Blackbird dives through, rattling out its alarm chuckle and everything stops abruptly. The silence is tense with alertness and suspense. A palpable change in the atmosphere and my sense of being there. Sparrowhawk? Tune in to the dynamic flow of the world on the bird sound network.

I started on this path because I wanted to recognise and understand all the bird sounds I heard when out and about. That and because, as a recording musician, I found them very beautiful. Gradually experience builds up: time spent listening to recordings feeds back into live listening until you reach a point where almost everything you hear is familiar. And the unfamiliar sparks curiosity and intrigue. The world is different: there's an intimacy beyond the visual. In the sound world you don't need to keep squinting through optics. Presumably, if you're reading this, I don't need to tread water trying to convince you of the intrinsic pleasures and beauty of birdsong. I take it you have arrived here because something in you has been touched by the subject. But let me tell you that we are caught in a fascination that goes back a long way and I've tried to convey something of this in the section on historical context.

The would-be author on the topic of bird sounds is faced with something of a challenge with a good title for the subject: bird sound lacks a sense of intention from the animal and, in pursuit of accuracy, the populist 'birdsong' soon needs to be expanded to 'songs and calls', but even this does not literally include the drumming of woodpeckers, the aerial wing thrum of Snipe or the wing-claps of Nightjar and Long-eared Owl. So the full and accurate title for the subject has to be 'acoustic communication in birds'. So dry. This is by way of apology for a certain looseness in my use of terms: so when you see birdsong (run together as one word), it's usually shorthand for bird sounds in general, whereas bird song literally refers to song as opposed to calls.

I've generally used the names I've grown up with: so it's a Dunnock, rather than a Hedge Accentor, and a Shore Lark, rather than a Horned Lark. I've got used to them now, though I've had to brush up on a few since childhood: a Waterhen is now a Moorhen, though I just occasionally slip back in a sudden response. The scientific and current international names for each species are given in the species account. I hope I've tidied up my spelling too, but, if some anomalies have slipped through the net, I'm sorry. My excuse is that I read a lot of old books and bird names have gradually evolved over the years: sometimes I see the older versions in my mind.

A preface is the customary place for an author to apologise for his inadequacies and acknowledge his debts and his superiors. Well, I have plenty of all of these and have already made a few apologies, so on to a brief word of thanks. Myles Archibald at HarperCollins took a risk on me with the first edition and has been a great source of encouragement ever since: thanks, Myles. Andrew Stuck has also been a source of great support over the years and has become a good friend.

There is a welcoming community of wildlife sound recordists out there, many of whom are members of the Wildlife Sound Recording Society: all have been keen to share their experience and given advice over the years. But I'd particularly like to thank Kyle Turner, Derek McGinn, Roger Charters, Lang Elliott and Andrew Skeoch. Many others have been very supportive with advice, assistance on projects and general enthusiasm for my pursuits: Roger Manning, John Steele, Kevin Redgrave, John Wilson, Harriet McDougall and Marcus Coates locally, Roy Dennis in Scotland, Marek Borkowski in Poland, Marcial Yuste Blasco in Spain, and a host of anonymous reserve wardens, who have been very patient in dealing with my enquiries and requests over the years. All your contributions to my ongoing preoccupations have been greatly appreciated and find some expression in this work. The staff at the BTO have been very helpful and enthusiastic in various dealings; in particular, the late Chris Mead was always so encouraging, with his encompassing interests and knowledge, and his unaffected verve is missed.

Special thanks are due to my colleagues and friends – Roger Boughton for allowing me to use his photos and recordings, and Simon Elliott and Heather and the late Charlie Myers for use of their recordings. Not to mention spirited and inspiring company.

And of course I doubt I would have managed to get through the work without the steady patience and equanimity of Jane.

Northumberland: January 2010

CD CONTENTS

CD 1

1 Intro
2 **House and Garden**
House Sparrow song and calls
3 Collared Dove song
4 Starling song
5 Carrion Crow calls
6 Pied Wagtail calls and song
7 Magpie calls
8 Blackbird calls and subsong
9 Blackbird full song
10 Wren song
11 Blue Tit song
12 Great Tit song
13 Pheasant male (sub)song and female calls
14 Dunnock song
15 Robin song
16 Song Thrush song
17 Chaffinch song
18 Greenfinch song
19 Goldfinch song
20 Swallow song
21 Black Redstart song
22 Jackdaw calls
23 Swift calls
24 House Martin and Swallow calls and song

25 **Farmland**
Skylark song
26 Corn Bunting song
27 Quail song
28 Yellow Wagtail song and calls
29 Yellowhammer song
30 Lesser Whitethroat song
31 Red-legged Partridge display calls
32 Linnet pair song
33 Yellowhammer calls and Tree Sparrow song
34 Rook calls
35 Grey Partridge display calls
36 Carrion Crow calls
37 Lapwing display calls
38 Barn Owl calls
39 Little Owl calls and song

40 **Hedges and Scrub**
Nightingale song
41 Blackcap song
42 Garden Warbler song
43 Willow Warbler song
44 Long-tailed Tit calls (Whitethroat calls)
45 Whitethroat song

46 **Woodland**
Woodcock roding calls
47 Redstart song
48 Nuthatch song
49 Chiffchaff song
50 Marsh Tit song
51 Red Kite calls
52 Jay calls
53 Green Woodpecker calls
54 Kestrel calls
55 Great Spotted Woodpecker drumming and call
56 Treecreeper song
57 Spotted Flycatcher song
58 Wood Pigeon song
59 Stock Dove song
60 Bullfinch song (Robin song)

CD 2

PART ONE
INTRODUCTION

SOME HISTORICAL CONTEXT

In *Palaeontology: An Introduction* (1973), James Scott makes an interesting comment about birds: 'Although the Tertiary Era is often described as the age of mammals, it could also be called the age of birds, or the age of gastropods, for that matter. Birds, however, provide an unsatisfactory fossil record on account of their frail structure; unlike the mammals, with their heavy bones and close-to-the-earth living habits.' His point is that birds have proved a very successful animal group through this period and their success is evident not just in the diversity of species, but in the diversity of their lifestyles, behaviour and their ability to exploit almost all of the varied habitats of our planet. Despite their small brains, they encompass relatively complex behaviour, including expressive communication. They have cultural traditions in their groupings and the ability to learn.

While the power of flight is often considered the defining characteristic of birds and may well be the 'unique selling point' in their evolutionary success, it is not unique to birds, but shared with a large part of the insect kingdom (which they prey on extensively) and some mammals, such as bats. The lives of birds also involve relatively elaborate social systems ('birds of a feather flock together'), and suffusing the workings of their pair bonds, colonies, foraging flocks and migrations is an elaborate communication system. Much of their communication relies on a combination of visual and sound signals, but birds have taken the potential of acoustic communication further than any other group of animals apart from man. William Thorpe (1961) was one of the pioneers in the science of Bioacoustics and his thoughts are worth quoting in full:

> *I sometimes amuse myself by imagining an intelligent visitor from another planet arriving on this earth just before the differentiation of the human stock – say somewhere about one million years ago. If such a visitor had been*

asked by an all-seeing Creator which group of animals he supposed would the most easily be able to achieve a true language, I feel little doubt that he would have said unhesitatingly, 'Why, of course, the birds'. And indeed, if we now look at the birds together with all the mammals other than man, we have little hesitation in saying that the birds are by far the more advanced, both in their control of their vocalisation and by the way in which they can adapt them collectively and individually to function as a most powerful communication system.

Having talked a little in the Preface about the wonders of modern technology in relation to enjoying bird song, it might be pertinent to trace back some of the history of our interest in the subject. So here begins a potted history of birdsong's grasp on our hearts and minds. References in literature to bird song go back as far as writing; and oral histories, as conveyed in the subject matter of their mythologies, often involve an awareness (if not appreciation, in the modern sense) of bird songs and calls.

While the early signs of our cultural interest in birds, such as the so-called 'death of the bird-man' cave painting at Lascaux, provide no reference to sound, I enjoy pondering what our early ancestors might have made of bird vocalisation. Intriguing, surely, and suggestive of a secret language, maybe. Musical? That's a difficult one – when did music arise? Perhaps they found it useful as early signs of approaching danger, for locating avian prey in hunting and also, through imitation, as a way of drawing their quarry closer. No doubt an awareness of bird sounds was part of the knowledge and mythology of early hunter-gatherers, as an integral part of their environment; and an attempt to understand and predict the fickle and mysterious nature of their world would be a necessary part of survival.

CLASSICAL TIMES

By the first millennium BC and the spread of civilisation through the Mediterranean area there are indications of other sensibilities creeping in. In a Greek epigram from around 600 BC, Erinna, a poetess friend of Sappho, describes her lament at the loss of a pet singing insect; there are other poetic references from later centuries suggesting that crickets were well regarded as singers, but the song of cicadas was jarring (for example Longos of Lesvos, second century AD). Okay, these are insects, not birds, but it reveals a human appreciation of the sound communication of other species in a musical sense. It's likely that birds were kept for the enjoyment of their songs, too.

In Aristophanes' production of his play *The Birds*, staged at Athens' City Dionysia festival in 414 BC, the part of the Nightingale is thought to have been played by a special flute player, the Hoopoe's songs performed by a professional singer and the Chorus, covering an odd mix of species (the visual effect would have been important), by singers too. The Hoopoe calls on the Nightingale to 'set free the notes of the hallowed songs that pour divinely from you … your tawny throat throbbing with liquid music …'. (Penguin translation).

The awareness of variety in bird sounds is picked up by Aristotle, in many ways the father of our scientific tradition: in his *History of Animals* (written *c.*350 BC), describing a bird he calls acanthis, he says 'its plumage is poor, but its note is musical' (as translated by D'Arcy Wentworth Thompson). Of swans … 'they are musical, and sing chiefly at the approach of death'. Of jays … 'has a great variety of notes: indeed, might almost say it had a different note for every day in the year'. Of cranes … 'their leader, with his head uncovered, keeps a sharp look out, and when he sees anything of importance signals it with a cry'. Not only do we have a reference to musicality in bird song and the notion of alarm calls, but we have the beginnings of a field guide.

From a work of Roman literature another interesting idea creeps in. Writing in the first half of the first century BC, the poet and philosopher Lucretius produced his much-admired work *De Rerum Natura* ('On the Nature of Things'), from which come these lines:

At liquidas avium voces imitarier ore
ante fuit multo quam levia carmina cantu
concelebrare homines possent aurisque iuvare.
Imitating with the mouth the fluent notes of birds
came long before
men were able to sing together in harmony
and please the ear.

This tantalising hint at the possibility that human song was not only influenced by bird song, but may have developed from copying it, is an idea that crops up down the ages and still haunts many of us. My own feeling is that, whether or not there is a direct link between imitating birds and our own singing, the development of our musical aesthetic, particularly in relation to melodic phrasing, must have been strongly influenced by what we have heard from birds. Unfortunately I cannot see how the question will ever be settled; perhaps it's more satisfying and inspiring if some things remain obscured in history. But if we look at our closest relatives in the mammals, although some are very vocal, with loud and sometimes tonally rather pure calls, there's no evidence of melodic or rhythmic elaboration that might develop into something like our more traditional essays in music.

ENJOYING BIRD SONG IN THE EARLY MIDDLE AGES

I know of no reference to bird song over the whole of the next millennium; there may be some interesting references from elsewhere in the world, of which I'm unaware, but it's a period in which the windows on European culture in general are limited, let alone those on music or ornithology. Then from around the turn of the next millennium there are numerous fragments of rather romantic Celtic poetry (from the Celtic west and north of Britain), where the songs of local bird species were celebrated, particularly the thrush family. These fragments provide a naturalist with tantalising glimpses of the character of the land and culture of the people of these islands as they emerged from an obscure period. The following are a few examples of poetry from the period, taken from Jackson (1971).

> *May-time, fair season, perfect is its aspect then; blackbirds sing a full song, if there be a scanty beam of day. The hardy, busy cuckoo calls, welcome noble summer! … The harp of the wood plays melody, its music brings perfect peace; colour has settled on every hill … The corncrake clacks, a strenuous bard. A timid persistent frail creature sings at the top of his voice, the lark chants a clear tale – excellent May-time of calm aspect!*
>
> **IRISH, AUTHOR UNKNOWN, 9TH–10TH CENTURY**

When the wind sets from the north the dark stern wave desires to strive against the southern world, against the expanse of the sky; listen to the swans' song.

IRISH, AUTHOR UNKNOWN, 11TH CENTURY

There was a time when I thought sweeter than the voice of a lovely woman beside me, to hear at matins the cry of the heath-hen of the moor.

IRISH, AUTHOR UNKNOWN, 12TH CENTURY

They have sent forth their cry, the loquacious lads, yesterday they heard it under the green trees, pure and church-like, three lifetimes to the gentle laureate poets – the linnet from the brake, the blameless nightingale, solemn and celestial; the pure-toned thrush, sweet rascal; the blackbird, he whose zeal is greater; and the woodlark soaring wantonly, catching the skylark's tune; singing, scattering so much fancy, so gay, so fresh, the accent of true passion.

WELSH, EDMUND PRICE, ARCHDEACON OF MERIONETH (1544–1623)

It's difficult to say how much these poets were working within a literary tradition (or perhaps oral), as opposed to expressing personal experience, and an ornithologist might puzzle over some of the species (Nightingale and Woodlark in Wales?), but these quotes, and many others like them, make a good case for the existence in this culture of a deep appreciation of the music of birds and its pre-eminent role in the seasonal tapestry of nature.

While these poems often express a love of place, and the bird is part of the *genius loci*, it appears that urbane society in the south of England found enough in bird song per se, even stripped of context, to engage the soul. Bircham (2007) refers to prohibitions in the statutes of some Oxford colleges, where the 'keeping of larkes' was forbidden at Queen's (1340), keeping 'thrushes or other singing birds' was forbidden at Magdalene (1450), and at Corpus Christi it was forbidden to keep 'singing birds such as those thrushes called Song Thrushes, Nightingale, Starling and Blackbird within college or without'. However, this may also be the first literary evidence of bird song being an unwanted intrusion or distraction, breaking the potential silence of contemplation. 'Drum and bass' probably fills the same role for Oxford students these days; although it's nice to think that someone might be playing one of my bird song CDs, and, with judicious use of the volume control, circumvent the problems of that previous era.

NIGHTINGALE IN THE MIDDLE AGES

Nightingale song was already admired in ancient Greece, as is suggested by the quote from Aristophanes given above, or by the Tereus myth where Procne (or Philomela according to later versions – there are many confusing reworkings of the theme), who had such an enchanting voice, became a Nightingale. The bird's fame as a singer had already transformed the image of this bird into a symbol of sonic beauty and, through cultural tradition, into so much more. Even earlier, in Homer's *Odyssey* Penelope compares her own sorrow to that of the Nightingale singing in lamentation for the loss of her son. This idea that a singing Nightingale was female and expressing sorrow was very persistent in literature and dominates the association with violence in the Tereus myth.

By the early Middle Ages the Nightingale had come to represent the essence of bird song and had become a rather powerful symbol for a range of qualities, broadly covering poetry, emotion, love, lust and the rising sap of spring (Gellinek-Schellekens, 1984), encompassing joy as well as melancholy. Endowed with these attributes the Nightingale became a key figure in a strange literary genre, the Middle English bird debates, in which anthropomorphic birds discuss philosophical questions and moral issues. It reminds me of current celebrity culture magazines, where the views of some singing stars are offered on the importance of, say, love in marriage.

WILLUGHBY & RAY'S ORNITHOLOGY

By the seventeenth century we have an emerging scientific ornithology. The three-volume *Ornithology*, by Francis Willughby, a wealthy aristocrat, and John Ray, son of an Essex blacksmith, two biologists who met as students at Cambridge, was first published in 1676 (in Latin!), then in English in 1678. This was the first work to attempt a classificatory system for birds, largely based on physical characteristics (researched via John Ray's dissection of specimens), and it represented the culmination of many years' travel and observation of the birds of the region. In a sense they were the first modern birders. Whereas their approach to taxonomy seems to have concentrated on morphology and physical structure, the species account does include some references to voice. Of Bittern, '… they say that it gives an odd number of bombs at a time viz., three or five; which in my own observation I have found to be false. It begins to bellow about the beginning of February and ceases when breeding time is over … in the autumn after sunset these birds are wont to soar aloft in the air with a spiral ascent, so high till they get quite out of sight, in the meantime making a singular kind of noise, nothing like to lowing' (from Bircham, 2007). (For more about Bittern 'gull-calls' see the Species account, page 76.)

GILBERT WHITE

Just a short while later we have further evidence of keen observation of bird behaviour, from the writings of Gilbert White of Selborne in north Hampshire. And in this there is plenty to catch the interest of the ear-minded ornithologist. It's well known that he split what had been known as willow-wrens into three different species, largely on the basis of their songs (also on the size of specimens). Writing in 1768 (letter XVI to Thomas Pennant), he describes Wood Warbler and Chiffchaff: 'I make no doubt but there are three species of the willow-wrens; two I know perfectly, but have not been able yet to procure the third. No two birds can differ more in their notes, and that consistently, than those two that I am acquainted with; for the one has a joyous, easy laughing note, the other a harsh loud chirp.' Was this the first taxonomic split based on bioacoustic data?

Also in letter XVI, he makes an interesting reference to Snipe drumming. 'In breeding-time snipes play over the moors, piping and humming; they always hum as they are descending. Is not their hum ventriloquous like that of the turkey? *Some suspect it is made by their wings*' (author's italics). It took well over a hundred years before that question was sorted (see Snipe in the Species account, page 118).

There are many references in his letters to bird song and, which is rather pertinent, he frequently refers to birds 'singing', including Cuckoo (a non-passerine). In letter II, to Daines Barrington, he includes a list of the song periods of 30 species of songbird, which is remarkably accurate; but in it he separates out those he describes as having merely 'somewhat of a note or song, and yet are hardly to be called singing birds' – including Goldcrest, Marsh Tit, Chiffchaff,

Wood Warbler, Grasshopper Warbler and Bullfinch. This is good evidence that it's all a matter of musical taste – as in father to son saying, 'What, you call that music!' – and tastes change. Interestingly, Bullfinches have long been popular with bird fanciers for their propensity to learn tunes played to them on whistles (as well as for their looks).

White also notes the autumn resumption of song by many songbirds: 'hence August is by much the most mute month, the spring, summer, and autumn through'. But another interesting area he delves into is that of individual variation, based on the best bioacoustic tools of the period – well, it does provide a fixed reference point. I'll quote this passage in full:

> *From what follows, it will appear that neither owls nor cuckoos keep to one note. A friend remarks that many (most) of his owls hoot in B flat; but that one went almost half a note below A. The pipe he tried their notes by was a common half-crown pitch-pipe, such as masters use for tuning of harpsichords; it was the common London pitch.*
>
> *A neighbour of mine, who is said to have a nice ear, remarks that the owls about his village hoot in three different keys, in G flat, or F sharp, in B flat and A flat. He heard two hooting to each other, the one in A flat, and the other in B flat. Query. – Do these different notes proceed from different species, or only from various individuals? The same person finds upon trial that the note of the cuckoo (of which we have but one species) varies in different individuals; for about Selborne wood, he found they were mostly in D: he heard two sing together, the one in D, the other in D sharp, who made a disagreeable concert: he afterwards heard one in D sharp, and about Wolmer Forest some in C.*

Here he is touching on some of the same issues that torment contemporary birders. To what extent are such vocal differences reliable evidence for taxonomic splits, or dialects of different subspecific groups? Scottish Crossbill? The whole crossbill complex? *Phylloscopus* warblers? It's all great stuff from the 18th century for those of us who enjoy rummaging through connections in history.

At about the same time in Austria, a famous composer bought a pet Starling, which he kept for the three years until it died. No one can say for sure what influence the bird had on Mozart's music, if any, but there can be little doubt that he cherished the bird's company, since he held an elaborate funeral after its death. It seems, though, that there may have been some musical interaction between the two, since according to David Rothenberg (Rothenberg, 2005) he found the bird singing a fragment of one of his own piano concertos, which it modified slightly, changing a G to a G sharp, 'making the tune sound centuries ahead of its time'. Rothenberg also reports the suggestion that the work K.522, 'A Musical Joke', was a tribute to, and inspired by, the bird's singing.

Starlings may be a common urban bird, even a pest to some people, but the way they play with sound is fascinating and, I think, shows something we can almost recognise as musical skill (as opposed to vocal skill or the ability to learn). Mozart was not the only composer from those times to use bird song in his work: Clément Jannequin, Vivaldi and later Beethoven all wrote pieces inspired by and incorporating bird songs. I'm sure there were others and there certainly have been many since.

THE INDUSTRIAL REVOLUTION

This also marks a period when artists in other fields paid homage to the inspiring impact of bird song. The poets of the time were showing a rediscovered zeal for matters of nature: John Keats, Percy Bysshe Shelley, John Clare, Robert Browning and Gerard Manley Hopkins all wrote tributes to the voices of birds. Much of the poetry revels in the emotional impact of bird song and generally focuses on particular virtuoso species (Skylark, Nightingale); it tells us more about the poet than the bird and its music. To be fair, John Clare enjoys more intimacy in his relationship with nature and penetrates beyond the thicket of the literary and spectacular.

It's also a period when trade in caged songbirds seems to have flourished, as is evidenced by numerous references to bird-catchers in the literature of the time. No doubt this was nothing new and had a long history, but it could be that the influence of the Industrial Revolution whetted the desire to have a little piece of the natural world, live and singing, in the home. Subsequently humanitarian considerations and the advent of recorded music and radio have undermined the practice, but it has never quite gone away. From Kearton (1900):

> *A very strange thing about some species is that they sing better in one part of the country than another. Birdcatchers say that an Essex Chaffinch can beat one from any other part of the British Isles, and close observers with good*

musical ears have noticed that this bird's notes are stronger and longer in some districts than in others.

Singing competitions are still held amongst Chaffinch fanciers in the East End of London, and it is difficult to understand how the poor little prisoners have the heart to utter a note in their cramped cages, enfolded within thick handkerchiefs that make the air dark and stifling. German birdcatchers used to think that the blacker the darkness in which a singing Chaffinch was kept the better it sang, and were, sad to relate, guilty of the unspeakable cruelty of destroying the eyesight of their unfortunate little prisoners with red-hot wire.

INTO THE 20TH CENTURY

Then came the momentous occasion of the first technology for recording sound, with the invention of the phonographic cylinder by Thomas Edison in 1877. It wasn't long before someone was engaged in recording the music of birds. In 1889 in Germany, eight-year-old Ludwig Koch was given one of the new phonographs by his father. The two main interests of his life were music and animals; he was fortunate in having quite a collection of captive animals including some songbirds, a personal zoo in fact, and that same year he made what is thought to be the first recording of bird song – of a captive Indian Shama. Ludwig soon went on to record wild birds, as you will read later.

The imaginary (or possibly real) race to make the first wild bird recording must have been quite a close thing. At around this time in Britain the Kearton brothers were avidly using the latest technology to bring wildlife to a post-industrial society and popularise the natural world; Cherry Kearton was a pioneer in the art of wildlife photography and Richard Kearton provided text. But sometime before 1900 they made some attempts at sound recording. Again I think this is worth quoting in full (Kearton, 1900):

The vocal accomplishments of some Song Thrushes are as much superior to those of others as are the notes of an Albert Hall concert singer to those of a bawling yokel in a country sing-song. My brother and I have proved this in our attempts to secure records on the phonograph and comparing them. He used to get up very early in the morning, climb evergreens growing on a common not far away, wherein we knew Thrushes habitually sang, and fix the instrument in such a position that he could start it directly the birds commenced to hold forth at the first blink of day. We spent a lot of time and money in our endeavours to record bird songs, but to little purpose, as the records we did obtain of Thrushes' notes in the way described invariably split on account of the wax being so susceptible to atmospheric changes. When near enough to a bird to secure a really good record of its song, the grinding of the needle cutting the vibrations of its notes in the wax cylinder invariably frightened it away. We, however, made the interesting discovery that wild, free Thrushes sometimes sing under their breath, in the same way that human beings hum tunes over to themselves.

This above was possibly the first reference to subsong in literature.

We have arrived at the first ripples from the surge of the 20th-century electronic era. But before the effects of this washed through our experience and understanding of bird song, there were still some fascinating publications to put a seal on what had gone before. Walter Garstang, a professor of zoology at Leeds University, had his book *Songs of the Birds* published in 1922. It was described by David Rothenberg (2005) as 'one of the most unusual of all bird song books, … a work that walks the line between science and poetry'. It included some of the oddest, most avant-garde poems ever seen, presented as transcriptions of bird songs. Then in 1925 Witherby (the pioneering natural history publishers who drove the subject forward over the next 50 years) published the first (I think) proper field guide devoted solely to bird song: *Bird-song – a manual for field naturalists on the songs and notes of some British song birds* by Stanley Morris. It was also the last, and only, bird song guide to be published without audio.

By this time, Ludwig Koch, who was in Germany working for EMI, had already produced some educational works in the field of music, combining textbooks and gramophone records. But he also had other ideas. The following is from his memoirs (Koch, 1955):

As far back as the late 'twenties I was already thinking of the value of a [sound] book on birds and animals, illustrated by good recordings instead of by those musical notations and curves which mean nothing either to a scientist or to a bird-lover. The translation, too, into such words as tu, tu, tu or tse tse tse will never bring to the ears of the average listener the sweetness of the song of the wood-lark or the characteristic note of the marsh-tit. ... The success of this idea was so great in Germany that within four years I was able to publish eleven sound-books, three of them on animals.

It was a little later, in 1932, that his first sound-book of bird song was released: *Gefiederte Meistersänger* (Feathered Mastersingers).

In 1936 Ludwig was forced to leave Germany and went to London; within a short time he had met the Witherby brothers and teamed up with ornithologist Max Nicholson, and by the end of the year *Songs of Wild Birds* was published – a book with two records. It made the news and was so successful that the following year *More Songs of Wild Birds* was published.

Ludwig went on to become something of a household name with his radio broadcasts; I think it is a testament to the integrity of a genuine love of bird song that a refugee with a marked German accent could win the hearts of the British people around the period of World War II. This same sensibility helps me out when I'm recording up a remote back road in a foreign country and someone arrives, suspicious of what I'm up to with my assorted electronic gadgetry and coils of cable. I always learn to say, politely and formally I hope, in the local language: 'Hello. I would like to record the music of the birds here. Is that all right?' And it almost always raises a friendly smile and often an attempt at some advice or assistance. Unfortunately, beyond France, I rarely have enough grasp of the language to understand these often lengthy replies! But it's important to choose the right words: 'music', not 'noise', 'sound' or any other vague expression.

Witherby went on to publish further sound guides, including in 1958, the ambitious *Witherby's Sound-Guide to British Birds* by Myles North and Eric Simms, with the cooperation of the BBC. I have Part One and this includes seven records. But I don't think this had the impact of Koch and Nicholson's earlier work. It wasn't just that the earlier work had some novelty value or that culture had changed. The focus of the publication was different: whereas *Songs of Wild Birds* had an assumed musical theme, open to wide appeal, the latter work was a drier publication, with more the air of a reference catalogue for serious ornithologists.

And this marked a change of emphasis in the role of bird song in our culture, which lasted until recently, although I think the pendulum has been swinging back to a more balanced position recently. The false dichotomy: does one get more from bird song through art or science?

It's more than coincidental that the 1950s also saw the emergence of a new science. William Thorpe, a zoologist studying behaviour at Cambridge, got his hands on a new machine known as a sound spectrograph and began a pioneering study rearing Chaffinches under varying conditions and observing how their songs developed as they matured. The spectrograph analyses a sound signal and generates a graph of its frequency content against time, providing an accurate picture of the 'shape' of a sound sequence and thereby an objective reference against which other sounds can be compared. Also, it can reveal transient detail that is often hard for us to hear clearly. Thorpe had conquered time, and bird song could now be seen; he could point to a mark on a page and discuss its significance without subjective equivocation.

The Chaffinches provided some fascinating results, particularly in the fact that they learned the details of their songs from other Chaffinches. Chaffinches, with their brassy, repetitive cascade of chirps, have been well studied over the years since, notably by Thorpe's students Peter Marler and Peter Slater, and have contributed much to our understanding of bird song and its role in social co-ordination. But possibly most surprising has been the discovery, as researchers studied other species, that not only is there great variation in the sound of their songs between species, there is also wide variation in the behaviour underlying their singing and the way song fits into their lives. No single model fits the singing behaviour of all species.

I can't finish this section without mentioning Edward Armstrong's *A Study of Bird Song*, published in 1963, a comprehensive and very learned survey of the range of bird song in the world, well documented and balanced in its enthusiasm for both the scientific and musical approach. It still provides a great starting point and reference work for anyone drawn into the field and crops up in the references of most subsequent books on the subject, and even in current scientific writing.

THE SCIENTIFIC ACCOUNT

I should begin by saying I'm not a scientist: my recording and studio work have nothing of the rigour of a scientific study, though I'm full of admiration for and owe a debt of thanks to those who map the field of avian bioacoustics in painstakingly accurate detail. I try to keep abreast of the research, though occasionally it doesn't quite gel with the understanding I glean from fieldwork and careful studio listening. I suppose I'm primarily a musicologist (an ornithomusicologist at that, but I'm a bit shy of using such a grand term!); I have an interest in linguistic culture (Classics degree) and have completed a formal study in ecology. So, as a jack of a few trades, what follows in this section is a rather individual interpretation of the hard facts, as collated from various published sources, filtered through personal experience. My main source of reference for some time now has been the comprehensive review of the science of bird song provided by Clive Catchpole and Peter Slater (1995), to whom I owe a great debt of thanks, and probably a pint or two if memory serves.

Much of what we now know from the scientific study of bird song has come from controlled experiments testing hypotheses, beginning with Thorpe and his experiments with Chaffinch song-learning in the laboratory, leading to other researchers testing the reactions of wild birds to hearing the playback of recordings. As it has become apparent that the interactions of wild birds are rather subtle and a singer may vary his song in accordance with the reactions of listeners, both rival males and females, the most recent developments have involved interactive playback experiments. Here the choice of what is played is under the control of a computer programmed to perform in various ways depending on the response to the previous song that has been broadcast.

Another point that should be made clear at the outset is that birds are generally far more vocal than we are casually aware. We normally just hear the songs and calls they broadcast – those louder communications intended to be heard over some distance. But birds also habitually communicate with others nearby using quieter calls (and song) and it's a reasonable assumption that there are survival benefits inherent in not proclaiming your presence, identity or location to all and sundry unnecessarily. In fact the role of eaves-dropping has recently been attracting the attention of researchers. And note how those songbirds that sing from prominent perches all tend to have discontinuous songs (in verses) and look around intently in the intervals.

Voice permeates the social interactions of birds to a greater or lesser degree depending on species, but few birds are completely silent, even if it appears so to us, watching at a distance. This is particularly true of paired birds, in courtship, around the nest and when loafing or feeding together. A fellow recordist, Simon Elliott, who has made a special foray into recording raptors, grumbles when guides describe some birds of prey species as almost silent. But the brief summary in guides is of course very much from the context of average human encounters with those birds. Often the same species can be quite vocal when both of a pair are present and at ease at a nest site – but we do not visit raptor nest sites. And if we do stray into a nesting area, what we tend to hear are alarm calls, not the other bits and pieces of soliciting, chivvying and negotiation that go on.

IS IT SINGING OR CALLING?

In general discussion, bird song usually refers to the full song of males in the breeding season, and often in particular to the more elaborate vocalisations of passerine songbirds. Its purpose is often said to have a dual function: establishing and holding a territory (generally a male to male relationship), and attracting and stimulating a female.

Sometimes called territorial or advertising song, males sing to broadcast their presence and their character, to show off, to strut their stuff, to advertise their worth. This lets other males assess their rivals, thereby generally avoiding actual fights and the risk of physical injury, and lets females know where they are, and something of their character and status.

Songbirds often have elaborate sound patterns for this, and it's thought that the use of the term 'song' has arisen through the close analogy between human singing and the performances of these male songbirds. In other, non-passerine, species, although their territorial and advertising vocalisations may be much simpler in structure, they still tend to perform equivalent social functions. The booming of a male Bittern, the bleating and nasal fluting of a drake Teal, the whiplash whistles of a male Spotted Crake, the crowing of a cock Pheasant or the trilling of a Dunlin may or may not sound as much like song as the more melodic phrasings of the songbirds, but they are all performing with sound and sending out a similar message.

Sometimes such vocalisations in the non-passerines might be referred to as display calls, territorial calls or advertising calls, but in many ways they amount to the same as passerine song, even if not always delivered so formally. There are differences, discussed below, as there are differences between different species of songbird: one might question whether species such as Fieldfare, Long-tailed Tit, Lesser Redpoll or Hawfinch have a full male song, equivalent to that of Skylark or Song Thrush, but they still can be heard showing off and performing excitedly with sound in a way that could be described as singing.

Then there are a few species that perform with sound as territorial or sexual advertisement, but the sound is not produced vocally: the bill-drumming of woodpeckers, the feather-thrumming of Common Snipe, the wing-clapping of Nightjar and Long-eared Owl all convey a similar message to song. Sometimes these have been called 'song substitutes'. But males, and occasionally females, of many species 'sing' in other ways. In the songbirds, the less formal and quieter modes of song have generally been referred to as subsong; this has sometimes been used loosely as a catch-all term to include quiet 'practice', tentative early-season warm-up (leading to plastic song, then crystallising after a while on full song), intimate courtship, maybe even copulation 'rattles' and flock or communal singing.

Whereas song, particularly full song, tends to have a seasonal basis, is usually performed by males and is largely only of interest to other members of the same species, calls, on the other hand, tend to be independent of season, produced by either sex and can convey an important message to other species (for example, alarm calls in a mixed flock).

Calls also tend to be shorter vocalisations, often a single note, in response to a particular situation: birds call to keep in touch with each other, to mob and scold intruders, to warn others of danger, to threaten others who come too close, to solicit food and sex and to express excitement. They convey an immediate message about the mood and situation of the individual; though brief, they can be repeated rapidly and varied in pitch and voicing to cover a wide range of emotive impact and respond to changing circumstances. Notice how parental alarm calls will become more frantic as one approaches dependent young, rising in pitch and rate of delivery – the message is clear.

The distinction between calls and song is largely an intuitive one, which works well in practice; it's obvious that there is a clear-cut difference between the continuous trilling phrases of a male Wren singing and the hard repeated 'tak's of a Wren calling, both in the patterning of the sound and the nature of the performance, as well as in the social function of the vocalisations. But there is a grey area when it's not so clear-cut: when does excited and varied calling become singing?

Take Goldfinches: I've just watched a bird flighting around over some alders where several others were feeding, and pouring out an intermittent stream of varied call phrases. The behaviour appears to be song; but the sounds were those used in calling, without the formal continuity of full song, and it's December. Or was there some simple functional message 'come on, let's head off somewhere else'; one could still maintain that the improvisatory and semi-continuous nature of the vocalisation was akin to song and, rather like the communal singing of such finches, was intended to stimulate the flock, in this case into action. Who knows. The point I'm trying to make is that calls and song, calling and singing, are not as clear-cut as might at first appear – they are useful descriptive terms, rather than rigid categories.

Although generally much simpler in form than songs, calls are far more interesting than they initially appear. The manner in which they work, subtle variations in rhythm, repetition and voicing, even the sheer design and neat economy of the kind of sounds used, results in a far more flexible and adaptable system than the simple categorisation into alarm call, contact call and flight call actually implies. Furthermore, these aren't clearly distinct categories. The desire for social contact is connected with the feeling that there's safety in numbers and any particular alarm or contact call involves both information on immediate security and an invitation to collaborate, to varying degrees. Calls tend to seek a response and provide a kind of social radar, by which individuals not only keep in touch, but also keep informed of the current situation.

LEARNING TO SING

As mentioned earlier, it's now customary to define bird song as being all about advertising territory and attracting a mate. It's important to recognise what kind of a definition this is: it explains the evolution of singing in birds as a successful mode of behaviour in relation to its social functions and the benefits it confers. The danger here is in thinking that this is what the bird intends, when we really have no way of knowing what the bird thinks it is doing – in the sense of what its motivations and intentions are. It's a definition in terms of its evolutionary function – a form of behaviour that has evolved to serve this purpose in the biology of the species. In just the same way human courtship rituals can be reduced to such an explanation, but I'm sure most of us would agree that we act thus in pursuit of pleasure or to satisfy a deep-rooted need. And this really only fully applies to one kind of singing by some species, since there are other situations in which a bird sings that are not so clearly of sexual or status utility, and many species are not strongly territorial. But as the old Chinese proverb says: A bird does not sing because it has an answer – it sings because it has a song. A similar sentiment is expressed in the title of Charles Hartshorne's book *Born to Sing* (1973). The idea that a bird sings for pleasure and the scientific dual-function theory are not mutually exclusive.

The dual-function theory works well for many of the songbirds, where the male repeats a rather formal song from a prominent perch or regular circuit (Meadow Pipit, Robin, Blackbird, Willow Warbler and Chaffinch, even some of the waders, grouse and other gamebirds, all show clear territorial behaviour); but with Linnets and many of the other cardueline finches and some of the *Acrocephalus* warblers there seems to be less territorial importance in the male song. The particular role of song in performing these two functions varies between species and is related to the behavioural ecology of the species; in some, full song appears to be almost wholly about attracting a mate.

When William Thorpe conducted his research on Chaffinches in the 1950s (Thorpe, 1961), it was a major step forward to discover that, without hearing other adult males, a young male Chaffinch would only produce a very rough example of Chaffinch song. It was just recognisable as Chaffinch, but the syllables were simplistic and it lacked clear phrasing. When a bird was reared within the hearing of normal Chaffinch songs, it produced songs that were clearly based on those models; Thorpe tried various other species as tutors, but interestingly the only species that had any influence on the Chaffinches in his experiments was Tree Pipit (which has a rather similar song). This meant that, although there might be a rough innate blueprint, Chaffinch song development involved learning, and to a large extent copying, from adult males.

This set the ball rolling for much subsequent research on song development, and until recently it was thought that song learning was confined to the 'true' songbirds (the Oscines). Indeed, much of the research on bird song has been focused on this group, to the extent that for many academics the term 'song' is only really appropriate in the context of the Oscines, because of the structural complexity of their songs and the fact that learning was a necessary part in their development.

We need to get into some hard taxonomy here. The Oscines are a suborder of the passerines (properly Passeriformes), which include roughly half the living species of birds in the world and are characterised by having a syrinx with a complex system of muscles, as well as perching feet; the syrinx is the bird equivalent of our larynx (the 'voice box'). Whereas the passerine families are all grouped in the single order, the non-passerines fall into a range of different orders, from Struthioniformes (including ostriches) to Piciformes (woodpeckers). The other suborder of passerines, the Suboscines, includes such families as the Cotingidae (cotingas), Pipridae (manakins), Tyrannidae (tyrant flycatchers) and Pittidae (pittas) and are largely confined to the tropics of Central and South America (BWP, 2004). Since they do not occur naturally in our area, they aren't particularly relevant here; as far as our region is concerned, the important distinction in relation to bird song is passerine and non-passerine. However, recent research suggests that learning occurs in the vocalisations of parrots and hummingbirds (Catchpole & Slater, 1995), both non-passerine families, and at least one species of bellbird (suboscine), so is not entirely confined to either the passerines or the Oscines.

This is important because song learning gives rise to some interesting consequences, including, in particular, cultural tradition. It may be that this has played an important role in the evolution of diversity in the passerines. Cultural tradition sets the field for the development of dialects and subspecific social groupings, which may facilitate speciation over time. Dialect has become rather a hot topic in the world of bird song, but, if I understand it correctly, there are two rather different aspects to it. More on that later.

SONG DEVELOPMENT IN PASSERINES

The basic path for the way a male songbird arrives at its full breeding song begins early, as soon as it can hear other adult songs, round about the time of leaving the nest. Thorpe found that young Chaffinches, after hearing recordings of adult songs as juveniles, produced songs clearly based on the models the following spring. This entailed them retaining a detailed memory of those songs during the intervening period and matching their output to it. Birds that had never heard any kind of Chaffinch song only produced rudimentary examples.

The idea that birds could memorise tunes goes back a long way, but here was hard proof. John Locke's *An Essay concerning Human Understanding* of 1690 contains the passage: 'This faculty of laying up and retaining the ideas that are brought into the mind, several other animals seem to have to a great degree, as well as man. For to pass by other instances, birds learning of tunes, and the endeavours one may observe in them to hit the notes right, put it past doubt with me, that they have perception, and retain ideas in their memories, and use them for patterns.'

According to the literature (for example, Catchpole & Slater, 1995), most passerine males first start to sing when they are just under a year old, when the onset of spring with increasing daylight triggers a rise in their testosterone levels. There is anecdotal evidence that some young males sing a little in their first autumn, but the extent to which this occurs, or in which species it may be prevalent, remains to be answered. When they do begin singing, most young birds produce a rather meandering, quiet kind of song, exploring and extending the capabilities of their voice (the subsong). After a while this becomes louder and a little more formal, as they play around with the structure and syntax, but are still not quite there (the plastic song). Eventually the form crystallises on the patterns of full adult song. This is essentially the way an individual's song develops, although details may vary a little between species and perhaps between individuals.

During research on song development it's been found that, even in those species that will learn songs from pre-recorded models (and not all will), their behaviour may be different when learning from a live tutor. Social and vocal interaction plays a part; consequently the results of research based on playing young bird recordings of songs has been subject to review. For instance, in studies by Louis Baptista and others on White-crowned Sparrows (a well-studied north American species), while earlier research using recordings suggested they were highly selective in what they would learn, when social interaction was possible they would even learn the songs of certain other species. The timing of the learning period also was extended. Other research found that the presence of females could have an influence on song development, as they could learn from the females' responses to different phrases.

This all means that there is more to song development than simply matching one's output to a memorised model, and emphasises the importance of social interaction in behavioural development. In the wild, young birds can gauge the reaction of other birds to the songs they produce. Variation has also been found in which birds a young learner finally models his song on. MacGregor and Krebs found little copying of their father's songs in young male Great Tits; research on other species (including Marsh Tit) suggested that this did occur. This is related to the timing of the learning process and particularly the different influences from hearing adults (especially the father) in the early period on leaving the nest and from hearing neighbouring adults in the first spring when trying to establish territory. Obviously this has an important bearing on the idea of social groupings based on dialects and whether it's kin-based or neighbourhood-based.

Another interesting variation is in the extent to which individuals in a neighbourhood share the same repertoire of song types. Whereas neighbouring Chaffinches and Great Tits have been found to vary in their individual repertoires, and this is thought to be the usual way. Peter McGregor found that all the Corn Buntings of a neighbourhood tended to share the same two or three song types. Furthermore, learning is not entirely restricted to song and has been found to play a part in the development of some calls. For instance the 'rain call' and the 'spink' call of Chaffinches both appear rather rudimentary from birds reared in isolation.

There is no one model for song learning that works across all species, as there is no one model for almost any aspect of bird song one examines in detail. One important difference is in the period of learning. Some species have a restricted period in which they learn their songs, normally their first year, then remain singing those song types for life (with perhaps some minor modifications between years); though they will learn to recognise new songs heard from other birds. Other species such as Starlings remain lifelong learners, constantly changing or extending their repertoires.

REPERTOIRE

In assessing the variation in the song of any individual, the established method is to attempt to quantify how many different patterns of song (song types) that individual produces and this is considered to be the size of their repertoire. For the songbird species with stereotyped songs, it's a fairly straightforward matter to assess their repertoire size: in species like Great Tit, Chaffinch and Yellowhammer males may have a repertoire of roughly two to six song types. Typically a bird sings verses of one song type for a while, then changes to another song type, sometimes matching a neighbour's song with like (song matching), at other times without any apparent connection; species vary in whether they tend to match songs in counter singing or avoid it.

But for species whose song style is based on different syllables or phrases, which they combine in different ways to build a more varied collection of verses, it becomes problematic in defining what is a discrete song type and knowing when one has recorded the full range of a male's song variations. Clive Catchpole (1976) commented that a male Sedge Warbler may never sing exactly the same sequence of elements twice in his life. So a figure for the average Sedge Warbler repertoire size based on song would be very large, whereas birds were found to be working with a more limited repertoire of around 50 different elements, but in varying combinations.

Catchpole and Slater (1995) reviewed the estimates of repertoire size from various authors for a range of species. Some species are quoted as having only a single song type, such as (European) Redwing; presumably this is based on the first part of Redwing song, since the twittered ending appears highly variable. At the other end of the scale is the Brown Thrasher *Toxostoma rufum* of North America, which is reported to have a repertoire of over 2,000 song types. Song Thrush (138–219 song types) and Nightingale (100–300) are much more modest in comparison, though still impressive and at the upper end of the list.

The way in which a bird uses the different songs in its repertoire has also been found to vary between species. Nightingales are rather interesting in that their repertoires appear to be organised into 'packages'; though the same song type is rarely sung twice close together, when it does crop up again, it is often accompanied by the same associated song types, though not necessarily in the same order and usually with one or two omitted from the package. Thus Nightingale is building further variation and complexity into its singing through the way in which it sequences its song types. This is important since, as we'll see later, for many species females are attracted to complexity and versatility.

TERRITORIAL MATTERS

The idea of birds, particularly males, seeking to maintain an exclusive territory for breeding, and often feeding too, goes back a long way, and Gilbert White suggested a link between territory and song. Latterly, this has been tested experimentally in various ways, notably through the playback of male song in established populations and by observing the effect on other males seeking or holding territory. Research by John Krebs with Great Tits revealed that the areas where adult males were removed and replaced with the playback of recorded songs were slower to be invaded by territory-seeking males than control areas, though they were eventually taken over, leading to the conclusion that song is a cost-effective first line of defence.

Such vocalisation is an adaptable and dynamic way of maintaining social arrangements, through assessment and negotiation. Early in the season, song helps in setting up a territory: an individual male can broadcast his 'CV', listen to and assess the competition, perhaps increase his rate and volume, as a challenge to a potential rival, judge the response and either move on or continue to stake a claim. Later in the season, song may contribute more to the security of knowing your neighbours, maintaining the status quo, and holding the interest of your mate, or even attracting the interest of other females in the locality.

Further research has shown that in highly territorial species like Great Tit, individual recognition through song is important, and in a settled population males will respond more actively to the playback of an unrecognised song than to that of one of their neighbours; unless, that is, the neighbour's song is played from a different area to where it is normally heard. Then a male in an adjacent territory will investigate quickly. So individually specific song is working to maintain the status quo between territorial males, who thereby can recognise each other at a distance and do not need to rush off to investigate every other Great Tit they hear singing nearby. But it may go beyond the distinctiveness of the song pattern, since it has been shown through similar experiments that some birds (e.g. Great Tits in Weary & Krebs, 1992) can recognise a known individual, even if he is singing a song they have never heard before – in the same way that we can recognise someone by voice, even though we may never have heard them speak those particular words before.

But species vary in their territorial behaviour: some species, like Great Tit, Chaffinch, Yellowhammer, Chiffchaff, Dunnock and Wren, are quite aggressively territorial, but others much less so. There appears to be a rough correlation between stereotyped song and strictly territorial social behaviour. There are other species, typically the cardueline finches like Goldfinch and Linnet, whose territorial instincts are less strong; and they tend to have songs of a less formal structure. But it's not straightforward and variation between individuals can be confusing. Blackbirds are normally considered to maintain exclusive breeding territories. Yet in 2009 I recorded a male Blackbird singing from the hedge in my back garden soon after dawn; almost immediately after he vacated the song-post, what I'm sure was a different male arrived and sang from a very close position, but there was no antagonism between the two. Puzzling. The real world of song is rarely as simple as the underlying model system implies.

A few years ago I watched two Song Thrushes facing each other on the ground, separated by a footpath, heads lowered, both singing something like full song, but very softly. You can often see Robins facing up in the same way. It's odd that they sing quietly in such a situation of confrontation (cf. 'Quiet song in song birds: an overlooked phenomenon', Dabelsteen et al., 1998). The implication from the subdued character of this expression might be that it's just too much of a goad to action to hear another male showing off close to you, and the louder the song, the greater the challenge. And for much of the time singing seems part of the status quo of males settled in their own space, rather than the image that is sometimes flagged up of a 'sound contest'. It is a kind of reflection of the social geography of the species.

One might expect the loudness of a species' song to bear some relation to the usual size of a male's territory. This seems to be borne out in the case of the territorial passerine species, where a suitable tract of habitat is occupied by individuals who can hear their neighbours. But the non-passerines raise some interesting questions. Listen to the spread of cock Pheasant crows over an early-morning landscape and you can imagine a similar social system to the passerines, similarly with Tawny Owls after nightfall. But what of Long-eared Owls? The male's song is very quiet, barely audible at 150–200 metres (165–220 yards); the wing-claps in display flight may be heard a little further off. To what extent are these territorial signals or simply mate attraction and stimulation calls? And what of the formal calls of Carrion Crow, often referred to (I roll it out too!) as territorial calls, but given all over the place? They have a self-assertion and formal delivery similar to the songs of territorial songbirds, but is crow territory more mobile, something that they carry around with them?

LEKKING

An unusual development from territorial behaviour is found in the lekking systems of some grouse and wader species (Black Grouse and Capercaillie in Britain, Great Snipe in continental Europe). The term derives from an old Scandinavian word for play. The males of a local area gather daily to perform on traditional sites and the females visit the leks to mate. This is normally the only part the males play in breeding. The different males tend to have their own positions on the lek, with the top male, who tends to get the most matings, in the centre; all the males display with song, posturing and explosive flutter-jumps in ritualised aggression, during which the lesser males jockey for a better position. That's the usual description of what's going on, though at least in Black Grouse (the species with which I'm most familiar) it's never been easy to follow this in action.

With Black Grouse, the males tend to perform in pairs facing up to each other (or more accurately, heads down, tails up) and there's much shuffling about and changing of partners, so it's difficult to follow where the stance of a particular male is. Although two males come close and shuffle back and forth, as if about to engage, and explode into their sneezing jumps, I've never yet witnessed an actual fight break out, though it is supposed to happen occasionally. After the lek, you can often see the birds begin feeding in loose groups. The roo-cooing song is often produced by many of the males at the same time and may be more of a communal chorus to attract females to the lek and stimulate them, than a competitive signal. Capercaillie males are more solitary in their daily lives and tend to remain spaced on their individual stances on the lek; though I believe fights are more frequent between Capercaillie males.

In conclusion I would say that one needs a rather flexible concept of territory, advertisement and display to cope with the full range of vocal behaviour exhibited by different bird species. Our interest often emphasises the competitive and aggressive aspects of territory and display, rather than the cooperation involved, but, without wishing to deny the serious rivalry often involved, like sport, for the game to work and make a good play, there has to be a balance of both.

FEMALE ATTRACTION

The other side of the 'dual function' concept of bird song states that a male's song is attractive to females. This has been tested experimentally in a range of species, showing that the females are more attracted to dummies accompanied by the playback of song than a 'dumb male' (and other methods). In those species in which the male sings for a short period, then ceases or greatly reduces his output of song on pairing (for example, Pied Flycatcher or Sedge Warbler), it's been inferred that the function of song is far more biased towards female attraction than territorial maintenance.

So why does male song attract females? Many studies have investigated this in a range of species, looking at what aspects of song are attractive and why. In most cases females have been found to prefer males with larger repertoires and more complex songs. This has been observed in the earlier pairing of male Great Reed Warblers with longer songs and increased female display to the playback of more complex songs. In research on Great Tit and Sedge Warbler, females were also found to prefer singers with larger repertoires, in the latter case providing for more versatile songs.

In the case of Great Tit, a territorial species with a modest repertoire of stereotyped songs, it's been found that males with larger repertoires tend to occupy better territories, leading to better survival and more viable young. So it may be that such qualities in song are an honest signal of a fitter male and may also indicate a better-quality territory, as well as possibly better genes. Separating these variables is not easy and beyond my scope here. Certainly it's to be expected that a fitter male on good territory (with a good food supply) can invest more energy in singing; in this sense song is an honest signal of quality – a weaker male will simply not be able to afford the time or the energy.

Early experiments with budgerigars and canaries showed that it's not only a matter of female choice. The playback of male song was found to influence the reproductive physiology of females and to stimulate breeding behaviour. Music certainly is the food of love for such birds. More recent work with canaries has found that females are particularly stimulated by what's been called 'sexy syllables', which tend to be harmonically complex and considered to be difficult to produce. It could be that they are an honest signal of a clever or physically more capable male.

This all suggests that complexity in male song has evolved through sexual selection and female choice, though there is still much to be fully understood. For instance, it might be thought that, with increased male competition for successful mating in polygynous species, this should lead to larger repertoires than related monogamous species. Donald Kroodsma found this to be the case with the North American Wrens he studied, but Clive Catchpole and Peter McGregor found the opposite in the *Acrocephalus* warblers and *Emberiza* buntings they studied. They figured that, in the cases studied, the males held large enough territories to support several females who mostly reared the young alone; thus female choice might be based on territory quality, and male song – concerned almost wholly with territorial defence – has evolved with smaller repertoires.

In general there appear to be two main influences on male song: the male to male relationship, concerned with territorial defence, leads to loud, rather simple songs and a limited repertoire, whereas the male to female relationship, concerned with mate attraction, leads to complex songs and a wider, more versatile repertoire. But this is a gross simplification of the subtle variations found in nature.

DUETTING

So far we've considered song from male birds, but it's long been known that females of some species sing at times. Armstrong (1963) recognises four kinds of female song: first, where the roles of the sexes are reversed, as in Red-necked Phalarope; second, where the female sings to mark her own territory, as with Robins or Mockingbirds in winter; third, where the female sings as well as the male, but the performance is more concerned with the pair's relationship than territorial defence, as with Bullfinch, Crossbill and many non-passerines; and finally, where female song is rather exceptional, maybe in old age, when isolated or experimentally injected with male hormones.

In many non-passerine species both birds of a pair often vocalise together in a form of duet: one bird breaks into song and its mate joins in, in a kind of affirmation of togetherness or mutual territorial advertisement. Grebes, Fulmar, Water Rail and woodpeckers are some examples. Both sexes of a pair in many other species may vocalise at the same time in display and courtship, but it hardly seems like a duet: when drake Goosanders are displaying, their calls elicit responses from the females and the calls may overlap and mingle, but it's a more random kind of interaction with different calls from males and females. With the species mentioned previously both birds give the same kind of call and give the impression of joining together in a mutual display. It shows other individuals and pairs that they are an item (and may strengthen the bond between them) or sends a message that this space is occupied.

There are some species that have taken this a step further and sing in a rather special kind of duet, with a strict formal arrangement to the two parts, such that it almost appears to be a single vocalisation. Classic examples of this are found in the African bushshrikes of the *Laniarius* genus or the Eastern Whipbird *Psophodes olivaceus* of Australia. This phenomenon is commonest in the tropics and I'm not aware of any such duetting species in our region. It tends to be associated with species that form long-term monogamous pairs and are often monomorphic; it's thought that the more constant conditions of the tropical environment, which enable pairs to settle on year-round territories, underpin the evolution of this behaviour.

Peter Slater and colleagues have recently been studying the singing behaviour, including duetting, of a number of species of wrens in the tropical Americas (Mann et al., 2009). In one species, the Plain-tailed Wren *Pheugopedius euophrys*, which lives communally, they found that more than just the two birds of a pair may combine to produce a strictly formal group song. The song contains four components ABCD, where males sing A and C and females B and D; the different contributions are precisely timed and the song may continue for over 40 cycles of the sequence. This is very different from counter-singing between territorial male songbirds, who are effectively rivals.

We have nothing to match that in temperate northern Europe, as far as I know. But we do have species that sing together less formally, often in large groups, producing a dense volume of sound. On winter afternoons, you occasionally come across flocks of various finches, typically Goldfinch, Linnet, Twite and Siskin, perched up in a tree, where every bird seems to be giving a stream of varied calling. There appears to be no formal arrangement to the patterns and all the sounds overlap randomly; this has sometimes been called communal song (or corporate song in Armstrong (1963)) and is a kind of chorus. As well as the cardueline finches, one can hear a similar massed song from Fieldfare and Redwing in the spring.

MIMICRY

Birds have long been admired for their powers of mimicry, as is reflected in the phrase to repeat something 'parrot-fashion'. We find their voicing of familiar or deprecatory phrases amusing and wonder at the accuracy of detail. As Armstrong (1963) points out, mimicry is part of the process of learning and, as already discussed, we know that young male songbirds develop their songs partly by copying other males of their species; but many birds' songs also involve sounds mimicking other species' notes, in fact almost any sound they hear, if they're capable of reproducing it.

I'm not aware of any examples of mimicry in the non-passerines other than parrots, so it may well be a symptom of vocal learning in the Oscines. Out of our songbirds, some are particularly drawn to using other birds' calls and occasionally song phrases in their own songs – Starling, Whinchat, Song Thrush, Sedge Warbler, Marsh Warbler and the shrikes spring to mind. But many other species include mimicry in their songs to a certain degree: Skylark, Robin, Redstart, Blackbird, Reed Warbler, Whitethroat, Blackcap, the crow family, particularly Jay, and some of the finches, particularly Siskin.

There have been several attempted explanations for this phenomenon. One suggestion has been that, by including the vocalisations of other species in your song, you are giving the impression that your territory is more densely populated than it actually is, and this will act as a deterrent to rivals who might be seeking to invade. But it's not convincing and not clear why a male of one species should be deterred by hearing the voices of other species that do not compete with it for resources. It seems that mimicry may simply be a consequence of vocal learning that offers an easy way of developing a more versatile and complex song.

Jays are a rather interesting case, since as well as including mimicry in their subsong, they also have a propensity for giving isolated calls (i.e. not in continuous song) of predators like Buzzard and Tawny Owl. I do wonder if there is some rather different functional significance to this, such as flushing out small passerines, with the call acting as an invitation to mob; or possibly to confuse human intruders, since they've certainly confused me on numerous occasions. But it may just be a simple display of their vocal prowess or cleverness.

DIALECTS AND VARIATION

Variation is the spice of bird song and it occurs on many intermediate levels between the extremes of species and individuals with their repertoires. The middle ground is a fascinating, complex and disputed area that continues to provide a focus for research, for both its functional and taxonomic implications, where the search for patterns has often resulted in the use of the catch-all term dialect.

Variation over time must happen since evolution occurs and we appreciate the result in the diversity of vocalisations we hear in different species today. Studying it is not easy, since audio recording (to provide objective data for comparison) has been around for a relatively short period. Geographic variation, on the other hand, is easy to observe (or rather hear): go to Spain and you'll find the Blackbirds give a markedly different call at dusk than those in England. Around a disused quarry near the coast, about 16 kilometres (10 miles) from my home, some of the Blackbirds in 2005 had an odd distinctive phrase they added to alarm calls that I have never heard from birds nearer home. Variation in Chaffinch 'rain calls' has long been recognised, but the question is really what is the significance, if any. These are examples of calls but, as discussed earlier, there are patterns of sharing and divergence in song types that arise through learning from neighbours and much of the research has focused on song.

Nevertheless, the case of the Chaffinch 'rain call' is an interesting one. This is a call used by males in the breeding season, often given for long periods, and shows wide variation from area to area. Some birds call with a clear, rising 'weet', some with a more wheezy 'wee', some with a churring 'chree' (all these heard in Northumberland); on Lesvos most birds gave a descending 'tyoo' and last year in Northumberland I recorded a descending phrase 'wee-te-tu', occasionally just 'wee-te'. Learning is involved in the development of an individual's version of this call, and research cited in Catchpole and Slater (1995) found that all the birds of an area tended to call similarly, whereas a few kilometres off it could be different. However, if one went further afield the same forms of the call could be found again, so the distribution of the call is like a mosaic and any one form is unlikely to be unique to any one area. It may be that the form on Lesvos is more distinctive because this is an island population but, since it is close to mainland Turkey, without further research it's difficult to draw any firm conclusions.

In the case of song, there has been much research into patterns of shared song types; as a result of learning from neighbours, it's quite common to hear a similarity between some of the songs in any one area from a range of species, and one might expect this to be more marked in species with a small repertoire of stereotyped songs. But the research shows this to be an oversimplification, and the extent and patterns of sharing vary greatly. The two extremes are where neighbours tend to share the full repertoire (rare, but for example Corn Bunting) and where neighbours seem to avoid sharing (for example European Blackbird).

Most species in which there is sharing between neighbours tend to share just one or two song types from their repertoires and this allows for matched counter-singing.

The best examples of what might be called local dialect are provided by a few species that show sharp dialect boundaries on a microgeographic scale, notably Corn Bunting, Nuttall's White-crowned Sparrow *Zonotrichia leucophrys nuttalli*, found in coastal California, and to some extent European Redwing. In these species groups of males (typically 30–100 for Corn Bunting) have been found to share the same repertoires of two to three song types, where a neighbouring group will share a different repertoire; the boundaries between groups have been found to persist over a period of years. The function of such sharply defined local song dialects appears neither simple nor uniform; McGregor et al. (1988) found that dispersal across dialect boundaries is common. Furthermore, male offspring did not tend to sing songs of the same dialect group as their fathers, and female offspring did not tend to mate with males of the same dialect group as their fathers.

This is a kind of socially active dialect system; but the term is also used of geographical variation on a larger scale (macrogeographic), where there may be no sharp boundaries between song types and regional divergence has grown over time. In the case of Chaffinches, Catchpole and Slater (1995) comment that 'there is no single feature that all males in an area share, which is distinct from those in other areas'. It seems that over time it's normal for geographical variation to occur through compounded errors in song learning.

What of the well-known case of the Great Spotted Woodpecker-like 'kit' syllable found at the end of some Chaffinch song types in continental Europe? Whereas it appears to be limited to birds of that region and has only once been recorded in Britain (presumably from a continental migrant), Catchpole and Slater comment that since it's not heard from all birds of the area, it should not strictly be considered a dialect feature.

THE DAWN CHORUS

Set your alarm clock for 4am (BST) in Britain during the first week in May and step outside (after an invigorating hot drink, of course). It may not yet be light enough to see clearly, but you will be amazed at the sheer volume and complexity of bird song all around, particularly in gardens and around villages, which approximate to the woodland edge ecotone. The dawn chorus is now widely recognised as a thrilling natural phenomenon and the term has become a byword for bird song. It is particularly spectacular in the temperate latitudes in spring, where breeding has a pronounced seasonal bias; in the tropics, where the seasonal climatic oscillation is more even, breeding rhythms can be less focused on spring and sunrise is rather sudden. Closer to the polar regions, breeding is rather later and, with lighter nights, dawn becomes less definable, with far more spread; many bird species sing at night in these areas. Where so much of nature seems at its most spectacular in exotic tropical locations, this is a phenomenon to be witnessed on our doorsteps. But why dawn? And in what sense is it a chorus?

The impression that many species sing most intensely in the early morning has been confirmed in various studies, such as Clive Catchpole's work with Sedge and Reed Warblers; he found that song output was highest in the early morning, gradually declined to midday, then picked up again somewhat towards dusk. Other studies, particularly by Kacelnik and Krebs with Great Tit, have led to the idea that there are three ways in which dawn singing might be advantageous: sound transmission, feeding conditions and territorial acquisition (Catchpole and Slater, 1995).

Wind turbulence has a distorting effect on sound and sound travels further in cold air than in warm air. So the calm, cool conditions that generally prevail at dawn, and through the early morning, help a sound signal to cover a greater distance more clearly; evidently this is a good period to get the message across, if broadcasting a complex sound signal.

Low light could make it difficult to find food by sight; and the cool conditions will inhibit activity in cold-blooded prey, including insects and other invertebrates. So it's likely that early-morning foraging will be less rewarding than later in the day. It's also been pointed out that birds will normally have some surplus in the energy reserves they've stored to get them through an unpredictable night. Cuthill and Macdonald found that supplementing the food supply of paired male Blackbirds resulted in them singing earlier, longer and at a higher rate the following dawn (reported in Catchpole and Slater, 1995). This is further evidence that dawn singing is cost-effective.

The early morning will also present the first opportunity for taking over any territory that has become vacant, through overnight mortality or other reasons. It's also been pointed out that, in the case of nocturnal migrants, dawn is the first opportunity for attracting any newly-arrived females. There is evidence that for some species mate-guarding with song plays a role, since females are at their most fertile at dawn.

There do seem to be territorial advantages to staking an early claim – as they say, the early bird gets the worm. In a study of Wrens (Amrhein & Erne, 2006), the playback of song to simulate an intruding male was found to have a pronounced influence on the dawn songs of the neighbouring territorial males even on the day after playback: they significantly increased their song output before sunrise, implying that dawn singing is particularly important in territorial defence.

All these factors contribute to making dawn and the early morning a good time for singing. On the other hand, if everyone is singing, there is a danger that you will not be heard and will be drowned out by the general clamour. There are various ways in which the patterns of singing have evolved to help deal with this, which contribute to the impression we get of a chorus, rather than just synchronous sound.

Firstly, not all species sing at the same time, there is something of a movement as different species join in and drop out. In our garden-woodland habitat, it's generally appreciated that the first wave includes Robin, Blackbird and Song Thrush – what I think of as the turdine chorus. After a while other species gradually join and soon the output of the turdines becomes less dense; with Wrens, Blue Tits and Treecreepers involved there's a sibilant trilling phase, and at around this time, maybe half to three-quarters of an hour after the first song, the chorus is at its densest and, in a well-populated habitat, really does approach cacophony – quite a phenomenon to experience and a challenge to pick out individuals, but not necessarily the best time to appreciate bird song.

With all this competition for the available acoustic space, we can imagine some of the possible acoustic factors that may have influenced the evolution of the various patterning of different species' songs. With limited acoustic bandwidth, to a certain extent there has been selective pressure in any particular ecological community for different species' songs to work together symphonically. Much of this is speculation on my part, but Catchpole and Slater (1995) point out: 'There is now some evidence to suggest that the singing behaviour of males is affected not only by the songs of conspecific neighbours but also by the songs of other species with whom they share their habitat'.

One way of avoiding the masking effect of other species' songs would be through using different frequency bands: and there is a certain amount of frequency-range separation in reality between species' songs, but with so many songbird species' voices (even in the same community) occupying more or less the same rather restricted bandwidth (2–8 kHz), there is a great deal of overlapping.

What contributes far more to the chorusing effect is timing separation and particularly the pattern of singing in verses with intervening space. Within species a certain amount of counter-singing occurs where neighbouring males alternate their songs (though in some species, such as Nightingale, certain individuals have been found to deliberately overlay their neighbour's song). Such counter-singing gives the impression of a theme being repeated, with more or less variation, into the distance, though it has to be said that some species (for example Blackbird) frequently sing at such a high rate at dawn, with such short intervals between verses, that the effect is smeared.

There is also a certain amount of time-sharing going on between species, presumably to avoid being drowned out. It was noticeable in the recording work for Marcus Coates' Dawn Chorus project (see page 55) that this was happening with a Robin singing near a Blackbird. It appeared that the Robin was fitting its verses around those of the Blackbird (i.e. the Blackbird was leading); with the Blackbird verse ending in high-pitched twittering and the Robin song beginning with roughly similar pitch and phrasing, it was very difficult to hear where the Blackbird song ended and the Robin began. Multiply this across all the individuals of various species singing in our arena and it became a real problem to get clear separation of individual singers, even with 14 microphones spaced around the area.

These various factors all contribute to the impression of themes flowing in continuity, intertwining and repeating with variation and counterpoint – very much a symphonic chorus rather than a randomly synchronous mass of unrelated patterns. The way that it all fits together so well, and the blend manages to sound musical, is something that interests me greatly and I think makes the use of the term chorus appropriate. But this should not be taken to imply that the birds are intentionally joining together in harmony; there's no evidence to suggest that each individual performance is motivated by anything other than self-interest, getting his message across within the whole.

CULTURAL CONNECTIONS

Until the 20th century and the proliferation of bird books, I think there can be little doubt that the bird most celebrated in literature was the object of so much attention not because of its looks, but because of its voice and its singing habits. The Nightingale acquired iconic status that still makes waves today – the history of our fascination with the Nightingale, its role in literature and music, is the subject of a comprehensively researched and fascinating book by Richard Mabey (1997), first published in 1993 as *Whistling in the Dark*.

It's not surprising to find the Romantic poets of the 19th century latching onto bird song performances, such as the Nightingale's, as a paragon of the beauty and passion they found in nature – theirs was a pastoral ideal as the Industrial Revolution began to shape a more urban world. Alongside the Romantic poetry run the more lyrical attempts of many classical composers to convey the songs of birds in their works, usually hinting at the particular sound patterns and delivering an overall impression of listening at the gates of Eden. It's only to be expected that bird song would reach the hearts of composers and musicians since all share the same medium of expression: as Percy Scholes says in *The Listener's History of Music*: 'There are two musical races in the world – the birds and the humans'. Bird song finds its way into our music and art in the 20th century no less than previous centuries; we'll explore these connections a little in this section.

I mentioned earlier the idea of birds' influence on human musical sensibilities in the quote from Lucretius. This general theme was expanded in a book by William Gardiner, published in 1849, entitled *The Music of Nature; or, an attempt to prove that what is passionate and pleasing in the art of singing, speaking, and performing upon musical instruments, is derived from sounds of The Animated World. Nature's Music* (subtitle: The Science of Birdsong) also happens to be the title of a book edited by Marler and Slakkeboorn, published in 2004, that reviews our knowledge of bird song through progress in the field of bioacoustics. I take this as a sign that the old false dichotomy of either listening to it as music or studying it as science can now be seen for what it is: the two perspectives are complementary, approaching the same subject from different objectives and, more importantly, one can inform the other.

BIRD SONG IMPRESSIONISTS

The quote from Lucretius talks of imitating bird song with the mouth, but it's not clear whether he means whistling or singing; in the context, it doesn't really matter. Although we can reproduce the songs of songbirds most accurately by whistling, the birds actually produce these sounds vocally. There are physical constraints on the frequencies they can produce determined by the size of the resonant volume in the syrinx, so the resultant tones from songbirds are at a pitch way above most people's vocal capabilities, but more or less within the range of our whistling.

I've no evidence of how far back the tradition goes, but certainly by the late Victorian era and into the 20th century, there was enough demand in variety halls to support a number of professional bird imitators, known as siffleurs (from the French for 'whistle'). Examples of this in other cultures are probably well known to ethnomusicologists: Tuvan musicians traditionally include bird imitations as well as all sorts of other sounds in their repertoires. Jeremy Mynott (2009) recounts a fascinating tale involving a famous siffleur, Maude Gould (performing under various stage names including Madame Saberon), who actually produced the sound from her throat through an 'inherited condition', rather than whistling with the lips as most did. Mynott's detective work suggests that it may have been her and not a Nightingale that accompanied Beatrice Harrison on her first broadcast by the BBC.

Possibly the most famous siffleur of recent times, and perhaps the last in the line, was Percy Edwards, who gained fame through the radio and regularly performed music hall with Max Miller. According to his obituary in the *Independent* (10 June 1996), his repertoire included 153 bird species. There's also a lovely sequence in Dennis Potter's *The Singing Detective* where the boy's father is entertaining in the back room of a pub with his whistled impressions of bird song. The packed audience is depicted as listening in a silence of rapt attention.

BIRD SONG AND MUSIC

Aside from questions of how much it has shaped our nascent musical aesthetic, we have seen something of the long history behind listening to the music in bird song, and drawing inspiration from it, in the examples of early composers using particular bird songs as themes in their work. Possibly the most popular classical piece associated with bird song, Vaughan Williams' *The Lark Ascending*, written in 1914, appears not to have been directly inspired by bird song at all, but was conceived while watching troop ships crossing the English Channel at the start of World War I, or so the story goes. The image of the lark ascending (in its song-flight), as expressed in the music, is one of nostalgia for the lost innocence of peace. Delius' *On Hearing the First Cuckoo in Spring*, written about the same time (1912), is more direct and uses Cuckoo song as an opening musical theme.

The French composer Olivier Messiaen (1908–1992) follows in the tradition of taking inspiration, and actually using motifs, from bird song, but takes the process far more seriously; he developed his own system for transcribing bird songs and would go on walks into the French countryside, noting down what he heard. Following a more oblique path into the landscapes where he hears the various styles, he discovers a deeper mystery in his response to these places (perhaps as a result of having spent time as a prisoner of war). His music is not easy listening and I struggle to hear the representations of bird songs that others hear; but I do hear the influence of the landscapes and the bird songs in the strange harmonic developments and individualistic use of sound in his compositions. The exploration of bird song in his music peaks with the *Catalogue d'Oiseaux* (Catalogue of Birds), with 13 pieces named after the birds they represent, and it's an odd collection, beginning with Alpine Chough and including Buzzard, neither of which are really singers.

Meanwhile, with the progress of audio technology during the 20th century, the use of concrete examples begins to creep in. Ottorino Respighi was probably the first, when he specified the use of a Nightingale recording in his piece *The Pines of Rome* (1924). Nevertheless it's not something that appears to have cropped up a great deal until later in the century, possibly with the development of better recording technology. The other notable example in classical music comes in 1972 with Finnish composer Einojuhani Rautavaara's concerto for birds and orchestra, *Cantus Arcticus*, which includes recordings of Curlew, Crane, Shore Lark (brought down two octaves) and Whooper Swan. It's interesting that both works use the bird song essentially as an evocation of place and mood.

The use of birdsong recordings has spread, rather prolifically, to other genres of music in recent decades. In 1968 the Beatles song *Blackbird* was produced, with a recording of a Blackbird featured; Paul McCartney has said that the song was inspired by the racial tension rising in America at the time. Pink Floyd used more ambient nature recordings, as well as featured birds (for example, Skylark, Bewick's Swan) on their albums *Ummagumma* and *Meddle*. In jazz, Mike and Kate Westbrook's *Chanson Irresponsable* takes as its starting point the song of the Sedge Warbler. A limited-edition series of CDs from Treader features several solo musicians improvising to bird recordings, such as (on saxophone) Evan Parker with *Birds*.

In the dance music of the late 1980s and 1990s the whinnying call of Great Northern Diver became a much copied motif, as well as synthesised 'bird song' phrases, which I believe was regarded as 'cooler' than using a recording of the real thing.

But for me the most interesting in this area was Kate Bush's double CD album *Aerial*, released in 2005. Not only does the album cover comprise a landscape derived from a waveform that looks remarkably like a bird song, the whole of the second CD, *A Sky of Honey*, uses bird song as a central theme in concept, in lyrics and in sound, both as ambience and in featured spots. This comes together on a short piece where Kate duets in unison (more or less – not at the same pitch) with a singing Blackbird (recording). It's a remarkable vocal performance that captures the vibrant nuances of Blackbird song beautifully and is the most intimate and successful marriage of bird song and human music I've come across, though I rather suspect that the timing of the Blackbird song has been modified slightly to give it a more human rhythm.

Scottish/Dutch composer (and a member of The Sound Approach) Magnus Robb's piece *Summoning Dawn* also features a female singer performing a bird song in literal imitation. In this case, though, it's based on a recording of a Siberian Rubythroat, slowed down and scored out.

Following on in the footsteps of Messiaen there has been quite a surge of interest in recent years from composers and musicologists keen to explore the musical syntax, thematic development and harmonic relationships revealed in bird song. Canadian-American composer Emily Doolittle is one such practitioner in the field of zoomusicology, a term first used by composer and musicologist François Bernard Mâche, himself a student of Messiaen, in his book *Music, Myth and Nature*. Emily's doctoral research was on the relationship between bird and other animal songs and human music. In a presentation to the 'Listening to Birds' symposium at Aberdeen University in 2009, she outlined common features and differences between birds' and human music. This showed much shared ground, but with a few important aspects restricted to our music; I look forward to reading more on this, when her work is published.

Also at the symposium was Stephen Preston, a flautist who has researched and specialised in the performance of early European music (Baroque to Romantic periods) using original instruments. More recently he has developed a musical system he calls ecosonics, deriving from his passion for bird song. In reaction to traditional Western music's 'more rational than physical inclination', he describes ecosonics as providing a medium for exciting improvisations and techniques based on unstable scales.

These are just a few of the many contemporary musicians finding something inspiring and relevant in bird song that feeds into their desire to take their music into new areas. The fascination with bird song is still growing, yet the source remains as enigmatic as ever. Ornithomusicology, zoomusicology and biomusicology are all trying to get a grasp on the musical aspects, as opposed to the functional systematics researched in science, but it is not easy.

BIRDS RESPONDING TO MUSIC

So far we have had examples of composers borrowing themes from birds, of more impressionistic attempts to convey the performances of birds, of musicians using recordings of bird song in their work and of musicians using the musical framework of bird song to take their own work into new areas; there are also instances of musicians playing live in an attempt to elicit interaction. Mostly we think about our own responses to the music of birds. What do we make of it? Is it music? But what do the birds make of our musical essays?

No doubt there are many unrecorded instances in the past, but the first ones that come to prominence, and possibly the most famous, are the cello recitals of Beatrice Harrison in her Sussex garden to the accompaniment of a Nightingale. These were broadcast by the BBC and proved incredibly popular and moving to listeners. There is no doubt that singing birds will interact with other sounds around them in terms of the timing of their songs, that they can be stimulated to sing by hearing other sounds and that many species will copy sounds they hear and even modify them, but I'd be wary of considering it musical interaction.

Recently, David Rothenberg has been pursuing a similar line improvising with birds in zoos and in the wild and relates some of his adventures in *Why Birds*

Sing; though again it's a very subjective matter as to the extent you consider the concerts a two-way musical interaction. I still think this is a valid area of genuinely experimental music and David is to be applauded for taking on the challenge; but the psychology of birds is very different from our own and I think this needs to be appreciated if one is aiming at musical interaction. Why would any particular species of bird be interested in singing with another musician of any species? And in what circumstances? On the whole it's not something they do.

I'll wind up this brief theme with a few teasing anecdotes. Firstly from W. R. Mitchell (1973):

> *George Logan [a forestry worker] tells me that it is possible to sooth a caper [Capercaillie] by music. He parked his vehicle during a mid-day break while working in a pinewood and, switching on the radio, listened to the strains of classical music. A cock caper approached, stopped and moved its head from side to side as though in appreciation of the music. The head movements stopped when George switched to another radio station and jazz (then a current craze) blared out through the wood. When a return was made to the radio station providing classical music, the caper advanced almost to the door of the car. (The effect of jazz on a roe doe was to make the animal advance to the car and stand with ripples of excitement running along its spine!)*

The second is from Keith Atkin, quoted in Jim Flegg's compilation of British Birds extracts (1981):

> *In March 1976, while attempting to photograph Red-legged Partridges* Alectoris rufa *from a car at Grainthorpe, Lincolnshire, I found that these birds were affected to a remarkable extent by music from the car radio. Although a close approach was frequently possible, most started to run away as soon as I switched off the car engine. When I then experimented by leaving the car radio on, so that the change in noise level was less noticeable, I was able to photograph several partridges feeding normally. To my surprise, however, some seemed attracted by the 'pop' records being played and, on two separate days, one particular individual approached closely and stood listening intently under the car window for about ten minutes. Others sang*

in accompaniment to the records, with a subdued, twittering warble. The rarer Partridges Perdix perdix *were less approachable and seemed completely unaffected by the music.*

Of course it's well known that dairy cows relax to classical music!

BIRD SONG AS PRODUCT

Bird song has recently been used in more functional ways to provide a service. Snatches of bird song, as well as other sounds from the animal world, have proven quite popular as ring-tones on mobile phones. There's something quite ironic in this, since some species (such as Starling and Blackbird) have been found to mimic electronic ring-tones; it goes full circle. More ambient bird song has been used as piped music in airport washrooms, Metro stations and elsewhere for its relaxation and stress-relief benefits – presumably not the clarion outbursts of Song Thrush which might function better as an alarm clock.

DAWN CHORUS WALKS

In recent years the phenomenon of the dawn chorus has even been hijacked as an official cultural event. Of course rising on a May dawn to experience the ambience is nothing new. But the modern version seems to need the input of human cultural significance. People gather together, at an advertised point in space and time, to go on a dawn chorus walk, in a gang accompanied by an expert guide (like me!). And the first Sunday in May for some years now has been International Dawn Chorus Day; the cynic in me feels this is more about PR for the conservation organisations that promote it, than creating a deeper appreciation of bird song, but hey, it's all in a good cause. Unfortunately the majority of the walks begin after 5am, so it's not actually the dawn chorus the participants are listening to; in Britain at any rate that initial surge of sound is about past its peak by 5am, but nevertheless it's a very pleasant time to go out and listen to bird song. The significance of the first Sunday in May is that the next day is a Bank Holiday, so you can have a lie-in to make up for the previous morning.

In Finland they do things differently: they have a songbird serenade late in the evening to hear the night singers, and it tends to be a little later in the year. It's rather nice listening to birds into the darkness, where sound becomes intensified in our minds. But then Finland has some great night-time singers – Thrush Nightingale, Marsh Warbler and Blyth's Reed Warbler in the south (where I got quite a surprise at the Siikalahti nature reserve car park filling up at 11pm).

BIRD SONG AND ART

Aside from the world of music, bird song has also attracted the attention of contemporary art. If I remember rightly, what did they play at the opening of Tate Modern but bird song. I get the feeling modern art doesn't know quite what to make of it, at least in terms of critical theory, and I'm sure that's why many artists find it attractive.

Marcus Coates is an artist whose practice explores the inherent ambivalence in our status as human animals, and he has produced a number of works that translate bird song into a human context, notably the video installation *Dawn Chorus*, on which we worked together. For this we spent two weeks recording an actual dawn chorus with a 14-microphone array to try to get the individual parts recorded separately but synchronously. From this we took the individual parts of a suitable section and slowed them down to bring them into the range of the human voice and trained selected singers to perform the score. Marcus filmed the singers performing in their particular habitats (a dentist in his surgery, a taxi driver in an underground car park, etc.), then sped the film up so that the sound was again back to the speed and pitch of the birds' songs. For the installation, the various singers had their individual screens placed roughly as the birds' song-posts had been during the original recording, resulting in a human performance of an actual dawn chorus.

The songs were so clearly identifiable that quite a few visitors did not grasp that the sound was produced by the human singers. But the visual effect is even more striking; human movements become 'ornithomorphic'. The fact that the singers are in their normal daily settings adds to the unsettling effect. If this account makes it sound rather dry, the feedback from staff at the Baltic Centre for Contemporary Arts, Gateshead, where the show opened, was that they had never seen so many smiling faces come out of one of their exhibitions. Marcus treads a fine line between the serious and the frivolous; in fact his work usually manages to be both at the same time.

I've also worked with another visual artist, Harriet McDougall, on projects involving bird song. She began by producing site-specific works using sonograms generated from birds recorded in the Eden valley in Fife. On another project she produced some abstract pieces, again site-specific, based on graphs charting the singing rhythms of different bird species during a 24-hour period in June round a meadow in Cambridge.

IS IT MUSIC?

As we've seen in the section on the historical context and this section on cultural connections, all through the ages bird song has been heard as music and has been discussed in musical terms. Bioacoustic researchers have traditionally avoided musical terminology, as being too much in the realm of the subjective and more importantly because musical parameters are not easily measured. Nevertheless, I think many of the scientists currently working in this field would agree that bird song shares much ground with our human music, in the arrangement of sound patterns, its performance and social functioning.

But still the question of whether it is music continues to nag away. From the world of sound art, critic David Toop quotes a lecture by soundscape composer Michael Rüsenberg:

> *This is the voice of my favourite music philosopher, Peter Kivvy (from Music Alone, Ithaca 1990). "However much bird 'songs' may sound like music, they cannot be music – unless, of course, we ascribe to birds a mental life comparable to our own, which few of us will want to do."*

And yet, what is staring-in-the-face remarkable is that so many musical figures are shared between our music, in a traditional sense (i.e. not including what might more accurately be described as sound art), and bird song. For instance, consider how many bird songs and calls use note intervals that strike us as melodic, particularly the major and minor third and the slides between (blue notes). Cuckoo, Great Tit's 'teacher', a common Blackbird phrase, even the pitch change of a churring Nightjar all approximate to that third. Instead of pondering why bird song sounds musical to us, let's accept for a moment the hypothesis that our human musical aesthetic has been heavily influenced by our long evolution listening to birds (and remember that our closest animal relatives show little in the way of vocal elaboration): then the reason becomes clear, but we have to accept that birds beat us to it!

I don't really want to get bogged down by the question – I think it's enough that many people, including musicians, find bird song musical. Now, in the 21st century, our understanding of bird song has come a long way, as well as our concepts and practices in music. There is a sense of metaphor in calling the sighing of the wind or a babbling stream musical: the experience of the listener may be akin to musical, but I doubt many would propose that there was any intention on the part of the 'musician' to produce the sound. It's accidental. The sound communications of animals are a different matter, reaching their most challenging in the songs of the passerine birds.

Kant's old question crops up here: What if we found that bird song was produced by a machine? Would it affect our enjoyment? Yes and no. Like all music, and art, knowing something of the background to a piece enhances one's appreciation. If they were produced by a machine (and surely someone must have programmed it, or are we to assume it's a happy accident like the sound of running water), some of the more elaborate bird songs would still be arresting sequences of sound and even simpler calling phrases would strike us as beautiful sounds. But the sound patterns are produced intentionally, by a living creature.

Knowing the identity behind the performance, understanding something of the significance in the vocalisations (through the scientific research), the fact that we are hearing a creature perform something that is the current expression of an ancient tradition – all these add greatly to the appeal of the sound and our hearing it as a 'musical' communication. It's interesting to note that so many of the most dedicated bird-song recordists are musicians.

Whether it is music or not depends on how you define music and that seems to differ according to your conception of man's place in the animal world. I await Emily Doolittle's analysis through her studies in zoomusicology to clarify the issue. I'll leave you with a quote from Olivier Messiaen: 'I doubt that one can find in any human music, however inspired, melodies and rhythms that have the sovereign freedom of bird song.' I think you can, but … another time.

THIS GUIDE

FIELDWORK

Like most wildlife sound recordists, I'm an opportunist and I've made a lot of recordings wandering discreetly in good habitat with a parabolic reflector at the ready. When you hear something of interest, you record it. If it's something of value, you record it straightaway, even if it's distant; then you try to work closer, stopping every now and then to record another, closer and clearer sequence. This works reasonably well for most of the passerines, but for warier species you end up with mostly rather distant recordings. And even with the songbirds there is a certain point at which the bird may tolerate your presence enough to sing, but is a little uncomfortable and maybe sings more hesitantly, with longer intervals, or drops the endings. In my early days trying to get a good reflector recording of Chaffinch song, I was constantly frustrated by birds not quite delivering complete songs, typically petering out without a 'terminal flourish'; and I figured this had to be down to the bird's concern at the strange lurking behaviour of the human with odd contraption nearby.

As well as fieldcraft concerns about recording natural behaviour, unaffected by one's presence, and the drawbacks of humping around a cumbersome satellite dish, there are some sound issues intrinsic to reflector recordings. It's called a reflector because it reflects sound waves, and the curvature (a parabolic curve) is designed to bounce the sound waves travelling straight into the concave face of the reflector, inwards to a focal point, which is where the microphone capsule is placed. Sound waves coming from other directions bounce off elsewhere; because it is gathering the on-axis sound energy into one point, the reflector acts as an acoustical amplifier, boosting the loudness of the on-axis sound relative to surrounding sounds. This boost, in a sense also narrowing the directionality of the microphone pick-up, works well for the separation of an individual subject from a general ambience – useful in densely populated habitats like woodland or wetland. It's the same principle as cupping a hand over the ear: sound from in front is collected and sound from the rear rejected.

The problem is it doesn't act evenly across the frequency spectrum. One ends up with a large boost in the upper mid frequencies, tailing off into the higher frequencies and dropping out altogether in the lower mid (the exact point being determined by the width of the reflector). Most of the harmonic content in bird sounds is in the frequency range of the boost, so this performs well in bringing the detail 'closer'; it also covers most of the energy range in the songs of songbirds. Obviously, without a ridiculously large dish, a reflector is not going to be much good for recording the hoots of larger owls, the full range in the voice of geese, larger gulls and others. But I've also noticed that it makes the songs of most songbirds slightly jarring on the ears; that peak in the boost is in the frequency area where our ears are most sensitive and it gives the birds' songs an unnatural harshness. I have a love-hate relationship with the reflector: I'm grateful for the quick and ready results, but they're a bit cheap, lacking in nutrition and the aural vitamins of reality.

I much prefer to work with stereo microphones, set up on a tripod (not in a reflector) at the end of a long cable (anything from 20m to 150m) running back to the recordist operating the recorder. The microphone set-up I use has roughly a 270-degree pick-up, so even where I have the microphones placed close to an individual bird, they still pick up the surrounding ambience. This produces a much more natural-sounding recording and I like having the ambience to give context to the individual. But it also means that all the surrounding sounds get recorded, whether that be the rest of the bird community, farm animals, traffic noise or whatever. So the choice of location and exact positioning of the microphones become crucial factors in making a good recording. This is essentially the same method as Ludwig Koch used many years ago, though not with stereo microphones.

Aside from recording ambiences and choruses, using the remote microphone technique to record individuals involves predicting where an individual is going to perform. Rarely can you walk up to the spot, place the microphones then back off without causing the bird to scarper. I spend a lot of time investigating sites, considering their ambient noise patterns, observing the behaviour of individual birds, pairs or community, and thinking about how I might get a worthwhile recording. I have regular sites that I work, some of which I have returned to repeatedly over the last 20 years. In fact I sometimes say I work sites more than subjects. In compiling the first two CDs of this guide, where I have tried to convey habitat communities, although they comprise sequences of recordings made at different times, many were made at the same site or in the same general locality.

Working with a long cable is quite laborious and time-consuming compared to the immediacy of wandering with a reflector or any other microphone and simply recording what you come across. But the rewards can be thrilling – when the action pans out just as you hope, as well as when the unexpected occurs. There's an intimacy to it. One great benefit is that generally the birds are unaware of your presence, so the behaviour and performances are uninhibited. Then there are the cases where the opposite happens: I'm lying in the heather, mics 50 metres (55 yards) away recording the displays of Arctic Skua, and a hunting Hen Harrier comes across me (CD 2:31). Or the mics are out in the field to catch Grey Partridge activity and a pair of Carrion Crows arrives – one soon suspects something is fishy (CD 1:36).

One drawback is that I often can't see clearly what's going on around the microphones; but then I'm not doing bioacoustic research on species and I actually enjoy trying to interpret the activity purely from the sound information.

THE AUDIO WITH THIS GUIDE

As you've probably gathered by now, in my approach to my work with bird song, from recording fieldwork right through to selecting passages for a guide like this, aesthetics is an important consideration. For me the sounds of birds are not merely indicators of species, but a source of great beauty. The subtle intonations of voice, the rhythms and cadences of phrasing, the ecstatic performances of individuals, the context of natural acoustics and the quasi-symphonic interplay delivered through the long-evolved genesis of the various specific patterns, all combine to make listening to bird song a singular musical experience. It's not enough to just pick a clean example of vocalisation for any species; I want something that encompasses an individual or group of a species at their best and conveys something of their particular magic. What that is, makes for some difficult choices and gives rise to some thorny dilemmas in a guide where there is only room for brief examples. Do I use a recording of a Blackcock lek taken close-up to convey the full richness of the chorusing, or at a little distance to deliver the feel of how their bubbling suffuses a soundscape?

Now consider selecting those recordings from my library. I'm not really a species collector: it's less a matter of adding new species to my recordings library (though that's always welcome) than covering a species' vocal range well, including examples of singing individuals that show the species at its best, as well as documentary recordings of the bird communities (habitats) at classic sites. For a guide like this, I have 1–2 minutes I can allot to the endless variety of Blackbird or Marsh Warbler, or the slow build of Greenshanks courting. I have hours of each of them in my library covering numerous individuals. How do you go about selecting a few short passages that convey the full glory of the vocal expression of one kind of bird within those constraints? So essentially what you are getting is headlines; or to use another metaphor, just the highlights from the full match.

In the first edition I tried to maintain the illusion of an ideal walk in a particular habitat: with this edition I've been less concerned with such an illusion. It would be an extraordinary thing for a full community of moorland birds to call or sing in sequence before the microphones over a 10-minute period! But by selecting recordings from the same or similar locations, I hope the feel of continuity in the context is maintained. For instance the Red Grouse sequence was recorded in February 2003 on Wooler Common; the Whinchat and Ring Ouzel by the Hawsen Burn, around 2 kilometres (1 mile) away, in May 1998 and April 2008 respectively, so the sequences are from the same community of birds broadly speaking, and certainly can be heard at the same time in that area.

The first two CDs, covering species in habitat groupings, are more focused on song and display, and I've used open stereo recordings as much as possible to keep it natural and contextual. On the third CD the emphasis is more on identification, including both songs and calls, and features a mix of both open stereo and mono reflector recordings. The third CD begins with the basics of learning to recognise bird sounds (for beginners), moves onto discriminating between similar-sounding species and winds up with a reference section on calls. While individual species recordings, clear of context where possible, work well for reference, I think the habitat approach, with more natural ambience, helps in honing listening skills and makes for a more enjoyable session when listening for longer periods, whether purely for pleasure or to build familiarity with the subject. It's good practice to try to pick out background species in the more ambient sections, since this is generally how we find birds in real life.

The habitat groupings should not be taken too literally. Within the range of habitats in which a species occurs, it's largely been a practical consideration that's determined where I've included it here. So you may find species cropping up in what appear to be 'wrong' habitats. For instance Cormorant appears in the riverside sequence: 'What,' you say, 'but this is a species of the coast, or maybe still waters, particularly southern gravel pits.' Nevertheless, the recording of the Cormorants was made on my local river, at a group of alders where there is a regular roost of five to ten birds all year round, very close to where the Kingfisher and the Common Sandpiper in the sequence were recorded.

Certainly there are species that are largely restricted to a single habitat: Ptarmigan, pelagics like the petrels and shearwaters, Bearded Tit and Bittern all spring to mind. But many species use a whole range of habitats; not just the obvious generalist scavengers like Carrion Crows, but Wren, for instance, can be found from gardens in the centre of London to nooks and crannies on the sea-cliffs of the Scottish Islands, taking in most habitats between, from hedgerow scrub, woodland, marshes, coastal dunes, river banks to lowland and upland heaths – anywhere there is a little cover.

It's a balancing act: I've tried to make this as much a guide to the music of birds as a guide to identifying species. Sometimes the two concerns pull in different directions, but for much of the time they are complementary. Putting a name to a species is part of recognising its unique characteristics, which contributes to one's enjoyment of that particular bird.

THE SPECIES ACCOUNT

For species I'm familiar with in local habitats or I've spent numerous sessions recording at different times of year, the textual coverage is strongly influenced by my own experience. When making recording trips further afield, I may have spent much time with several different individuals of a species, but often only for a limited period and at a particular season (usually spring!). In these circumstances it's rarely possible to make more than an informed guess at the status of a bird in terms of its pairing and breeding phase, its age or social context, nor its behaviour at other times of year. I've relied more heavily on other sources for such species (mostly BWP, 2004), even when they don't quite agree with the impression I've formed from experience – impressions can be wrong. For instance in the case of some of the Icterine Warblers I've recorded and listened to in Poland, often singing for much of the day, I formed the impression that they had mates; yet BWP comments 'song much reduced after pair-formation'. Nevertheless I've followed BWP here, since when it comes to bird sounds it can be all too easy to misinterpret behaviour.

One has to be a little wary in interpreting the voice sections of BWP. The editors have made great efforts to provide a comprehensive account and have collected material from many sources. But in collating the notes from different observers (listeners), they often make distinctions that aren't real: frequently vocalisations are treated as separate categories where the same sound has been heard and described in different ways, or maybe the particular voicing has varied.

In the end there is only so much you can say about a sound: you need to hear it. In the case of this guide, it's only an example, one particular instance from the seasonal flow and variety of individuals that occur in reality. But hearing a good recording can really focus the mind on a bird's voice and provide a mental blueprint. So I've tried to avoid too much sound description in the text.

Interpretation of behavioural context varies too between different observers. I'm rather wary of ascribing functional significance to calls without good evidence for that being the case when I make a recording. For instance the explosive 'chidou' call of Moorhen may be an alarm call, but I've rarely had evidence of this being the case when I've recorded it. And even if a call appears to be given in a certain context in a particular instance, it's still difficult to be sure that it is consistently given in that context. What's more, contexts overlap – the same call may be given in alarm and excitement.

Despite the quote from Ludwig Koch given earlier in which he's critical of the value of phonetic transcriptions of bird sounds, I think they are still necessary as descriptive labels. It's a rather thankless and frustrating task trying to be exact with such terms and largely unnecessary in a guide with audio examples. It's useful to be able to refer to the 'tak' or 'tchk' call of Blackcap to distinguish it from the 'sweer' call; and it does differ from the similar 'tsuk' call of Sedge Warbler. But I wouldn't place too much importance on the exact expression used: it's an approximation to act as a reference – listen to an example of the sound for closer scrutiny.

As I said earlier, I'm not a scientist. I don't expect to make any breakthroughs in our understanding of language, acoustic communication, ornithology or any of the other fields that this subject touches on. I continue to develop my understanding of how the vocal systems of birds work, though it's not always easy to match theory to observation in the field or the evidence of recordings. I suppose I see my own role as a facilitator of the enjoyment of bird song. But above all I do it because it fascinates me and provides a deep intimacy with the natural world that is its own reward.

IDENTIFICATION TIPS

Learning to recognise bird songs and calls and identify between different species doesn't happen overnight: it's a case of continued practice and building up experience. Nor is listening to recordings enough in itself, but it does help in learning what to listen for or conversely in checking something you've heard in the field. It can be a great help with distinctive sounds – once you've heard a recording of Quail or Nightjar song, there is a good chance you will know what it is if you do hear one out in the countryside. They are unique sound patterns, at least in our area. It's rather different when it comes to distinguishing between similar sounds, especially with brief, ephemeral calls and the complex songs of some of the songbirds, but recordings can help here, by providing a side-by-side comparison.

With songs it's generally a case of recognising the structure of the song. In the case of calls, there are a number of different parameters that may contribute to a confident identification, though many help with song also:

1. pitch of the voice – a low sound implies a larger bird; though the opposite is generally true also, and some larger birds have some rather high-pitched calls
2. tone or timbre of voice – is it thick and scratchy or pure and clear?
3. pitch inflection – does the call hold an even pitch, rise or fall in pitch?
4. rhythm – does the call tend to be given in rhythmic phrases?
5. tempo – in the case of song, note the speed of delivery
6. habitat – eliminate the unlikely for the particular habitat
7. season – likewise eliminate the unlikely for the season

I find phonetic renditions helpful for remembering the rough shape of a call. Syllables without vowels tend to be staccato calls, with a percussive, often harmonically complex, waveform. Vowels tend to be an indication of a definite pitch, with two vowels indicating a change in pitch: 'ui' suggesting a rising pitch change, 'eeoo' a descending one. A hyphen between the vowels would suggest there are almost two separate syllables or notes. A 'y' is often an indication of a sudden slide in pitch; thus 'whee-yoo' should refer to a disyllabic call holding a high pitch briefly, then with a quick slide a lower one, sustained briefly. So 'hooeet' (Willow Warbler) implies a steady, rather pure-toned note, possibly disyllabic, rising at the end; 'hweet' (Chiffchaff), a single ring syllable. I say the sound to myself to help fix it in my mind. The use of associative terms can be helpful: think how melodic phrases in music can have a particular air to them. Golden Plover calls are often described as plaintive. Robin song tends to sound bitter-sweet to me. Skylark calls tend to be chirpy and cheerful.

For species with less fixed patterns to their vocalisations, or with a wide range of call variations, it's a matter of building familiarity with the sound of their voice and a feel for the kind of rhythms and phrasing they use, rather than learning any particular phrases; although often there may be a few particular call types or classic song phrases that crop up consistently and serve well as mental references for the species. Remembering sounds is not easy for most of us, so whatever works best for you is the way to go.

With individual variation or awkward circumstances, it can be very difficult, if not impossible, to get a confident species identification from calls. Summer into autumn can be a difficult period, with half-formed calls of juveniles to confuse the issue. Likewise migrants can often crop up in unusual habitats – almost anything can appear on the coast in the autumn. Sometimes it can be quite easy to get the family or genus, but difficult to fix the species, for example terns, gulls, grey geese, pipit calls or finch calls. But this is still useful information and makes for good progress on the learning curve.

TYPES OF SONG STRUCTURE

This is a kind of key, not categorically different kinds of song but useful structural distinctions.

NON-PASSERINES

1. Excited rhythmic repetitions:
   e.g. grebes, Fulmar, terns
2. A simple formal call, sometimes repeated:
   Black-throated Diver, Bittern, many duck species, owl species, woodpeckers
3. A motif that's looped:
   many wader species, Cuckoo, pigeons and doves

PASSERINES

1. A simple motif that is looped:
   Great Tit, Chiffchaff, Nuthatch
2. A formal pattern of distinct phrases, repeated at intervals (stereotyped):
   Chaffinch, Yellowhammer, Wren
3. Verses of a set form, but varied in sequence:
   Robin, Blackbird, Willow Warbler, Redstart
4. Continuous warbling, no obvious structure:
   Skylark, Swallow, Sedge Warbler

Late winter through to early spring is a good time to start with song because there are relatively few species singing. By May it's bedlam, at least in the early morning. Start by building confidence with the familiar, practising on the birds that sing in your garden or on a regular walk; then gradually extend to the songs you think you can recognise, but cannot put a name to. Some of the common garden bird songs are quite difficult ones to get the hang of, and conversely there are many rarer species that are much more distinctive. When you can recognise Robin song with confidence, that's a significant achievement.

NOTES

Audio refers to tracks on the CDs: e.g. (2:15) indicates track 15 on CD 2, which will take you to the point in the moorland sequence where you will hear Short-eared Owl. There may be some other sounds, often more song or calls from the bird on the previous track; the voice-over will point out the relevant sound at some stage during the track.

The bar charts against some entries indicate the song period for that species, with darker colouring for more frequent singing. This is mainly relevant to the passerine songbirds, but I have included a few for some of the non-passerines, where it may be of interest. There is no chart where it's less relevant or in cases where I haven't been able to find information and my own experience is limited.

PART TWO
SPECIES ACCOUNTS

DIVERS – GAVIIDAE

Rarely heard during the winter months, which they generally spend at sea, divers become much more vocal on their breeding grounds in spring. Their vocabulary ranges from mewing wails to rather harsh croaks.

RED-THROATED DIVER

RED-THROATED LOON, GAVIA STELLATA

AUDIO: CD 2:33

J	F	M	A	M	J	J	A	S	O	N	D

Rather vocal during the breeding season, particularly when several birds are gathered or when other birds fly over a territorial pair. Family parties that have moved onto the sea in summer can be quite vocal at times, but are rarely heard during the winter.

The wailing call, like a loudly mewing cat, is given by both sexes, often together, as part of courtship and territorial displays, as well as singles calling for company; another diver flying over elicits these calls and apparently may also be stimulated by a predator flying over. Red-throat wails are single drawn-out notes, descending slightly in pitch. Pairs also indulge in duets of raucous cackling, which may accompany the wailing calls.

Red-throats frequently call in flight, at least during the breeding season, on their trips to and from the sea. Single terse hard croaks are given at intervals and occasionally the pace is quickened into a longer series in rapid-fire repetition with a few long moaning croaks.

BLACK-THROATED DIVER

BLACK-THROATED LOON, GAVIA ARCTICA
AUDIO: CD 2:24

This is a much less vocal species than Red-throated Diver, or at least much less prone to giving loud calls, though paired birds frequently give soft crooning calls to each other on breeding lochs. This may be because of the low density of breeding pairs in Britain, since pre-breeding gatherings in Scandinavia are said to be rather vocal.

Birds call more frequently when first arrived on breeding lochs, then again when young are hatched. Also birds are reported to call when other Black-throats enter their breeding territory or if a predator flies over. Otherwise for much of the time they are not often heard. I have spent long hours observing singles or pairs floating on the water without hearing anything (though pairs are often communicating with very soft crooning calls). Sound recordists have been known to resort to playback to stimulate the birds and get some recordings.

The male's equivalent of song is a yodelling wail, usually given in a short series, typically two. It can be distinguished from similar wails of Red-throat by the break in pitch (hence 'yodelling'). It is often accompanied by a splashing and a sharp yelping call (sometimes given separately).

Calls include a pulsed (almost trilled) croak, reminiscent of Raven, reported to be given as a warning and in territorial encounters (BWP, 2004). I've not heard any calls in flight.

GREAT NORTHERN DIVER

GREAT NORTHERN LOON, GAVIA IMMER

Wintering birds are almost always silent. Some birds linger into early summer in northern waters and even gatherings at this time are quiet. Roger Boughton reports that the only time he has heard louder calls (the manic laugh), from May birds in Colonsay, was when a gathering in the harbour in westerly gales was stimulated into calling by the warning beeps from the ferry ramp being lowered. Otherwise he has only heard soft grunts when two birds approach each other.
It has bred.

GREBES – PODICIPEDIDAE

Vocal behaviour shows some affinities with the divers: rather silent in winter and a tendency for pairs to indulge in excited duets (cf. Red-throated Diver). The braying calls fall between the divers' wails and croaking croons of families lower in the systematic list.

LITTLE GREBE

LITTLE GREBE, TACHYBAPTUS RUFICOLLIS
AUDIO: CD 2:60

Though rather vocal and fairly obvious during the breeding season, mainly through the advertising call, wintering birds are rarely heard to call.

Their advertising call is a loud tittering trill, often given as a loose duet between paired birds. Each burst usually lasts from around three to six seconds, quickly building to a crescendo and fading a little at the end; but excited birds, for instance when neighbouring pairs are displaying, may prolong this appreciably and one burst leads into another. The calls of female Cuckoos are rather similar sounding. More subdued variations are heard as breeding progresses. A brief, rapid titter of three to five syllables is given as a contact call, generally between paired birds. The usual alarm call is a monosyllabic, sharp, very terse squeak, high-pitched and with a slight metallic ring.

GREAT CRESTED GREBE

GREAT CRESTED GREBE, PODICEPS CRISTATUS
AUDIO: CD 2:57

Often described as vocal birds during the breeding season (e.g. Mullarney et al., 1999), isolated pairs may be less so, though display and calling (possibly rather subdued) might still be expected intermittently during the day in spring. They are not often heard in winter habitats.

Courting birds 'chak' at each other for lengthy periods and this accompanies the head-shaking display. Every now and then they will break out into groaning moans, though not necessarily that loud. I have heard a pair in the early spring break out into loud moans, after settling into their roost and again before leaving in the morning – slightly eerie, but ethereal on a calm night.

The main advertising call is a loud, rolling bray, usually given in a sequence of three or four; also used for longer-distance contact with mate. The most frequently heard calls are the sharp, staccato 'yak's, usually repeated in sequences of three or four and often in duet between a pair; voicing is variable from a softer 'hew-hew-hew' through to loud barking 'chak's.

RED-NECKED GREBE

RED-NECKED GREBE, PODICEPS GRISEGENA

Very vocal during the breeding season, though rarely heard in winter. Even single birds that linger into spring can be noisy and sometimes display to Great Crested Grebe.

The main advertising call is a loud wailing bray, like a donkey, high-pitched and more squealing than the similar throaty call of Great Crested.

Often a call sequence subsides in more subdued stuttering in a similar voice. Also gives rather raspy 'chak's and moans, not easily separated from Great Crested.

SLAVONIAN GREBE

HORNED GREBE, PODICEPS AURITUS

Not noted as vocal outside the breeding season. Display tends to be in the early morning, peaking an hour or two after dawn. Pairs spend lengthy periods wikkering to each other, building to crescendos of trilled squeals. Established pairs display excitedly with much water splashing and surface runs, when visited by neighbouring pairs and individuals.

Display on territory includes quite a range of sounds: repeated down-slurred calls, like sighs, which can be more or less trilled, through to sequences of a fast bubbling trill, vaguely reminiscent of Little Grebe; all of these are often produced as duets between paired birds or even as song matches against neighbours. There is also an extraordinary low, drawn-out croaking note.

Other calls include a thick 'tchik-tchik', maybe in irritation, sometimes a clearer 'wik-wik' (maybe different voicing of previous call) and a sharp 'wheeo'.

BLACK-NECKED GREBE

BLACK-NECKED GREBE, PODICEPS NIGRICOLLIS

Generally only heard at breeding sites when the pair, particularly the male, can be vocal with display calls. The usual display call is a wheezy 'wee-ta' repeated (from example in Roché & Chevereau, 2002). According to BWP, birds call mainly at night and are not heard often in daylight. Other calls include various soft 'peep's and a deep crooning sound.

TUBENOSES: FULMARS, SHEARWATERS & PETRELS – PROCELLARIIDAE AND HYDROBATIDAE

These are colonial breeders, and not considered vocal outside the breeding season. As with previous families, there is a tendency for paired birds to display with loose duets. Calls tend to be rhythmic crooning, churring and cackling.

MANX SHEARWATER

MANX SHEARWATER, PUFFINUS PUFFINUS

Apparently quiet at sea, birds become vocal when visiting their nesting sites in the dark. Calling is just occasional (BWP, 2004) when birds are gathering in rafts near colonies.

Display calls given in flight are a repeated rhythmic motif in a thick wheezy voice. Two to three coughing notes are followed by a drawn-out wheezing note, sometimes almost a squeal, as if on the intake of breath. Adults also call in their nesting burrows, often at a higher pitch in excitement, sometimes for long periods and occasionally during the day. Calling activity is much subdued on clearer nights with moonlight.

There are many stories of visitors spending the night on deserted islands and leaving the next day because of the demoniacal laughter heard during the night.

FULMAR

NORTHERN FULMAR, FULMARUS GLACIALIS
AUDIO: CD 2:83

Fulmar can be quite vocal on their breeding ledges, which can be occupied from early in the year; otherwise they are rarely heard. Paired birds usually perform a loose duet in display to other individuals or pairs and in greeting when one of the pair returns. A bout of calling builds to a crescendo of rhythmic cackling, interspersed with snorts, and gradually subsides, often to finish with soft, drawn-out crooning notes. Although usually silent in flight, they occasionally call with a soft, snorty 'cough'.

STORM PETREL

EUROPEAN STORM-PETREL, HYDROBATES PELAGICUS

Like Manx Shearwater, birds appear silent at sea but become vocal around their breeding colonies at night. The main display call is a rather high-pitched, squeaky purring, emerging into a brief wheezy gulp every 2 seconds or so, and repeated continuously. Birds also call in phrases with a thick scratchy voice, typically something like 'chikka-cher-chick'. A rapid 'wick-wick-wick' is also occasionally heard during aerial chases.

LEACH'S PETREL

LEACH'S STORM-PETREL, OCEANODROMA LEUCORHOA

Vocal behaviour is generally similar to Storm Petrel (and Manx Shearwater), though the voice is relatively purer, with a less coarse wheezing timbre. Display calls include a sustained purring note, rising to a brief soft yelp at intervals – on intake of breath (BWP, 2004); interspersed with this is a rather squeaky chattering phrase, something like the laugh of Woody Woodpecker, also given frequently in flight at colony. Recent research has been looking at sexual differences in certain phrases of the calls, to help with more accurate surveying for breeding females. The overall impression is very comic, with no offence intended to the seriousness of Leach's nuptials.

GANNETS AND CORMORANTS – SULIDAE AND PHALACROCORACIDAE

Colonial breeders, and generally quiet away from breeding sites and roosts. Voices tend to hoarse, guttural croaks.

GANNET

NORTHERN GANNET, MORUS BASSANUS

Like the tubenoses, Gannets are rarely heard away from breeding colonies, though occasionally they have been heard calling offshore. Colonies are bustling and raucous. Calls are in a gruff, throaty voice, with a rolled, guttural 'r', and usually repeated in a steady sequence. There appears little variation in the patterns of calling, but possibly courting birds may elaborate the rhythms.

CORMORANT

GREAT CORMORANT, PHALACROCORAX CARBO
AUDIO: CD 1:81

I don't think I've ever heard a Cormorant call away from a social gathering – either a breeding colony or a roosting site; so for much of their time they are silent and, to a large extent, solitary hunters. Birds arriving at our riverside roost usually call briefly when they arrive, claiming a perch, and sometimes others present a call asserting their position.

The call is a kind of gruff croak, in a fuller voice than Shag's hollow grunt, often sustained briefly into a rhythmic whinnying. At breeding colonies the whinnying croak is sometimes heard in chorus; displaying birds also give deep grunts, similar to Shag. Cormorants have deep, rich voices that we rarely have the chance to appreciate close up.

SHAG

EUROPEAN SHAG, PHALACROCORAX ARISTOTELIS
AUDIO: CD 2:86

Not a particularly vocal species, Shag are rarely heard away from breeding sites. Pairs call when courting, and nesting birds respond to intruders (human or neighbouring birds trying to pinch nest material) with a thrusting call; the calls don't carry very far, as they are mainly concerned with the birds' immediate proximity. Voicings are based on deep, hollow, guttural croaks and clicks. Displaying birds tend to repeat the croak and click over in a rhythmic series, 'hucca-hucca-hucca …'.

HERONS – ARDEIDAE

Quite a vocal species, especially at breeding colonies, though Bittern has a different breeding system. Heron calls encompass croaks (including Bittern flight call), shrieks and bill-clapping. The unusual booming calls of Bittern may have some parallel in the bubbling calls of egrets.

BITTERN

EURASIAN BITTERN, BOTAURUS STELLARIS

AUDIO: CD 2:39

J	F	M	A	M	J	J	A	S	O	N	D

Best known for the male's advertising call, or song, which is given regularly, if not prolifically, during the breeding season. Other calls are only heard very occasionally. Over a two-day period recording Bitterns at Leighton Moss in late May, their song-rate was highest between two and four in the morning, at around one series per minute.

Male Bitterns provide the bass in the bird song choir: their song is probably the lowest-pitched of all British species (aside from infrasonic components in Capercaillie song). The low-frequency signal works well in their dense reed-bed habitats. Each sequence begins with a series of soft gulps, as the bird inflates its resonant air sac, leading into a series of usually three to five evenly spaced booming notes (with softer notes of breath intake between). The shape of the note is distinctive to each male – listen to the difference between the two males in the recording.

Birds sometimes call in flight with a hoarse 'kwaa'. I've been told of an interesting phenomenon, where birds give gull-like calls; these calls only seem to be heard from birds soaring to gain height on a spring evening when they are leaving a wintering site, but there's no mention in BWP (2004). This may also be the phenomenon and vocalisations referred to in Willughby and Ray's bird guide of 1676, but here linked with autumn behaviour: 'in the autumn after sunset these birds are wont to soar aloft in the air with a spiral ascent, so high till they get quite out of sight, in the meantime making a singular kind of noise, nothing like to lowing.'

LITTLE EGRET

LITTLE EGRET. EGRETTA GARZETTA

Little Egret colonies can be quite noisy places, but otherwise birds are fairly quiet, occasionally calling if disturbed. Around colonies, and occasionally elsewhere during the spring, a throaty bubbling call is heard; this appears to be a display call (BWP, 2004, suggests the advertising call of male). They also give rather harsh shrieks and croaks, similar to but not as deep as Grey Heron, and this is usually the kind of call heard from a flushed bird.

GREY HERON

GREY HERON. ARDEA CINEREA
AUDIO: CD 2:58

Grey Herons usually give voice to their irritation when disturbed and put to flight; they are also prone to call when disputing fishing sites. Nesting colonies can be quite raucous, though much of the time at small colonies quiet prevails – until the young hatch, that is, then they chitter away almost incessantly.

The usual call when flushed is a rough short shriek, sometimes singly, but frequently in a decrescendo series of three or four. Calls in disputes over fishing sites are similar, but occasionally birds give long, drawn-out unearthly shrieks. Nervous alarm is expressed with monosyllabic short croaks, in a voice similar to Great Crested Grebe or a diver.

Shrieks, both long and short, are heard around the nest site, generally at the return of an adult, as well as deep throaty croaks, varying in force. Some calls are voiced with bill-snapping. The young call in rapid sequences of short calls 'chi-chi-chi …' rather thin and hissy or squeaky to begin, gradually becoming deeper and more throaty.

SWANS, GEESE AND DUCKS – ANATIDAE

Though Mute Swans are generally rather quiet, the other swans and geese tend to be highly vocal. The voice ranges from more tonal bugling calls, through yapping and gabbling to full raucous honks. Though their vocalisations may initially appear limited and the voices frequently rough, variations in delivery enable a versatile and expressive communication system. The equivalent in ducks is their quacking, croaking and growling calls (mainly females), but male ducks also have some very subtle and diverse display calls, with a tendency to tonally rather pure whistles and fine wheezes.

MUTE SWAN

MUTE SWAN, CYGNUS OLOR
AUDIO: CD 2:53

Mute Swans are more vocal than their name implies, though they do remain silent for much of the time. The heavy thrum of their wing-beats distinguishes them in flight from either of the other two swan species in our area. According to Cosima Wagner (Koch, 1955) it was the sharp rhythm of swans' wings that inspired Wagner to compose the *Ride of the Valkyries*.

The commonest call is a quite soft, but explosive, snort. When alarmed they yelp, but I think I have mostly heard this from immature birds. Young of the year maintain a lovely, soft, musical cheeping while following their parents.

BEWICK'S SWAN

TUNDRA SWAN, CYGNUS COLUMBIANUS

Vocally very similar to Whooper Swan, the voice is lightweight and generally higher-pitched, as one might expect from a smaller bird. Calling patterns are broadly similar to Whoopers, with louder trumpet calls (Bewick's more of a yelp), softer crooning and gabbling chatter. But overall the timbre is possibly purer, with less of the bugling edge that can sometimes sound harsh in Whooper's calls.

WHOOPER SWAN

WHOOPER SWAN, CYGNUS CYGNUS
AUDIO: CD 2:52

Whoopers are generally very vocal birds, pretty much throughout the year. Parties on spring and autumn migration usually call in flight, more occasionally mid-journey and more repeatedly around takeoff and landing. Family parties and flocks on the water or ground can be vocal much of the time, though when settled roosting or feeding, rather quieter. I expect pairs are intermittently vocal on breeding waters, but I don't have experience there. The voice is rather fuller and deeper than Bewick's Swan, though similar in many ways; calls can also sound rather similar to Canada Goose, sharing a rather 'musical' bugling timbre.

Louder calls are resonant 'honks' in a full trumpeting voice, with a variable hint of creaking. Birds calling repeatedly vary the pitch and voicing. Adult pairs display to each other vocally, almost in a duet during the 'Triumph Ceremony'; and BWP (2004) makes reference to Kirkman & Jourdain (1930) for the male's song, a 'musical series of 7 notes'.

A flock calling in flight is often a single 'hoop' from different birds, interspersed with individuals repeating more subdued notes. A pair in flight will often have one bird giving a double figure. In alarm, often a single rather more barking honk is repeated. Quieter, closer communication is often rather high-pitched, though varied in phrasing, but all in much the same voice, ranging from soft, rather pure 'hoop's to low chattering with much of the creaky timbre.

BEAN GOOSE

BEAN GOOSE, ANSER FABALIS (FABALIS)

The small wintering flocks in Britain are mainly *fabalis*, breeding in European taiga. There is no evidence of any discernible difference in voice between the two subspecies and they are treated together here. BWP (2004) suggests this is the least vocal of the grey geese and certainly there are not many recordings of their calls available; Scottish sound recordist Derek McGinn has worked on the flock near Falkirk and found them 'difficult'.

In voice they are somewhere between Greylag and Pinkfoot: possibly most similar to Pinkfoot in call patterns and voicing, there is a hint of Greylag's harsh nasal timbre, but not so coarse in Bean Goose. The calls also generally sound slightly deeper or fuller than Pinkfoot.

PINK-FOOTED GOOSE

PINK-FOOTED GOOSE, ANSER BRACHYRHYNCHUS
AUDIO: CD 2:78

Pink-footed are possibly the most vocal of all our grey geese, although that impression could be down to the fact that a large flock winters where I live, and large numbers pass through the wider area. As well as the general hubbub of a flock feeding and moving around, single birds and small groups on the move tend to call at intervals.

The two voicings of louder calls are pretty typical of the grey geese; a full-voiced honk and thinner, rather shrill 'wink', both calls often repeated as doubles. In sound Pink-feet are not as harsh and raucous as Greylags, nor quite as lightweight in voice as White-fronts.

WHITE-FRONTED GOOSE

GREATER WHITE-FRONTED GOOSE, ANSER ALBIFRONS
AUDIO: CD 2:79

White-fronted are vocally very similar to Pink-footed Goose, both in behaviour and sound. I'm not aware of any consistent vocal differences between the European White-fronts and Greenland birds. The calls tend to be of similar structure to Pink-foot, with perhaps a tendency to intersperse doubles with triples: 'ungh-ungh-ungh' and 'wing-wing-wing'. The voice is more lightweight, gentler or less harsh than either Pink-foot or Greylag, although this impression is something that varies with distance to the listener.

GREYLAG GOOSE

GREYLAG GOOSE, ANSER ANSER
AUDIO: CD 2:77

Probably the most familiar goose vocally in Britain, Greylag flocks can be very noisy when taking off or coming in to land, as also are pairs or even single birds joining up with a flock. Like the other grey geese, the loud calls can be roughly divided into full honks and squeakier 'wink's. Pitching and phrasing are variable, but Greylag's voice is harsh and rather coarse compared to the smaller grey geese and often has a whining tone or nasal timbre. The 'wink's can be really sharp and squealing.

CANADA GOOSE

CANADA GOOSE, BRANTA CANADENSIS
AUDIO: CD 2:59

Often a very vocal species, in voice Canada Goose is probably closer to Whooper Swan than any of the grey geese and at a distance calls might be confused between the two species. It has a similar musical trumpeting timbre, though generally rather lower-pitched, and if anything less harsh harmonically.

The full call opens with a deep reedy croon and breaks into an abrupt trumpet note at a higher pitch, with a smooth zipping transition, but birds often converse with just the crooning note, adding the ending as excitement rises; and sometimes birds repeat a short call, more akin to the trumpet ending, without the croon or upward inflection.

BARNACLE GOOSE

BARNACLE GOOSE, BRANTA LEUCOPSIS
AUDIO: CD 2:76

Flocks are generally very vocal, whether feeding or in flight, and the calls merge into a rippling mass of sound. Birds settled into feeding can be quieter, but often give lower-pitched calls that merge into a murmuring hum from the whole flock. In aggressive encounters calling is higher-pitched and squealing.

The basic voice of Barnacle Goose is a rather hoarse, squeaky yelp, quite high-pitched for such a large bird ('aow'). At a distance the hoarse timbre is not so noticeable and the sound is something like a yapping terrier.

BRENT GOOSE

BRANT GOOSE, BRANTA BERNICLA
AUDIO: CD 2:75

A flock of Brent Geese is rarely silent: feeding, roosting or in flight, individuals keep up a fairly constant stream of calls, maintaining the unity of the flock. The sound carries well and a feeding or marching flock may be audible at over 1 kilometre (two-thirds of a mile) on calm winter marshes.

Their voice is probably the most distinctive of the geese, with a marked throaty burr. Calls tend to fall into one of two groups: slightly longer calls in full voice are strong on the distinct rolled 'r'; shorter calls, often given casually in flight, are little more than a short grunt 'rrup'.

EGYPTIAN GOOSE

EGYPTIAN GOOSE, ALOPOCHEN AEGYPTIACUS

In voice somewhere between a grey goose and Shelduck in general sound. The main calls are a repeated rather coarse honking 'agh-agh-agh …', short syllables, and 'aarr-aarr-aarr…', with more drawn-out syllables from the female and a low, gruff call from the male, something between a Mallard drake and a Grey Heron. Alarm is a repeated, sharp, quacking 'eck'.

SHELDUCK

COMMON SHELDUCK, TADORNA TADORNA
AUDIO: CD 2:71

A rather vocal species, Shelduck calls show hints of both geese and ducks in their range and voicing. Birds are confrontational, and meetings between an established pair and others can be noisy affairs at any time of year, though flocks in autumn and winter are more sociable. Display is regular through winter and spring. Males' display calls are based around a whizzing whistle, repeated, rather thinner and sweeter than Wigeon: pitch rises and tempo increases with excitement, and is occasionally delivered as emphatic singles or a quick trill. The main call, also given in flight, is a rich, raspy 'arrk', rather goose-like, sometimes becoming slightly disyllabic in 'arrak'. In alarm and excitement (females in display) birds give a quickly repeated, chattering 'ack-ack-ack …', in a similar rich voice to the previous call.

MANDARIN DUCK

MANDARIN DUCK, AIX GALERICULATA

Generally very quiet birds, I've only heard very soft indistinct calls from females on the water. BWP (2004) suggests they only tend to be vocal during communal display and when disturbed. Roché & Chevereau (2002) give examples of male and female calls that include a rather thin, nasal, disyllabic quack, 'coo-eh' and brief, squeaking 'ook', but it's not clear which is which. I suspect the quack is the female and the whistled squeak the male.

TEAL

EURASIAN TEAL, ANAS CRECCA
AUDIO: CD 2:51

Although heard all year round, this vocal species goes rather quiet while nesting. Family parties gathering in the autumn can be vociferous and display is frequent on finer days through the winter and early spring. Birds often call when flushed. Teal drakes call with a high-pitched, almost bell-like bleep, sometimes referred to as a 'bleat'; single males calling formally repeat the note usually in series of three to six at regular intervals. Males in communal display repeat sequences of rather softer, breathier versions (sounding like whistled snorts), varying the pitch a little and almost becoming melodic; a good gathering gives off a chorus that could pass for pixie flute music.

The female's quack is similar to Mallard's, but higher-pitched and much thinner sounding; they call in the same sort of rhythms to Mallard including the decrescendo sequence, like raucous laughter. Females also give low scratchy calls, often in chittering rhythms.

WIGEON

EURASIAN WIGEON, ANAS PENELOPE
AUDIO: CD 2:70

This is one of the more vocal species of duck, and the males tend to be heard more than females, although this impression may be biased by the males having a more distinctive call. Winter flocks can sometimes be very active with display and, when disturbed, flight around calling. Scattered birds or a pair on a potential breeding site seem to call more occasionally.

The drake's full display call is a loud and distinctive wheezy whistle, 'whee-yoo', rising in pitch through the 'whee' and subsiding on the 'yoo', and normally preceded by a softer introductory wheezing syllable, the latter less audible at any distance: so the full phrase is 'wup whee-yoo'. Excited birds are often heard repeating monosyllabic variations on a shorter version of the phrase. Females call with a rasping growl, often drawn-out and given in rhythmic phrasing in display.

GADWALL

GADWALL, ANAS STREPERA
AUDIO: CD 3:53

Not a particularly vocal species, birds call in aerial chases in the breeding season and sometimes when flushed. The male has a distinctive quack that sounds like a sharp, hard snort, sometimes accompanied by thin whistles in display. Female quacks are rather like a female Mallard, though rather thinner and higher-pitched.

MALLARD

MALLARD, ANAS PLATYRHYNCHOS
AUDIO: CD 2:64

Mallard, our commonest duck, are generally the most frequently heard; the female's call is the model type for a duck's 'quack'. Birds can be vocal throughout the year, though breeding females and pairs tend to be quiet. There does not appear to be much difference between the vocalisations of truly wild Mallards and those living a feral existence.

Drakes call in a low, almost croaking quack, with a liquid rippling quality; in display the quacks may be accompanied by a few thin whistles, but not often heard. Females' calls tend to be louder, full 'quack's, higher-pitched than the drake, and often given in a decrescendo series, sounding like a full-on laugh. Both sexes give shorter, stuttering sequences of their calls in closer interaction.

PINTAIL

NORTHERN PINTAIL, ANAS ACUTA
AUDIO: CD 3:54

Though in general not a particularly vocal species, on mild days in the early spring I've found gatherings to be quite vocal affairs. Gatherings might not be the right word, since my experience has been of small scattered groups spread out across the Lindisfarne mud flats; as the birds move around there tends to be calling from courting pairs, as well as display when pairs and singles meet up.

The drakes give a tonally pure short 'prüp', rather like a drake Teal, which carries well, and is usually enveloped by softer wheezing calls. Females have a coarse quack, which often opens out into a decrescendo series in display, somewhere between Mallard and Teal in pitch and tone, and similar to both in patterns of calling.

GARGANEY

GARGANEY, ANAS QUERQUEDULA
AUDIO: CD 3:53

Garganey can be quite vocal at the start of the breeding season, but I have no information or experience of their vocal behaviour outside that period. The drake's advertising call is an unusual dry crackle, delivered in short rhythmic phrases, like running a card briefly back and forth on a deep brittle comb. Females (and perhaps males too) call with a thin, high-pitched quack, rather like a female teal, most often heard in flighting courtship chases.

SHOVELER

NORTHERN SHOVELER, ANAS CLYPEATA
AUDIO: CD 3:54

Occasionally males can be quite vocal in late winter and into spring, and females with dependent young readily give alarm calls, but they are not generally considered very vocal (BWP, 2004).

The male's call is a short, rather percussive, wheezy 'phut', often given as a double. Softer variations, like 'huc', more or less wet or raspy, are also heard in domestic situations, either in more subdued calling or perhaps from younger birds.

The female's quack is similar to a female Mallard, but a bit rougher and more strained, and at a slightly higher pitch. The wing sound of drakes is quite distinctive, with a fast, hollow beat, especially at takeoff.

POCHARD

COMMON POCHARD, AYTHYA FERINA

A rather quiet species, but the male's call is one of the most beautiful of all the duck sounds. The male's full display call is a rather whizzy, drawn-out 'wee-ooo', with a gradual rise and fall; not a high-pitched whistle like a Wigeon, more like a cross between a clarinet and a kazoo in tone. Females have a raspy growl, typical of *Aythya* ducks.

TUFTED DUCK

TUFTED DUCK, AYTHYA FULIGULA
AUDIO: CD 2:65

Though not a particularly garrulous species, males can be heard giving their display calls at almost any time of year, probably most often in winter and spring.

Females call occasionally in group displays, but otherwise are mostly heard calling in flight, especially when flushed or coming in to land.

The drakes' calls are a soft, rapidly whinnying whistle, which you could imagine as a fairy's chuckling laugh, with a sound something like a squeaky toy. In display the female calls are drawn-out crooning quacks, giving a sense of yearning. The calls given in flight are a raspy growl, in common with other *Aythya* ducks.

EIDER

COMMON EIDER, SOMATERIA MOLLISSIMA
AUDIO: CD 2:81

Quite a vocal species in that they can be heard on occasions virtually all year round. Even while females are sitting on their nests a group of males on the sea may get into some communal display with calling.

The male's display call is a very distinctive full cooing 'aa-ooh', quite loud and audible up to perhaps half a kilometre (a third of a mile) in calm conditions. Voicing varies and birds sometimes give just the low half or the high half, but the full call starts low and slightly throaty and breaks into a high, tonally rather pure 'oo', with a languid fade. Lovely. Females call with low, staccato grunts, in a frothy voice, rising in pitch, loudness and rate of repetition with excitement and alarm ('ug-ug-ug-ack … ack … ack').

SCAUP

GREATER SCAUP. AYTHYA MARILA

Not often heard, the male is described in Mullarney et al. (1999) as mostly silent. The male's display call is a neat wheezing whistle, 'wu-poo', very similar to Pochard, but generally not so drawn-out. Females have a growling quack like other *Aythya* ducks, possibly a little lower and drier than the others.

LONG-TAILED DUCK

LONG-TAILED DUCK. CLANGULA HYEMALIS
AUDIO: CD 2:82

Although quiet for much of the time when busy feeding, birds can be very vocal at times, particularly when in a flock and as spring approaches. Display from a flock has famously been described as sounding like distant bagpipes (Witherby et al., 1938–1941).

Displaying males call with a yodelling phrase, typically something like 'ah ah aa-oo-eh', in a voice slightly reminiscent of Whooper Swan, though higher-pitched and of a more nasal intonation. Females and probably males give a rather Shelduck-like 'ack-ack-ack' call, as well as other low short calls in close contact and alarm.

COMMON SCOTER

COMMON SCOTER. MELANITTA NIGRA

Common Scoter are not heard often, but this may largely be due to the observer's distance from an offshore flock. It's difficult to say how often birds call, but communal display is reported from birds on the sea in calm conditions during the autumn and winter months and this presumably continues into the early spring, leading up to the birds' dispersal to breeding sites. BWP (2004) suggests this is more vocal than other scoter species and makes reference to the loud whirring of a male's wings on takeoff, 'likened to trilling of Alpine Swift *Apus melba*'.

Calls heard during display are piping bleeps, 'pyu, pyu…', rather like a Teal or Pintail, but with a fuller voice and generally repeated in sequence. Pitch and voicing are variable and sometimes the calls become disyllabic. Mullarney et al. (1999) describe this as a common call from migrating flocks on spring nights. Females are reported to have a growling quack, something like the *Aythya* ducks.

VELVET SCOTER

VELVET SCOTER, MELANITTA FUSCA

Described in BWP (2004) as much less vocal than Common Scoter, the calls of Velvet Scoter are not well known and there is doubt about whether some sounds are vocal or non-vocal wing sounds. BWP includes references to a confusing range of calls varying from croaking and growling to purring, piping and whistling, but all are described as brief and crude. Published recordings (Roché & Chevereau, 2002) include a rhythmic whinnying 'vraa-a-a-a', probably from the female, and a sharp, thick repeated quack, probably from the male, sounding very like the courtship calls of Great Crested Grebe.

GOLDENEYE

COMMON GOLDENEYE, BUCEPHALA CLANGULA
AUDIO: CD 2:55

Goldeneye have a distinctive whistling wing-beat; otherwise drakes tend to become vocal with their display calls and upright salute posture as winter approaches spring.

The drake's formal display call is an abrupt double ratchet, I suspect, accompanied by tossing a splash of water in the air. Display takes place on water and is also often accompanied by a low, drawn-out croaking, sounding a little like a fly reel.

Females, and possibly also males, call with a fast, raspy growl, almost a soft bark, usually given in flight and quickly repeated; it's very similar to the *Aythya* ducks, though a fraction lower-pitched and slightly less squeaky than Tufted Duck.

SMEW

SMEW, MERGELLUS ALBELLUS

I believe Smew are rarely heard in Britain and usually described as mostly silent (e.g. Mullarney et al., 1999). The drake's display call is a ratchety phrase, with a dry sound reminiscent of Garganey, but of a form similar to Ruddy Duck, the clicks accelerating to an abrupt double hiccough ending. Females are said to have a harsh rattling call and a low rapid 'wok' (BWP, 2004).

RED-BREASTED MERGANSER

RED-BREASTED MERGANSER, MERGUS SERRATOR
AUDIO: CD 2:92

Red-breasted Mergansers are rarely heard and voice plays little part in either their identification or their detection.

Nevertheless the drakes can often be observed displaying when small groups are gathered on the water in winter and through spring; this display involves a bobbing movement where they stretch their neck out and lower their head to water level. They open their bills wide and let out an odd soft, wheezy croak; but usually you need to listen very carefully to hear it. BWP (2004) refers to calling in more complex phrases, which I have never heard.

Occasionally birds call when flushed, or in other situations of alarm, with a cackling croak very similar to their close relative Goosander.

GOOSANDER

COMMON MERGANSER, MERGUS MERGANSER
AUDIO: CD 2:62

Goosanders are not heard very often: sometimes when flushed a bird calls a few times, but social gatherings can be quite vocal, though the calls are not particularly loud. Birds congregating at a roost in the winter months, usually a regular site, indulge in communal display at dusk, with the males giving their 'salute' pose and both males and females calling intermittently. I've also seen this occasionally during the day, notably at a site where there is a build-up in numbers in the late winter and small parties often work together in what appears to be a synchronised hunt. I've also watched females in breeding areas circling in flight and calling repeatedly, either prospecting for a nest site or nervous about coming in to an established one.

The males' display includes an odd, rather electronic-sounding, nasal croak or beep, usually given in sequences of two different see-saw motifs; the beeps are interspersed with soft grunts. Females respond to the males' advances and each other with short cackling sequences (similar to the calls when flushed) and little lunges on the water. There is much demonstrative wing-flapping in brief bursts; and birds coming in to the roost mark their arrival with a loud rush of air on their wings as they make a sharp descent to the water.

RUDDY DUCK

RUDDY DUCK, OXYURA JAMAICENSIS

A rather quiet species and certainly not heard much in Britain recently! The males do call regularly in display with an accelerating series of soft notes leading into a low croak, or so it sounds. BWP (2004) reports that this has been found to be a mechanical sound produced by beating the bill against the chest, though possibly there is a vocal component in the final note. Certainly there is a resemblance in timbre to the calls of male Garganey. Both sexes occasionally give other vocal calls, but rather nondescript.

RAPTORS – ACCIPITRIDAE, PANDIONIDAE AND FALCONIDAE

Not noted as particularly vocal families, with a few exceptions, nevertheless most species (not all) call readily in alarm when disturbed at the nest site. Display can be vocal, and paired birds often call in the vicinity of the nest with quieter calls. In many species, males bringing in prey to the nest call to the female, who then comes to take the food from them. Young birds can be vociferous, both in the nest and for a while after fledging. Voices are often thin and high-pitched for the size of bird. Calls tend to fall into three types: 1) drawn-out wailing, mewing, whistling or 'eeping'; 2) rapid repetitions of a syllable in yikkering or chattering; 3) short and sharp syllables, like the falcon clicks or some of the eagle and Osprey calls.

HONEY-BUZZARD

EUROPEAN HONEY-BUZZARD, PERNIS APIVORUS
AUDIO: CD 1:73

Honey-buzzards are generally quiet and rather secretive birds, only calling much in display in spring and later in alarm around the nest site.

Nevertheless the calls are fairly distinctive, thin, plaintive whistles with a pronounced rise and fall in the pitch; it's almost disyllabic, the first note rising, then breaking to a lower-pitched note 'whey-you'.

The voice is rather similar to a kite and could even be confused with a wader (Stone-curlew in my experience, which I had just been listening to and I thought the Honey-buzzard calls might be a juvenile Stone-curlew). Beware also of recently fledged Common Buzzards, whose hunger calls to their parents are rather similar, plaintive squeals.

RED KITE

RED KITE, MILVUS MILVUS
AUDIO: CD 1:51

Birds can be quite vocal at the start of the breeding season, otherwise more occasionally. In an area of high numbers, in the Chiltern Hills, there was much vocalisation in the early mornings around the end of March and into April and a certain amount in the evening.

Calls are based on a drawn-out whistle with a hint of sibilance: the main call rises and falls in pitch 'whee-you', and birds sometimes call with just this, but usually add a repeated syllable ending like 'whee-you, hi-hi-hi', but variable. Unusually for a raptor, the calls sound quite melodic to us and with the whinnying ending can suggest a miniature horse in the distance.

Black Kite *Milvus migrans* is vocally very similar to Red Kite, but calls have a faster modulation, producing a more pronounced high-pitched whinnying. Where the Red Kite whinnied ending has 2–3 syllable repetitions, Black Kite has a sustained modulation with around 6–12 repetitions.

WHITE-TAILED EAGLE

WHITE-TAILED EAGLE, HALIAEETUS ALBICILLA

Quite a vocal species compared to Golden Eagle, at least around the nest site and particularly so in the early part of the breeding season (BWP, 2004). The female's voice is lower-pitched and hoarser than the male's, especially apparent when calling in duet. There's a creaky timbre to the voice, when heard clearly, often a shrillness and more or less of a squealing element to softer voicings.

Display involves a sustained series of strident, short yelps, rather similar to the trumpeting calls of the larger gull species, but at a faster pace and harder in sound, and could even be compared to the yaffle of a Green Woodpecker. Alarm calls are rather similar to display calls, but sharper and less strident. Closer communication involves squealing chucks, rather similar to Golden Eagle.

MARSH HARRIER

WESTERN MARSH HARRIER, CIRCUS AERUGINOSUS

Marsh Harriers can be quite vocal around their breeding sites, but less so outside the breeding season. Even so, their calls are easily overlooked, being rather weak and inconsequential for such a large raptor. As with the other harrier species, single birds on potential breeding territory may display quite frequently, hoping to attract a mate (in all three species, the single birds I've observed in display have been males).

Displaying males rise to a fair height above a prospective nesting site, then descend in a series of shallow dives accompanied by sequences of a monosyllabic call (a brief, whining 'queoo'). In courtship a squealing whistle may be heard and the male uses a similar call when visiting a female at a nest. Birds are said to call in alarm at an intruder with a rapid kekking; the alarm call I have heard from a female near her nest was a thin, wheezy 'weep, weep'.

Juveniles in summer and autumn can be vocal with a very thin high-pitched squeal, quite far-carrying, though rather insignificant, sounding like a Reed Bunting or even a Coal Tit calling in the distance.

HEN HARRIER

NORTHERN HARRIER, CIRCUS CYANEUS
AUDIO: CD 2:31

Hen Harriers are rarely heard calling other than in display and in alarm at an intruder near the nest site. Display involves aerial 'sky-dances', where a prospective bird or a pair rise up sometimes beginning at a considerable height, but often at around 15–30 metres (50–100 feet), and cover the nesting moor in a series of twisting dives with much elaborate wing show. In my experience in the Borders, display tends to peak around mid-morning and mid-afternoon. There's also a brief exchange of calls between male and female on food delivery.

In display two different calls are heard: from both sexes a subdued chattering (i.e. not in a regular timing) yikker and a slightly sibilant squeal, descending in pitch at the end, repeated a few times, more associated with the female (BWP, 2004). The latter also serves as a food and soliciting call from the female. In alarm, birds give a call rather like the display yikker, but higher-pitched: 'chit-chit-chit'.

MONTAGU'S HARRIER

MONTAGU'S HARRIER, CIRCUS PYGARGUS

Rather similar to Hen Harrier in general and vocal behaviour, the species' voice may be more similar to Marsh Harrier. Though considered a less vocal species than Hen Harrier (BWP, 2004), birds can be quite vocal in display and in setting up breeding territory. I've come across quite vocal birds in Spain at the end of April and beginning of May.

The main call is a rather subdued, but audible up to *c.*300–400 metres (330–440 yards) in display, brief 'chew', with a distinct nasal twang, usually repeated. This is what I've heard from a 'sky-dancing' male. It may be given singly, but in display is usually given in a short series. Tonally it bears some similarity to the display calls of Marsh Harrier, though the voicing is different.

Both sexes apparently use a rather pure squeal, or whistle, in association with food, as well as from a soliciting female, though in the excitement of the food exchange there may be a few chatter-calls. In alarm, birds give a sustained chittering in a voice similar to the first call.

GOSHAWK

NORTHERN GOSHAWK, ACCIPITER GENTILIS
AUDIO: CD 2:02

Though rarely heard to call in casual sightings, Goshawks can be very vocal around their nest sites, particularly in the early mornings in spring. After fledging, juveniles are conspicuous in the surrounding area from their regular hunger calls.

The usual call given in alarm and excitement is a sharp kek, quite like a Jackdaw, given both in monosyllabic renditions and frequently rattled off in a lengthy rapid series, but fuller-sounding and more deliberate than a Sparrowhawk. These calls can easily be mistaken for Jackdaw or Green Woodpecker (particularly a juvenile Green Woodpecker). Females also have a drawn-out, wailing yelp when calling for food from the male (and possibly when soliciting copulation).

The hunger calls of the young are like the female's food call, but thinner-sounding, becoming a little more of a squeal, but still rather fuller than food calls from a juvenile Sparrowhawk or Common Buzzard.

SPARROWHAWK

EURASIAN SPARROWHAWK, ACCIPITER NISUS
AUDIO: CD 2:07

Sparrowhawk is rarely heard calling away from the vicinity of the nest site; dependent young can be quite vocal with their hunger calls, but they are still likely to be within the general vicinity of the nest.

The main call is a rapid kekking, rather strident in alarm at an intruder into the nest area, but rather quieter from a male returning with food. The female responds to the male's food call with a few thin squealing calls, and the hunger calls of the young are similar squeals, possibly even thinner and shriller.

BUZZARD

COMMON BUZZARD, BUTEO BUTEO
AUDIO: CD 1:65, 3:09

Buzzards are generally the most vocal of all the hawks and falcons and can be heard throughout the year, though they go rather quieter during the nesting period.

The main call is a hard, rather shrill mewing, trailing off towards the end, but with variable voicing. Sometimes it's rapidly modulated and then sounds rather similar to a kite call. I've also heard Buzzards occasionally give a repeated 'kek' call, not really distinct from similar calls of other hawks.

Care needs to be taken between July and October, when young Buzzards are out of the nest but still dependent on their parents; their hunger calls are something between a whistle and a squeal and can sound very similar to some of the calls of gulls, Honey-buzzard or even young Goshawks: note that there's usually a rather shrill sibilant element.

Rough-legged Buzzard *Buteo lagopus* is vocally very similar to Common Buzzard. It's been suggested that Rough-legged may be more whining or piercing in voice, and calls may have a more emphatic drop in pitch (Mullarney et al., 1999).

GOLDEN EAGLE

GOLDEN EAGLE, AQUILA CHRYSAETOS

Wild adult Golden Eagles are very rarely heard calling; this could be down to the fact that most encounters are at such a distance that they are unlikely to be heard, but it is also very likely that they are silent birds for much of the time, particularly away from nesting and roosting sites.

The young can be vocal prior to fledging and, once fledged, while they are dependent on their parents and remaining in the area of the nest site. The usual call, and the only one I've heard, is a yelping 'kiya', or heard more closely 'ss-yok'. Other calls have been reported from various observers, including a bubbling call. And some pairs have been described as rather vocal (Crane & Nellist, 1999).

OSPREY

OSPREY, PANDION HALIAETUS

Osprey can be quite vocal around the nest site, but only heard occasionally on passage. The voice is rather thin and high-pitched, described as 'feeble', yet quite sweet sounding.

The main calls include a brief, descending 'chew' ('piu' BWP, 2004), which is easily mistaken for a finch or a wader, and generally given in mild alarm or contact; full alarm (e.g. from female at nest) a short, repeated whistle 'tü-tü-tü …'; and in sky-dancing display or intense alarm (conspecific intruder near nest site) a drawn-out, squealing whistle 'pee-ao'.

KESTREL

COMMON KESTREL, FALCO TINNUNCULUS
AUDIO: CD 1:54

Kestrel can be quite vocal at times around the nest site and in family parties with recently fledged young in the summer. Otherwise they are heard only occasionally.

The most striking call is a brief yikkering phrase, quite rapid and shrill, 'ki-ki-ki …', given in alarm and excitement in courtship. This is the most commonly heard call away from the nest site (which may be because it's the loudest). A querulous, squealing call is given by both birds of a pair around the nest site, particularly in food exchanges, as well as by the female in aggressive displays and a threat to conspecific intruders (BWP, 2004). A very terse, squeaky clicking call, generally repeated for a while, is mainly used by the female (BWP, 2004) and often accompanies the previous call or may be given alone. I've recorded this call from a bird at nightfall in March, just possibly in response to the presence of a pair of Long-eared Owls in two lone pines, who were the focus of my attention.

MERLIN

MERLIN, FALCO COLUMBARIUS
AUDIO: CD 2:18

Merlin can be quite vocal in the area of the nest site, but otherwise are rarely heard calling. Calls range from a rapid, rather thin 'ik-ik-ik …', generally brisker and more drawn-out than Kestrel, to a squealing 'eep-eep-eep …', less modulated (querulous) than Kestrel and more regular in repetition; typically in a food pass, the male gives the former and the female the latter. In alarm, calls veer somewhere between the two extremes, typically an accelerating 'eerrrp-errp-eep-ep-ep-ep'. BWP (2004) also reports a repeated gutteral 'kak' for excited males and from females a clicking call, similar to Kestrel (but a soft ticking on arrival at the nest by both sexes).

HOBBY

EURASIAN HOBBY, FALCO SUBBUTEO

They are considered highly vocal around the nest site during courtship and after young hatch, otherwise quiet (BWP, 2004). The main call recognised is a repeated, descending, shrill note 'kew-kew-kew …', quite similar to Wryneck song. Vocal range appears to be broadly in line with other small falcons (but I'm not very familiar with Hobby).

PEREGRINE

PEREGRINE FALCON, FALCO PEREGRINUS
AUDIO: CD 2:19

Peregrines have quite a range of calls, usually only heard around the nest site and sometimes at a roosting site. Family parties with recently fledged young can be quite vocal in summer and into the early autumn. Generally you only tend to hear Peregrine calling if you've strayed too close to a nest site, when the bird calls readily in alarm with a deep, hoarse screeching, made up of a single, drawn-out rasping 'crraak', repeated insistently. This can be given rapidly in a more subdued form from a bird nervous on the nest, where it sounds a more goose-like cackling, 'crik-crik-crik …'. In courtship and food-calling, a squealing wail is given. Another call is a squeal-click sounding something like 'shlie-uch'.

GROUSE – TETRAONIDAE

The breeding systems of the grouse differ between the first two species, of the *Lagopus* genus, birds of more open habitat, and the next two species, woodland grouse of the *Tetrao* genus. The latter two species can genuinely be said to sing and are very vocal at their leks, much less so away from the lek; calling, or the equivalent of singing, is more sporadic with the *Lagopus* species males, but these tend to be more vocal birds in other situations. Calls tend to be rather guttural or crooning (dove-like cooing in the case of Black Grouse and including elaborate wheezing in the case of Capercaillie); wing-beats also tend to play a part in display.

RED GROUSE

WILLOW PTARMIGAN, LAGOPUS LAGOPUS
AUDIO: CD 2:13

Red Grouse males are vocal at dusk and dawn throughout the year; given reasonable conditions, they can often be heard during the day through spring and into summer. At other times of year it can come as quite a surprise when an area that has appeared devoid of the species during the daylight hours reveals their scattered presence in the twilight. Birds also tend to call when flushed.

The formal advertising call is a hard, chuckling phrase slowing at the end, to the rhythm of 'hey, go on get out of here', usually followed by 'go back, go back'. The sequence is usually given as a kind of song-flight: when perched, birds give a simpler accelerating series of 'bek's. Courtship and possibly territorial disputes are accompanied by variations on a low throaty, crooning 'kow', repeated in short series. Keepers have told me that a yikkering call I've heard quite frequently comes from young birds. It's not clear to what extent females are vocal.

PTARMIGAN

ROCK PTARMIGAN, LAGOPUS MUTUS
AUDIO: CD 2:22

Intermittently rather vocal, though birds can remain silent for long periods. Birds usually call when flushed, often after flying a little distance.

Calling in display is common on fine mornings in the early spring: in May just a few calls at dawn, but much more between 8 and 11am once the sun had begun to warm up the corrie. By early summer calling appears more restricted to dusk and dawn: on 2 July in the Cairngorms birds were only heard at around 11pm, then again between about 3 and 3.30am, and not at all before or after. I suspected it was males coming in to roost on the crags and screes, then leaving again at dawn. I have also heard birds calling well in September gatherings in mild weather and sheltered spots, which I took to be social interaction between family parties meeting up.

Most calls (at least from males) are in a distinctive, deep, croaking voice and sound like a rich belch; the female's voice is reported as higher-pitched and cooing (BWP, 2004). The full display call, usually given in a short flight out from a hillside, is a rhythmic phrase at a slowish pace to the lilt of 'here comes the bride', often followed by a few more subdued notes. But single drawn-out croaks are also heard as well as staccato series. Other calls include whimpers in courtship and a whickering purr in alarm from females with dependent young.

BLACK GROUSE

BLACK GROUSE, TETRAO TETRIX

AUDIO: CD 2:01

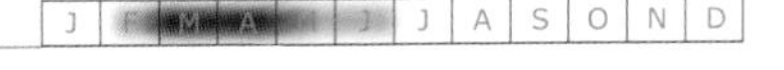

Generally rather quiet much of the time, the males make up for it on their traditional display grounds or 'leks' (probably from a Swedish word for 'play'). Lekking begins at first light and carries on till well after the sun has risen, then again a little in the evening. Birds may turn up at the lek at any time of year, but display is most intense from late winter through the spring.

The male's song is a rather dove-like cooing on a 2–3-second motif cycled round. The pose is head down, find a partner and pirouette a safe distance apart; the excitement builds and one or both birds will explode into the sneezing call and maybe leap into the air fluttering (perhaps a move homologous with a cock pheasant's crow and flutter display). Every so often there is a more prosaic conversational interchange of their general call 'cu-curroohu'.

Occasionally the 'cu-curroohu' call is heard away from the lek site, especially from birds flying in from lekking. I've heard a low clucking from a female visiting the lek; females also apparently call with a loud 'tchuk' when excited (BWP, 2004).

CAPERCAILLIE

WESTERN CAPERCAILLIE, TETRAO UROGALLUS

AUDIO: CD 2:09

J	F	M	A	M	J	J	A	S	O	N	D

Like Black Grouse, Capercaillie are rarely heard to call away from the lek, and their lekking period is shorter. Lekking males fan their tails, droop their wings, raise their heads up high and, shuffling around a small area, with pulsating iridescent, green breasts, repeat their strange song for several hours. They have more widely spaced stances than Blackcock; it's more of an individual affair, performing solo, without the partnering that goes on with male Black Grouse.

Each song begins with a series of spaced, double clicks, gradually accelerating to a clear, cork-from-the-bottle 'pop', followed by a wheezing, frenetic warble. Each rendition usually lasts between 6 and 10 seconds, depending on the amount of introductory clicks. The final warbling, though ostensibly high-pitched with a thickly slurred sibilance, has a low frequency component, audible as a thrumming low drone but extending into the infrasonic.

Display begins in the near-darkness of early dawn and peaks in April, but can take place any time in the spring when conditions are favourable. Despite being a rather shy species, males get so fired up during this period that very occasionally 'rogue' birds emerge, prone to display at any time, even away from the lek, and can attack humans or vehicles. Females observing a lek are reported to give a cackling in excitement. Occasionally birds of either sex give a terse, throaty 'kuk-kuk-kuk …'.

PHEASANTS, PARTRIDGES & QUAIL – PHASIANIDAE

Males of this family tend to have rather loud territorial calls and much softer calls between the sexes. Like grouse, wing-beats play a part in Pheasant display.

RED-LEGGED PARTRIDGE

RED-LEGGED PARTRIDGE. ALECTORIS RUFA
AUDIO: CD 1:31

A rather vocal species with a rich voice and varied repertoire; heard more often during the day than Grey Partridge. Display calls can be heard all year round at any time of day, though particularly on spring mornings. Where Grey Partridge usually repeats a short formal call several times and then leaves quite an interval before calling again, Red-legged Partridges display with continuous sequences of rhythmic chuffing, something like an old steam train. BWP (2004) recognises two forms: repeated sharp 'chuk's build and are interspersed with a more emphatic 'chukarr' in the rally call, becoming a more continuously repeated 'ker-chuff-chuff-chuff …' from a male in full display. But there is much variation within the basic theme. When flushed, birds give a wheezy squeal, usually repeated several times.

GREY PARTRIDGE

GREY PARTRIDGE. PERDIX PERDIX
AUDIO: CD 1:35

Not quite so vocal as Red-legged Partridge: territorial calls, given by both sexes (BWP, 2004), are frequently heard around dusk and dawn for much of the year, less so during the day. Usually calls when flushed. The voice has a scratchier timbre than Red-leg.

The display call, heard more from males, is a more stereotyped repetition than Red-leg: a drawn-out, scratchy or grating note which often becomes a disyllabic 'chirrrr-ick' usually given in sequences of up to half a dozen at intervals, which can be quite lengthy. There is much variation between individuals in the voicing and it's quite easy to identify individuals by ear. The same call in a more clipped version, repeated but not in a formal series, serves for more general contact and mild alarm.

Territorial and courtship displays are often accompanied by short aerial chases: when flushed, or in these excited display flights, birds usually call with a very clipped 'chik', often rapidly repeated, as well as a few short 'chirrik's.

PHEASANT

COMMON PHEASANT, PHASIANUS COLCHICUS

AUDIO: CD 1:13, 3:09 (AND MANY OTHER PLACES IN THE BACKGROUND)

Intermittently a very vocal bird during much of the year, Pheasant calls are mainly based on short, explosive crowing notes with a wheezing croak to them. Females are less vocal, certainly seldom heard.

Displaying males usually stand with head held high on some prominence and give a loud, distinctly disyllabic 'kurr kuk', usually followed by a brief but powerful and rapid beating of their wings; this is performed at variable intervals. During the breeding season, when the sap is high, males repeat soft mewing notes, often in distinct phrases, between their crowing outbursts, particularly in the presence of females.

Males taking flight often give a repeated 'kurruk, kurruk …' to accompany the clatter of the rapid wingbeats; females sometimes give a few thin squeaks. Males going to roost often call a single 'kurk', repeated at short intervals, then settle with softer clucking; females call with a repeated squeaky whistle.

Males in confrontations and fights sustain a subdued purring rattle, exploding occasionally into a cackle; nervous females give a similar call, though higher-pitched. The cheeping of juveniles, especially those reared in pens and then released, can be insistent in late summer and sounds rather like Bullfinch calls.

QUAIL

COMMON QUAIL, COTURNIX COTURNIX

AUDIO: CD 1:27

Quail are heard far more often than seen: the birds are usually hidden in herbage and difficult to see, but the male's song is very distinctive and fairly loud (audible at 1 kilometre (half a mile) in calm conditions). Song is regular through the breeding season, particularly at dawn and dusk, and can be heard through summer even to September. I don't have any information on vocalisation outside the breeding season.

The song is a staccato, 3-note, whistled phrase, 'whit-ter-whit' or 'wet-my-lips', repeated four to six times in sequence. Heard closely, it is introduced by two low, nasal mewing notes, 'mau-wau'. When flushed, birds give a trilling 'whreee', reminiscent of a wader (Mullarney et al., 1999); there are other soft calls between paired birds, as well as subdued alarm calls.

GOLDEN PHEASANT

GOLDEN PHEASANT, CHRYSOLOPHUS PICTUS

Not often heard apart from the crowing advertising call of the male in the breeding season, which could only be mistaken for a Common Pheasant with a sore throat – a loud squawky shriek, often repeated once quickly, otherwise at lengthy intervals (about 20+ seconds). Between shrieks birds give occasional softer cheeps, with a liquid melodious quality. There are other occasional calls. According to BWP (2004), Lady Amherst's Pheasant *Chrysolophus amherstiae* is similar to Golden Pheasant in voice, though distinguishable.

CRAKES & RAILS – RALLIDAE

Tend to be highly vocal birds, some species with a wide range of calls, often loud in territorial proclamation. Voice varies from hard, creaky or explosive notes to the squeals and croons of Water Rail and the finer whistles of Coot.

WATER RAIL

WATER RAIL. RALLUS AQUATICUS
AUDIO: CD 2:46

Birds can remain elusively quiet for long periods, yet at times they can be very vocal, calling incessantly. They can be heard all year round, at any time of day or night, though it seems that when a pair is settled on breeding territory, particularly if they are an isolated pair on a marsh, they only call occasionally. On a small bog I watched in April, there were at least five birds at the start of the month and on a warm Sunday afternoon there was much vocalisation; by the end of the month when there only seemed to be three birds present, I could wait for long periods without hearing them call. This pattern has been similar in previous years. They have a wide and varied vocabulary.

Paired birds express their claim to the territory with a short series of calls known as sharming. Each series begins suddenly with loud, shrill squeals and subsides into throaty groans, like one's stomach squelching; they can be given by an individual, but are often delivered as a kind of duet. There tend to be quite long intervals between subsequent bouts of these calls, though if one bird or pair calls, it usually triggers neighbouring birds into calling. In fact other sudden noises, such as farmers' gasguns or a crowing Pheasant, can stimulate Water Rails into calling. Sometimes the calls subside into soft thrumming rhythmic runs of something like guttural clucks; this sound can also be given in isolation, where it seems to serve as a kind of stealthy contact call between paired birds.

A repeated hard 'kek', often given insistently for long periods (especially during night), is said to be male song (e.g. Mullarney et al., 1999); several 'kek's ending in a drawn-out, trilled 'kerrr' (sometimes just the trill is given alone at intervals) is thought to be from the female (BWP, 2004).

Birds calling in the early spring produce a wide range of variations on the kind of calls used in the sharming sequence; sometimes individuals call with just the subsiding ending of the sharming sequence. Sharp squeals, repeated at short intervals, are given by nervous birds. I'd love to watch a Water Rail calling sometime, to get an idea of how they physically produce some of their calls, but given their secretive habits I wonder if anyone has had the chance to watch one of these gems vocalising.

CORNCRAKE

CORN CRAKE, CREX CREX
AUDIO: CD 2:50

Corncrakes are best known from the song of the male, well encapsulated in its scientific name *Crex crex*, repeated like this at short intervals for long periods. Usually the bird is hidden in herbage, but sometimes his head might be prominent or very occasionally he may sing from a perch, such as a low wall. Well known until the mid-20th century through much of the farming areas of Britain, but now largely confined to the north and west, the song is heard from May when birds arrive, through to July; birds of passage are sometimes found singing at potential breeding sites. In the breeding areas song output is at a peak between midnight and 3am, particularly on balmy nights.

The bursts of two loud ratchety notes are repeated often endlessly, at short (less than 1 second) intervals; calling birds broadcast in all directions by slowly turning their heads, giving rise to a reputed ventriloquial quality, and can be heard up to almost 1 kilometre (about half a mile) away in quiet conditions. There are other softer calls more rarely heard, including a growling mew from the male and a cheeping from the female.

The recording is from Tiree, where there is a dense population in an area on the west end of the island. Being out there in the darkness at midnight, surrounded by the pulsating rattles of countless males in full voice, all slightly out of time with each other, was a mesmerising experience and a little unsettling.

SPOTTED CRAKE

SPOTTED CRAKE, PORZANA PORZANA
AUDIO: CD 2:48

'Singing' males can be very noticeable in the spring, but otherwise Spotted Crakes do not appear to be particularly vocal birds.

The male's song is a loud whiplash note repeated at short intervals (sometimes less than 1 second) with insistent regularity. The sound can carry up to around 1 kilometre (half a mile) in calm conditions. Heard close, it is preceded by a soft grunt. According to BWP (2004), females also use a softer version of this call, sometimes in a loose duet with the male.

Birds are not often heard calling as opposed to singing, but seem to use quiet versions of the song note as call (BWP, 2004). I also have a recording of a singing male, with a very soft thrumming call almost certainly from this bird, very like the throat-drumming call of Water Rail.

MOORHEN

COMMON MOORHEN, GALLINULA CHLOROPUS
AUDIO: CD 1:82, 2:61

Intermittently this is quite a vocal species but it can remain silent for long periods. It is heard all year round. There are two loud calls, each given in an occasional single outburst, which often reveal a bird's hidden presence. The rolling 'prrt', 'kurruk' (BWP, 2004) or 'kyorrrl!' (Mullarney et al., 1999) are all renditions of the advertising call, although the actual voicing does vary a lot; and a hard, very terse 'chid', or often 'chidou', which may be an alarm call.

Nervous birds call with a more subdued 'huc' repeated at short intervals, often heard at dusk from birds going to roost; this is similar to the 'keuk' calls of Coot, but has a less percussive beginning and generally a less creaky timbre (I think of them as 'corky'). Sometimes it is also given as a short spluttering run in moments of high drama and then may be harder and more creaky. There are other softer calls used in close communication between birds.

COOT

COMMON COOT, FULICA ATRA
AUDIO: CD 2:54

Coots are generally very vocal birds for much of the year, probably more so than Moorhen during the breeding season. They gather in winter flocks, where they are rather quieter, and often tend towards socially, quite crowded breeding, where territorial and status displays are frequent and vocal.

The most obvious calls are the loud territorial 'keuk's, repeated at short intervals in often fairly long sequences. The sound is explosive, variable from hard and creaky to higher-pitched and squealing and sometimes tends to be disyllabic. Display includes tapping the foot on water and often goes in a skimming, half-walking flight over the water, with a rapid, regular beating of the wings on the surface.

Also heard from birds on breeding sites are several kinds of very short calls, unobtrusive though still quite loud. A very terse explosive 'phut', repeated in sequence, is said to be a contact or enticement call of the male (BWP, 2004); a short, thin, high-pitched 'zit' or 'zing' is also said to be a male call, given in combative mode or alarm. As with the 'keuk' calls there is much variety in voicing. Birds on the move call with a plaintive, high-pitched soft trumpeting call, generally given in a two-note phrase, and may be heard at night ('pe-peuu').

CRANE

COMMON CRANE, GRUS GRUS

Intermittently a very vocal species; birds on the move tend to call regularly, a large flock being vociferous, and settled pairs display vocally sometimes for long periods with very loud trumpeting calls which can be heard at several kilometres distance.

The advertising calls are mainly a repeated single note about a second in length, but in excitement may become a shorter, rapidly repeated note. Birds on territory are most vocal in the early morning (the 'reveille') and evening, and paired birds tend to call in duet, where the two notes, at different pitches, can often sound like a single disyllabic call. Calls, especially in flight, are on a drawn-out, rolling creaky note, which may end in a clearer, trumpeted voicing.

GREAT BUSTARD

GREAT BUSTARD, OTIS TARDA

Rarely heard calling and apparently not particularly vocal. Displaying males give brief snorts and a soft, throaty braying call. Alarm is signalled by a short, nasal bark (Mullarney et al., 1999). Young call with a quite distinctive squeaky yelp, reminiscent of some calls of Red Fox *Vulpes vulpes*.

WADERS – HAEMATOPODIDAE, RECURVIROSTRIDAE, BURHINIDAE, CHARADRIIDAE AND SCOLOPACIDAE

In general, the waders tend to be very vocal birds, but a few species are rather quiet. Many have display vocalisations that can well be described as song. Their voicings range from piping and fine-toned whistling to the stridently creaky, croaking and crooning. Trilling and the cycling of a motif (rather like some of the Paridae tit species) crops up frequently and there are some rather unusual sounds to be found among them. There is a tendency to sing and display in flight, and wader songs encompass some of the most beautiful of our bird sounds.

OYSTERCATCHER

EURASIAN OYSTERCATCHER, HAEMATOPUS OSTRALEGUS
AUDIO: CD 2:25

A vocal and garrulous species heard all year round in breeding and wintering areas. Display is on the ground, with long piping sequences, and takes place all year, but particularly from winter into spring. Once birds are paired and settled on a breeding territory they tend to advertise with a flight round and repeated calling and, when nesting is under way or with dependent young, adults are quick to call loudly and insistently in alarm at any intruder in the area.

In flight, they frequently call a 't-peep'; when alarmed and scolding an intruder this becomes a piercing 'peep-peep-peep'. In display, lengthy passages of bubbled piping and trills build out of the more usual calls and often include more creaky chittering passages. Though their vocalisation is highly varied, it all tends to be of a similar voice, so is difficult to separate into distinct calls.

BLACK-WINGED STILT

BLACK-WINGED STILT, HIMANTOPUS HIMANTOPUS

Very vocal in breeding areas with a strident voice, otherwise considered rather quiet (Mullarney et al., 1999). Calling is mainly in short, repeated notes in a voice varying form high and piercingly strident to lower and more grating, reminiscent of some 'keuking' calls of Coot.

AVOCET

PIED AVOCET, RECURVIROSTRA AVOSETTA
AUDIO: CD 3:48

Vocal in breeding areas, including family parties in summer, otherwise rather quiet. It readily gives voice in aggressive encounters and in alarm; 'constant chuckling or gobbling sound, audible only at short distance', characteristic of undisturbed colony (BWP, 2004). Calls are based around a short 'kleep' note, varying in voicing from a rather gentle weep (rather like Ringed Plover) from relaxed birds, to a more strident 'klup' and 'kleep' from anxious birds.

STONE-CURLEW

EURASIAN STONE-CURLEW, BURHINUS OEDICNEMUS
AUDIO: CD 1:71

Intermittently vocal on breeding grounds. Display calls peak at dusk and before dawn, and can be heard at night. Breeding pairs may be less vocal than social groups and non-breeders (BWP, 2004).

The main call is a drawn-out, strident whistle, typically a disyllabic 'cour-lee', with the second syllable at a higher pitch, vaguely similar to the calls of Curlew, hence the common name. Softer calls tend to have a slightly scratchy timbre. Display calls are something like an elaboration of the main call, with a hard trilling or churring note inserted, and often build from and subside into a rapid chipping note with a rather thick timbre. The louder calls, including display calls, are audible at a considerable distance.

RINGED PLOVER

COMMON RINGED PLOVER, CHARADRIUS HIATICULA
AUDIO: CD 2:35

Intermittently vocal, groups can be very vocal in display in the spring. It readily calls in alarm in the nesting area or in general when disturbed, although less insistently.

The main call is a brief whistle, in full form a disyllabic 'tur-weep', with the second syllable at a higher pitch; but often also delivered in shorter form as a single 'peep', usually repeated, in alarm and excitement. Birds gathered in the spring may repeat a short 'weep', of similar tone, over long periods, occasionally emerging into quicker rhythmic motifs and other clucking notes. And every so often a bird will break into song, a whistled 't-lee-u' becoming a buzzy whirring, repeated rhythmically and particularly given in a skimming display flight.

LITTLE RINGED PLOVER

LITTLE RINGED PLOVER, CHARADRIUS DUBIUS
AUDIO: CD 3:49

Intermittently vocal in breeding areas. Display can be frequent at the start of breeding, otherwise vocal in aggressive encounters and in response to any disturbance, but often calls at intervals (or just when you move!).

The usual contact and mild alarm call is a brief, hard, down-slurred whistle 'piü', usually delivered singly. In greater alarm and excitement a higher 'pree-pree-pree …', and in aggression low rasping calls. A high repeated staccato 'pri-pri-pri …' is considered a form of song (Mullarney et al., 1999); more obviously song is the rolling repeated 'krree-a, krree-a …' given in display flight.

KENTISH PLOVER

KENTISH PLOVER, CHARADRIUS ALEXANDRINUS

Possibly a little less vocal than its close relatives. The usual call in flight is a quick 'bi-bip', sometimes just 'bip'. In excitement, it may give a rattle with a hard version of this call and quite distinctive rising buzzy call of 'drreep-drreep'.

DOTTEREL

EURASIAN DOTTEREL, CHARADRIUS MORINELLUS

Not a particularly vocal species, the birds call in display in the spring and tend to call softly when someone crosses their breeding area. Nevertheless, they have a surprising variety of calls. Contact and mild alarm is a brief whistled 'wip', sometimes with a harder voicing 'kwip'. More distinctive and often heard from migrants (Mullarney et al., 1999) is a rather grating purr 'pjurr', also heard on breeding grounds. Various other short whistles are heard in spring, sometimes in rhythmic phrasing, particularly a lightly trilled 'pjuu'.

GOLDEN PLOVER

EUROPEAN GOLDEN PLOVER, PLUVIALIS APRICARIA
AUDIO: CD 2:21

Quite a vocal species, although birds settled on breeding territory can be quiet for long periods, until disturbed, when they call an early alarm. Winter flocks can be vocal at times, with a scattering of soft calls in flight and an occasional song; and a settled flock can sometimes give off a dense murmur of calls in a kind of communal song.

The main call used in contact and alarm is a straight, pure whistle, which may rise or fall just slightly in pitch according to mood. This is the plaintive call we hear when entering their moorland territories. In flight, birds often give a rather short, subdued version of this. There are two forms of song, both usually given in display flight. On breeding territories a mournful 'dur-deeyou' ('pü-pee-oo' Mullarney et al., 1999) is repeated at short intervals, often in a butterfly-like display flight, sometimes from quite a height; a rolling, slightly trilled 'yipiyu-yipiyu-yipiyu …', cycled three to four times, can be heard from birds at any time of year, but particularly in spring.

GREY PLOVER

GREY PLOVER, PLUVIALIS SQUATAROLA
AUDIO: CD 2:73

Wintering birds call occasionally in contact and every so often there can be a brief rally of calling from individuals scattered over some mud flats, then silence again. It is reported to be most vocal on breeding grounds (BWP, 2004), but song is rarely heard from wintering birds.

The main call in its fullest form is a drawn-out whistle, often described as trisyllabic, though continuous, but with a marked fall in pitch then a slurring rise ('t'looee'). Often shorter renditions are heard, just a rising 'looee', and can sound rather like a Curlew call. In fact the voice is generally rather similar to Curlew, both the usually clear whistle and the occasional huskiness that creeps in on occasion, perhaps in aggression or alarm. Male song is reported as a different whistle repeated in a butterfly-like display flight (Mullarney et al., 1999), and BWP (2004) makes reference to a trilling song.

LAPWING

LAPWING, VANELLUS VANELLUS
AUDIO: CD 1:37, 3:10

Generally, a rather vocal bird throughout the year, with one of the most characteristic sounds of farmland for my father and his generation in youth: 'peewit'. Display can be frequent among birds settling to breed, heard even in the darkness, possibly less so once breeding is under way, particularly after hatching. Display flights and calling are also sporadic from birds in winter flocks. Calls readily in alarm at intruders into nesting areas, and flocks on the move or during scattered feeding keep contact with calls.

The main call is a loud wheezing 'pwee-u' in alarm and with more varied voicing in flock contact. In display flight, birds thrum the air heavily with their wings, take tumbling dives and call with various motifs in a similar wheezing voice, 'pee-u-wee-a', 'wee-u-wee, wee-u-wee', as well as single, descending purring or crooning calls. Display is often a communal affair with all the birds of a site joining in. In courtship birds, possibly just the male (BWP, 2004), give a repeated raspy call. They are wonderful birds with unmistakable and vivid sounds.

KNOT

RED KNOT, CALIDRIS CANUTUS

Although a large flock can give off a loud murmur, Knot are otherwise not noticeably vocal outside the breeding season. Sound also plays very little part in their recognition and song is rarely heard in winter.

The main call is very nondescript, rather like Bar-tailed Godwit – low, brief and wheezy, while feeding. It tends to have a more whistled tone when calling an alert, a slightly hoarse 'knut' (Witherby et al., 1938–41). Birds do call frequently to each other when a group is feeding, with low wheezy squeaks, rather like Dunlin, but this is not normally audible at any distance and I've only heard it by listening through microphones placed near the birds.

Song is a lovely repeated two- or three-note motif in a full whistle, rather sad sounding; I've never heard the song in Britain. Alarm on the breeding grounds is a sharp, rather shrill note, usually repeated several times, 'kvee-kvee-kvee'.

SANDERLING

SANDERLING, CALIDRIS ALBA

Wintering birds feeding on the tide's edge call occasionally with soft, brief whistles, usually barely audible against the noise of the water. Calling becomes more excited when gathering to roost and with the onset of the breeding season. The main call is a brief 'whit', variable to a rising 'wheep'; in display birds give sequences of rather squeaky single notes, 'hyew-hyew-hyew …'.

TEMMINCK'S STINT

TEMMINCK'S STINT, CALIDRIS TEMMINCKII

Rather vocal during the breeding season, less so otherwise. The main contact and alarm call, often given when flushed, is a short, hard, clear 'tirr-tirr-tirr' (BWP, 2004), almost rattling.

In display, generally in flight, sings with a rhythmic tittering, rather like Common Sandpiper, with varied rhythms, peaking in a fast sibilant trilling with a gradually wavering pitch, compared to crickets (Mullarney et al., 1999) and Grasshopper Warbler (BWP, 2004). Overall the voice is rather sibilant.

LITTLE STINT

LITTLE STINT, CALIDRIS MINUTA

Singles may remain silent for long periods, but there is usually some calling from birds in a group as they move about, or in feeding encounters. Flushed birds usually call with a soft, rather indistinct 'peep'. Considered quite a vocal species with a varied vocabulary (BWP, 2004).

Heard closely, the main call is quite a thick, brief 'chit', similar to Red-necked Phalarope, usually repeated and maybe chattered. In display, song is in runs of a repeated, high-pitched, sibilant whistle 'tsee-tsee-tsee …', with a hint of Common Sandpiper and not so trilled as Temminck's, interspersed with an occasional tittering rattle.

CURLEW SANDPIPER

CURLEW SANDPIPER, CALIDRIS FERRUGINEA

Other than the usual flight call, which is not heard too often, there is little information on voice. Song appears to be a sustained trilling or tittering, with maybe a rising whistled 'twee' (from example in Roché & Chevereau, 2002). Occasionally it calls in flight with a soft, twittering 'chirrup'.

PURPLE SANDPIPER

PURPLE SANDPIPER, CALIDRIS MARITIMA

Wintering birds often give a low, rather indistinct call when flushed, though often not heard against a background of surf or swell. Soft calls, barely audible, are common among feeding birds with an occasional rattle, rather like Turnstone, in aggressive encounters. Reported to have a wide vocabulary in the breeding season, when 'song appears to be more an amalgam of vocabulary than discrete vocalization' (BWP, 2004).

The main call in contact and alarm, and often given in flight, is a brief 'quit'. In confrontations between birds sometimes a rather quiet, hard rattle. Song is in series of repeated short whistles, sometimes more trilled, occasionally breaking into sequences of crooning very like Dunlin.

DUNLIN

DUNLIN, CALIDRIS ALPINA
AUDIO: CD 2:34 SONG, CD 2:66 CALLS

Generally a rather vocal bird, feeding flocks in winter can give off quite a murmur of squeaky chatter; as spring gathers, display and trilling become more frequent and birds are intermittently very vocal on breeding grounds. Often calls several times when flushed and in ranging flight.

The main contact and flight call is a trilled whistle 'tseet', quite frothy. Feeding birds chatter with a soft hoarse squeaking. The main song is a prolonged trilling in a voice like the contact call, rising in pitch and speed, then falling away again. This often leads into the second form of song, a crooning trill, rising slightly in pitch and repeated. It can sound almost croaking like an amphibian, maybe Natterjack Toad but not so hard.

RUFF

RUFF, PHILOMACHUS PUGNAX

Considered a very quiet species, such as 'nearly mute, has only low grunting sounds' (Mullarney et al., 1999). The recording on Roché & Chevereau (2002) has a double-note call, 'euk-eu', sounding like a squeaky toy, with a nasal timbre.

JACK SNIPE

JACK SNIPE, LYMNOCRYPTES MINIMUS

Normally silent in winter, even when flushed, but reported to occasionally give a quiet, hard 'gatch' (Mullarney et al., 1999).

Display on the breeding grounds involves an odd, hollow rhythmic phrase, like the 'clip-clop' of a distant horse, interspersed occasionally with a sibilant, fizzy trilling, slightly reminiscent of Dunlin song. The rare flushing call is described in BWP (2004) as like the 'Scaipe-call' of Common Snipe, but shorter and lower.

SNIPE

COMMON SNIPE, GALLINAGO GALLINAGO

AUDIO: CD 2:38 SONG & DISPLAY, CD 2:63 CALLS

J F M A M J J A S O N D

Snipe become rather vocal in the breeding season, though remain silent for much of the time in winter, at least when perched. Display in breeding areas involves a high undulating flight, broadcasting a remarkably loud feather sound on dives, as well as a vocal figure, often repeated for long periods, given when coming in to land, from the ground or a more prominent perch. In winter at dusk and dawn birds often break cover into flight and give a rasping 'scarrp' call repeated at intervals; I'm never sure whether the birds are moving between feeding and roosting sites, or simply going for a fly around, maybe a low-key display. Flushed birds also usually give this call, repeated several times as flying off.

The display flight appears to be a male thing and the throbbing pulse, often called 'drumming', is a really eerie sound in the twilight, with no indication of where the sound is coming from – the bird is usually a speck somewhere above: I now think it was the source of a scary experience by some standing stones in West Scotland in my childhood – not supernatural at all. For a long time there was controversy about how the sound was produced, until apparently in 1907 when P. H. Bahr demonstrated the sound to the Zoological Society by fixing a Snipe's two outer tail feathers to a cork and whirling it round in the air. In a dive the bird fans its tail with the two outer feathers singled out, and winnows air over them with its wings.

The song is a steady ticking call 'tchuk-tchuk-tchuk …', but often given in two or three note motifs, hence description 'chipper-call' (BWP, 2004) or 'yikkering'; it is reported to be given by both sexes (BWP, 2004). The main contact and alarm call is the distinctive 'scarrp' (or 'scaipe' – BWP, 2004) call mentioned above, usually given in flight.

WOODCOCK

EURASIAN WOODCOCK, SCOLOPAX RUSTICOLA

AUDIO: CD 1:46

J	F	M	A	M	J	J	A	S	O	N	D

In breeding areas males display at dawn and dusk by doing circuits of their territories in what's known as 'roding' flight, with mannerised wing-beats and calling all the while. Otherwise birds are rarely heard calling. When flushed they sometimes give a subdued and indistinct call and migrants arriving on the coast in autumn have been reported as giving whistles (which I suspect is rather like the squeak part of the roding calls).

The male's song when roding is a croak and whistle motif repeated ad-lib: three to four croaks delivered at a steady pace explode into a resonant, squeaking, brief whistle, otherwise known as the 'snore-notes' and the 'sneeze-note'. Birds use both rapid wing-beats and slow-motion wing-beats as they cruise just below treetop height, often along the edge of a clearing or ride. When two males meet they break into a chase with a contest of excited squeaking notes. According to BWP (2004), the female may call down a roding male with soft sneeze-notes.

In alarm, they sometimes give a low breathy rasp as in my notes: 'call as flushed: a breathy rasp, "schurrup", like snipe in timbre, repeated several times quickly'. I've also a note of a soft whistle given by a flushed bird; and I have a recording of soft rasping calls, almost a subdued throaty growl, from a female with chicks. None of the calls is very loud, as might be expected from such a secretive and wary bird.

BLACK-TAILED GODWIT

BLACK-TAILED GODWIT, LIMOSA LIMOSA
AUDIO: CD 3:50

Though small parties may be rather quiet when feeding and roosting, birds tend to call occasionally in flight; becomes very vocal while breeding, with frequent vocal display flights and readiness to call in alarm at intruders.

Song in display flight cycles round a simple motif in a slightly reedy, or even husky, voice. There seem to be two forms: a quick, 'wicka-wicka-wicka …', quite Snipe-like, and a more drawn-out 'teu-wupoy', repeated. These can be in quite long sessions, with the bird rising to a good height before dropping swiftly.

The usual flight call is a quick 'vivivit' and in more nervous situations a repeated 'tveep'. Overall the voice is very reminiscent of Lapwing in timbre.

BAR-TAILED GODWIT

BAR-TAILED GODWIT, LIMOSA LAPPONICA
AUDIO: CD 2:74

I used to describe Bar-tailed Godwit as mostly silent, but having spent much time with microphones out on the mud flats somewhere near singles, groups and fly-overs, I've become aware that they are really quite vocal. You just don't normally hear much of it; calling is quite frequent, but not loud, usually in very brief syllables or otherwise not very distinctive to our aural grasp. Display flights in winter are rare, but occasional.

It's difficult to say what the usual call is, since there is so much variation in the recordings I have; calls in feeding encounters tend to be wheezy, rather like Dunlin, but fuller and lower pitched. Calls in flight are sometimes of this timbre, but often a clearer, brief syllable, or double 'kuwe', in a voice somewhere between Black-tailed Godwit and Knot. Song is a strident 'ku-we', stress on the second syllable unlike Black-tailed Godwit's 'wicka', delivered in display flight.

WHIMBREL

WHIMBREL, NUMENIUS PHAEOPUS
AUDIO: CD 3:50

Generally quite a vocal bird, particularly so while breeding: vocal display flights are quite frequent and birds call in alarm at intruders or in territorial encounters. Migrants call intermittently in flight, especially when looking to come down to land or after takeoff. The main call is a quickly repeated brief whistle, in a voice similar to but higher-pitched than Curlew; sometimes described as a trill, it's rather piped all on the same pitch after the initial note. It could be (and has been) mistaken for the anxious alarm calls of Curlew (a rather hard 'ku-ku-ku'), though it's normally longer sustained and in a higher-pitched voice.

Song is a drawn-out trilling, similar to the call, but faster and more ringing, interspersed with sequences of long clear whistles, each slowly rising and falling. It is every bit as captivating as its larger relative.

SPOTTED REDSHANK

SPOTTED REDSHANK, TRINGA ERYTHROPUS
AUDIO: CD 3:51

It's very useful to know the call for this species, though feeding and roosting birds are usually silent. In flight, particularly if flushed, birds tend to call and it's a clear signal to check out the assumed Common Redshanks.

We are listening for a quick, disyllabic 'chi-vee', often repeated at intervals; this is the usual call heard from migrants and wintering birds. On their breeding grounds, the alarm 'chip' (as other *Tringa* species) has a slight creakiness reminiscent of Black-tailed Godwit. This can be more or less apparent in the song, a repeated whistling motif, frequently 'tchew-wee-oo', with occasional trilling.

CURLEW

EURASIAN CURLEW, NUMENIUS ARQUATA

AUDIO: CD 2:30 SONG & CALLS (SUMMER), CD 2:72 SONG & CALLS (WINTER), CD 3:10

J	F	M	A	M	J	J	A	S	O	N	D

A vocal species all year round with some of the most distinctive calls of all the waders. Song is given in display flight all through the breeding season and in snatches occasionally from birds in winter. Birds call readily and loudly in alarm at intruders in the breeding area and usually call when flushed in winter; birds on the move, whether singly or in small parties, tend to call intermittently.

The usual call is the eponymous 'cour-li', generally repeated; often birds give a shortened version, usually as a double, 'cour-cour', but there is much variation in actual voicing. In winter there's often a huskiness in the voice, even grating, especially from more anxious birds; but on their breeding areas the voice tends to be clear-toned and the full alarm call (e.g. with dependant young) is a hard 'cu-cu-cu', though this is also heard from migrants (BWP, 2004).

The full song builds out of a sequence of 'sobbing' notes (one of the old names is 'whaup'), often prolonged, as the bird alternates a fluttering rise with shallow glides, then breaks into a series of ecstatic bubbling trills. Display is most frequent in the early morning and evening, but can be heard at any time of day and even in the dark hours. In the clearer breaks of stormy weather or after a shower has passed over, the whole moor can come alive with displaying Curlew (where there are still good numbers), then gradually subside to silence again (well, Curlew silence – the Meadow Pipits and Skylarks will still be going).

REDSHANK

COMMON REDSHANK, TRINGA TOTANUS
AUDIO: CD 2:36, 2:56 CALLS & SONG, CD 2:67 CALLS (WINTER)

A vocal species throughout the year, birds call readily at the slightest disturbance, even in winter – hence the description 'sentinel of the marshes'. Birds tend to call when moving around feeding areas and often a scattered feeding group will call intermittently. Song is occasionally heard through autumn and winter, but becomes more frequent into spring.

The main call is a clear, slightly drawn-out 'tyüü', often with an ending 'teuhühü', from relaxed birds; when anxious, the voice becomes more strident and clipped. There is quite an astonishing variety to the voicings of this basic call, as well as other rather different occasional calls. Full alarm, particularly from breeding birds, is a quickly repeated, short, sharp 'chip'.

Song is a lovely flutey phrase cycled round a few times, 'tuleeoo', normally given in flight or especially when alighting. Birds also display with a fly round repeating a single note 't'loo' or 't'luhu' excitedly at regular, short intervals.

GREENSHANK

COMMON GREENSHANK, TRINGA NEBULARIA
AUDIO: CD 2:37 SONG & CALLS, CD 3:51 CALLS

Very vocal birds during the breeding season, Greenshanks, although often quiet at other times when feeding alone, also tend to call when on the move, flushed or when individuals of a group are scattered feeding.

The main call is a rich 'tcheu', normally repeated in a run of two or three, quite like Redshank in form, but lower-pitched, fuller and with a richer timbre. The chipping alarm call is also lower and more clearly a sharp 'teu'. Occasionally, flushed birds give a raspy grating call on rising.

Song is a repeated, slightly clangorous motif 'kluhee-kluhee …', delivered in long passages in display flight over the breeding territory; shorter sequences are given when a pair take off or land and when individuals come in to feed and move around on feeding areas during the breeding season. Courtship involves sequences of a surprisingly full throaty chuckling and grinding trills. This basic vocabulary is supported by a varied set of other calls, particularly during the breeding season.

GREEN SANDPIPER

GREEN SANDPIPER, TRINGA OCHROPUS
AUDIO: CD 3:52

Fairly vocal all year round, particularly in the breeding season. Migrants frequently call when on the move and wintering birds usually call when flushed.

The main call is a short run of whistled notes with emphatic rising pitch, 'cleüy-cli-cli', sometimes just the 'cleüy'. Song, given in display flight, is a repeated motif similar to the call 'culeüy-clee …', often interspersed with some tittering phrases. Alarm is a similar chipping to other *Tringa* species, but thinner sounding.

WOOD SANDPIPER

WOOD SANDPIPER, TRINGA GLAREOLA
AUDIO: CD 3:52

Very vocal in the breeding season, otherwise tends to call intermittently and usually when flushed. Song is sometimes heard from passage birds in the spring.

The main call is similar in phrasing to Green Sandpiper (often given in a run of three notes), but of a steadier pitch, with a marked sibilance (slight shrillness) and notes usually lacking a hard opening, so although it could be described roughly as 'teu-teu-teu', it's more accurately transcribed as 'yiff-yiff-yiff'. When excited, the call becomes harder and shriller, and merges with alarm chipping. The main part of the song, usually given in display flight, is a repeated motif 'kli-hu', rather similar to Greenshank, but higher-pitched and quicker.

COMMON SANDPIPER

COMMON SANDPIPER, ACTITIS HYPOLEUCOS
AUDIO: CD 1:77 SONG & CALLS, CD 2:26 CALLS

Very vocal during the breeding season, less so otherwise, though calls are heard intermittently from passage birds. Voice is rather high-pitched and characteristically a slightly sibilant whistle.

The main contact and alarm call is a short run of high-pitched whistles descending slightly in pitch 'tseu-seu-seu-seu'. An anxious bird repeats at intervals a single drawn-out whistle, with a slight downward inflection at the end: very like blowing an alert call on a tin whistle. Song is in tittering sequences of a similar short piped whistle, with a pulsating rhythm, breaking into higher-pitched trilling in excitement, and can be given perched or in flight. In more aggressive confrontations, it becomes clipped and chittering.

TURNSTONE

RUDDY TURNSTONE, ARENARIA INTERPRES
AUDIO: CD 2:68

Turnstone are not especially vocal in winter, but do often call when flushed, and squabbles over food or foraging space can be quite noisy, as often is a roosting group.

The usual contact call, also given when flushed and in flight, is a quick 'teu', quite distinctive though variable in voicing from a short, sharp 'teuk', like pebbles knocked together, to a ringing, slightly raspy 'tchew'. In alarm, a short rattle 'teuk-a-teuk' is given; in squabbles and other aggressive situations birds call with a raspy, tittering rattle (based on fast repetitions of the contact call), which can be quite prolonged. It's not clear to what extent they have a distinct song or if excited versions of the rattling call heard in display serve the purpose. Breeding birds also call with a more distinctly phrased 'tuwhee-t'whee-tit-tit-tit', described as an alarm call in Roché & Chevereau (2002), but suggested as possibly also functioning as song in BWP (2004).

RED-NECKED PHALAROPE

RED-NECKED PHALAROPE, PHALAROPUS LOBATUS

Not a species noted for its vocalisation, calls can be useful for alerting you to its swift arrival at a feeding pool. The usual alarm and contact call is a rather thick, brief 'chit', sometimes an almost disyllabic 'chiwa'. Communal display involves much chattering, in a voice like the call as well as squeaky notes, but they do not appear to have a distinct song. The main call of Grey Phalarope *Phalaropus fulicarius* is a rather brief wheezing whistle, 'wheeo', reminiscent of Dunlin in the frothy timbre, and quite distinct from Red-necked Phalarope.

ARCTIC SKUA

PARASITIC JAEGER, STERCORARIUS PARASITICUS
AUDIO: CD 2:31

Generally, they are only vocal in display and in domestic interaction on the breeding grounds. Display flights can be frequent and often end in a spectacular dive from a height, with a loud wooshing of their wings. Display in flight is accompanied by a repeated, mewing yodel, rising in pitch and in a rather gull-like voice, like some calls of Common Gull (and quite easily mistaken for this species). Also heard in display (and perhaps other situations) are an abrupt, staccato 'kow' like Kittiwake or 'keu-ha', as well as a sharp, slightly squeaky 'kew', reminiscent of the terns, and short moans. These abrupt calls are also given at intruders.

GREAT SKUA

GREAT SKUA, CATHARACTA SKUA
AUDIO: CD 2:32

Considered silent outside the breeding season (BWP, 2004), birds give voice occasionally on and around their breeding areas, in display and in alarm. Display takes place at the nest site and loafing and bathing sites, usually on arrival, and involves stretching back the wings fully and giving a series of calls.

The display calls are a short series of hoarse, throaty grunts, sometimes given in flight as well as on the ground. Alarm is expressed in flight with an abrupt, rather hoarse and nasal 'aw', repeated at intervals; this is what an intruder in a breeding area hears from patrolling birds and in the lead-up to an attack.

GULLS – LARIDAE

Most of the gull species have a more or less similar vocabulary and, in distinguishing between the species, pitch and timbre become more important characteristics. The different species all give variations of short gruff calls and longer, squealing calls. Most species have a long (trumpeting) call, with a more formal structure, which acts like a song. Such display calls can be heard at virtually any time of year, outside the breeding season serving as status claims.

BLACK-HEADED GULL

COMMON BLACK-HEADED GULL, LARUS RIDIBUNDUS
AUDIO: CD 2:39

A very vocal species all year round and breeding colonies are very noisy. Most calls marked by a rather harsh rasp to the voice, and it calls aggressively in alarm.

The main call is a rather grating, drawn-out 'kearrr', trailing down in pitch at the end. In display, birds give a yelping repetitive sequence of this call, building to a crescendo; may subside into a softer mewing. In alarm and threat a short, staccato 'kuk' in a similar voice. Hungry birds patrolling in winter frequently give a subdued, breathy rasp.

MEDITERRANEAN GULL

MEDITERRANEAN GULL, LARUS MELANOCEPHALUS

Considered rather quiet in autumn and winter, though quite vocal in spring and the breeding season (BWP, 2004). Its nasal, whining calls sound like a child's voice in the distance – really quite distinct from either Black-headed or Common Gull, but with a similar reedy timbre to Lesser Black-backed Gull. Though rather brief, each call rises and falls in pitch 'aawu'. Males give a sequence of more drawn-out calls in display.

LITTLE GULL

LITTLE GULL, LARUS MINUTUS

Very vocal in breeding areas, otherwise rather quiet – though little information. Voice rather tern-like. The main call is a brief, hard and thin 'kew', often repeated. In display, it is given in see-saw rhythm, alternating short with even shorter 'kikew-kikew-kikew …'.

COMMON GULL

MEW GULL, LARUS CANUS
AUDIO: CD 2:29, 2:69

Generally a rather vocal species, sometimes very vocal, such as when gathered at a bathing site. Voice somewhere between Black-headed Gull and Herring Gull, lacking the grating timbre of Black-headed and higher-pitched than Herring. The main calls are based around a drawn-out 'kleeya', slightly squealing and occasionally just slightly hoarse in shorter, lower renditions 'klew'. In display, it gives a series of these calls, emphatically higher-pitched and more drawn-out, accelerating and subsiding towards the end. In threat and alarm, it may give a stuttering 'ka-ka-ka ...'.

LESSER BLACK-BACKED GULL

LESSER BLACK-BACKED GULL, LARUS FUSCUS
AUDIO: CD 2:28

Really quite a vocal species, probably more so than Great Black-backed and in voice somewhere between Herring Gull and Great Black-backed.

Calling patterns are generally similar to these other species, but Lesser Black-backed has a reedier voice than Herring Gull, giving a hollow, slightly nasal twang to its calls. It never reaches the pure, rather piercing squeals of Herring Gull. On the other hand it is not so deep and gruff in voice as Great Black-backed; it's actually quite light and pleasant as gull voices go, with a similarity to Arctic Skua.

HERRING GULL

HERRING GULL, LARUS ARGENTATUS
AUDIO: CD 2:28, 2:85

Overall a very vocal species and the classic gull sound of harbours and the seaside. The voice is loud, rather full, and generally lacks the raspiness of Black-headed or the reediness and gruffness of the Black-backs or Yellow-legs, though lower sounds can be a bit hoarse.

In display, it gives a trumpeting series of fairly clear, full and long 'keeya' calls, more or less of a clanging quality, introduced by a few hoarser low notes, then accelerating into brisker regular pacing; it sounds like the bird is having a good laugh. In alarm: a shorter squealing 'kiyow', a lower slightly hoarse 'kow' and a gagging staccato 'kow-kow-kow'.

GREAT BLACK-BACKED GULL

GREAT BLACK-BACKED GULL, LARUS MARINUS
AUDIO: CD 2:27

A rather vocal species at gatherings and especially around the breeding season. The voice is deep, hoarse and throaty and often sounds strangled.

Most frequently heard is the 'kaow' call, similar to Herring Gull and Lesser Black-backed, but deeper and gruffer; often accompanied by 'ow-ow-ow's in a similar throaty voice, especially when given in alarm at an intruder. The full display call is a repeated, laughing 'aow-aow-aow …', given as powerful, throaty half-squeals at a slower pace than Herring Gull. At bathing sites, various subdued, deep moans and groans are heard.

KITTIWAKE

BLACK-LEGGED KITTIWAKE, RISSA TRIDACTYLA
AUDIO: CD 2:84

A very vocal species around the breeding colony and at the nest. The subtle range in their voice is surprising – not so much the variety, but the gradations of pitch and timbre give wide expression to the calls within their vocabulary.

The main call is based on a reedy moaning wail 'oo-aah', but in its more formal expression has a staccato opening to give 'kitti-waaa'. Their other distinctive call is a terse, monosyllabic 'cow' or 'ha', usually in a fairly pure voicing.

TERNS – STERNIDAE

A very vocal family, and breeding colonies can be intimidatingly noisy places. The sea-terns (Little Tern excepted) tend to have similar vocabularies and similar grating voices. Separating the species by voice can be very difficult apart from several more distinctive calls. They share a tendency for rhythmic elaboration in display flights.

SANDWICH TERN

SANDWICH TERN, STERNA SANDVICENSIS
AUDIO: CD 2:80

Generally rather vocal through spring and summer with probably the most distinctive call of our sea-terns. The main call is a grating, emphatically disyllabic 'kay-rrick', sometimes a more hurried 'kirrick', rising to a higher pitch on the second syllable, in a slightly fuller voice than our other species. In alarm and excitement a short 'krik', in threat a fast, staccato 'kitukit' and in display rhythmic sequences, such as 'kukraa-kukukraa-kukraa …'.

ROSEATE TERN

ROSEATE TERN, STERNA DOUGALLII

Described as very vocal, though calls are generally quieter but sharper than Common Tern (BWP, 2004). The main diagnostic call is a brief 'chivik', like Spotted Redshank; otherwise calls tend to have a quite distinctive hoarser rasp than the two similar commoner species and tend to be evenly pitched, typically 'kraak'.

COMMON TERN

COMMON TERN, STERNA HIRUNDO

As other terns, very vocal around breeding sites. Calls are of similar form to Arctic (and to a certain extent other sea-terns), but the voice has a deeper more rolling rasp. It is not easy to distinguish from Arctic on voice without practice. In alarm and threat, a full 'keeaarr', though pitch and force are variable, and when settling a more subdued 'karr'. It also has a 'kip' call similar to Arctic, maybe fuller, as well as staccato attack calls. In display a higher 'kierri-kierri …' and rhythmic sequences in a more rasping voice.

ARCTIC TERN

ARCTIC TERN, STERNA PARADISAEA
AUDIO: CD 2:89

Very vocal, with breeding colonies a mass of noise. The calls are similar to Common Tern, but generally slightly higher-pitched and thinner, and reported as softer in BWP (2004), but my impression is that the voice tends to a more shriller, grating timbre where Common's has a rolling rasp, at least in alarm. But I don't have regular enough experience to distinguish between the two with confidence. The main calls are a sharp 'jip', a grating 'skeerr' and in display a cycled rhythmic motif 'kitikarr-kitukitikarr …'. In threat and mobbing, a terse 'krk', often repeated rapidly in staccato series, like a machine gun.

LITTLE TERN

LITTLE TERN, STERNA ALBIFRONS
AUDIO: CD 3:48

Vocal on breeding grounds, but generally less so than the larger sea-terns. Compared to the other terns the voice is much higher-pitched, shrill and thin, with little of the grating or rasping quality. The main call is a brief, slightly squeaky 'krik', similar to Black-winged Stilt calls, sometimes almost disyllabic as 'kir-k'. In alarm and display, chattering sequences are given in a similar voice. BWP (2004) reports a wide range of calls given in various specific breeding contexts and differing levels of anxiety.

BLACK TERN

BLACK TERN, CHLIDONIAS NIGER

Described as a highly vocal species in BWP (2004), Black Tern calls are quite distinctive, not as harsh as the larger sea-terns and a little reminiscent of Little Tern. The main calls are multisyllabic, usually 'kierr-da' and sometimes 'kierr-kitik'; there are other calls in line with the usual tern vocabulary.

AUKS – ALCIDAE

The auks become fairly vocal around their breeding colonies, some very vocal at times. Birds call in display and in disputes between neighbours. In the closer nesting species, like Guillemot, calling between one or two birds often sets the neighbours off.

GUILLEMOT

COMMON MURRE, URIA AALGE
AUDIO: CD 2:85, 2:88

Very social and vocal on their densely packed breeding ledges, but it's difficult to know whether birds at sea in winter are vocal or not; certainly I've never heard any reports to indicate either way. I have heard post-breeding birds in coastal waters in August calling loudly in calm conditions; but for much of the time offshore birds are unlikely to be heard by an onshore observer against the noise of sea and wind.

The main two calls are a drawn-out, crooning 'aaarr …', sounding almost as if they are gargling, and a shorter, repeated 'arr-arr-arr …', like laughing. The sound in different areas of a colony rises and falls as bickering and negotiation break out and excitement spreads.

RAZORBILL

RAZORBILL, ALCA TORDA
AUDIO: CD 2:87

In keeping with their more solitary breeding habits, Razorbills are rather less vocal than Guillemots. Pairs tend to occupy a gulley to themselves, so calling is more occasional; birds gather on the water in rafts near breeding sites and possibly these could be quite vocal congregations, but, as with Guillemots, it's difficult to know how vocal they are at sea.

Their voice is deeper, though possibly more hollow, than Guillemot, and calls are less powerful. The usual call is a growling 'aaawrr' with a distinct rolling 'r' to it, and, when the call slows or subsides, can sound ratchety.

BLACK GUILLEMOT

BLACK GUILLEMOT, CEPPHUS GRYLLE
AUDIO: CD 2:91

The voice of Black Guillemot differs markedly from the other auks of our region: where the others generally have rather full-voiced, crooning and moaning calls, Black Guillemot has a fine, high-pitched whistle, easily missed as the calls of a songbird, especially pipits. The sound of its voice is presumably behind the Shetland name 'tystie'.

Calling motifs are varied rhythmic repetitions of whistled notes, sometimes short, some longer, and repeated quickly in display, gradually rising and falling in pitch. There is often a hint of a two-note lilt.

LITTLE AUK

LITTLE AUK, ALLE ALLE

They are highly vocal at breeding colonies, which can be rather noisy places. Otherwise they're rarely heard; winter birds blown inland may call in alarm when disturbed (BWP, 2004). Calls range from a rather trilled, drawn-out 'brrrrr' to tittering and yikkering, often sounding like giggling laughter.

PUFFIN

ATLANTIC PUFFIN, FRATERCULA ARCTICA

As far as I know, Puffin are only heard at breeding colonies and even then only seem to call from within their burrows. Certainly birds loafing around on the surface are generally silent. They are described as 'less vocal in breeding season than other west Palearctic Alcidae' (BWP, 2004). The usual call is a rolling moan, lightly burred, but may be single drawn-out calls or shorter in decrescendo series.

PIGEONS & DOVES – COLUMBIDAE

A vocal family, though vocalisation is largely limited to song and mate attraction (with a few species this can be at any time of year). They also have a tendency to sounding off with their wing-beats. Collared Doves are unusual in having a wheezy flight call. Voice is purring, crooning and cooing, and the tonal purity is something they share to a certain extent with some of the following families, cuckoos and owls.

ROCK DOVE (FERAL PIGEON)

COMMON PIGEON, COLUMBA LIVIA

AUDIO: CD 3:07

Though guides often lump the two together, it's not clear to what extent wild Rock Doves differ in their vocalisations from feral pigeons.

Rock Doves are certainly vocal around breeding sites, but I don't know if gatherings away from nesting sites lead to vocalisation, as is frequently the case with feral pigeons.

Male advertising song is a repeated drawn-out note, a deep moaning 'coo'. The display call is a more rhythmic bubbling phrase, sounding something like 'bucket-a-coo'; the phrasing of birds recorded on Tiree, which should have been genetically close to wild Rock Dove, was very similar to that of the feral pigeons living in the town walls at Berwick.

STOCK DOVE

STOCK DOVE, COLUMBA OENAS

AUDIO: CD 1:59, 3:07

J F M A M J J A S O N D

Stock Dove song is one of the benefits of knowing bird sound, as it can be so easily ignored as the crooning of a Wood Pigeon; but the full song that builds to an ecstatic yearning is a real gem and still to me has something exotic about it, as if it's from a bird in a tropical rainforest chorus.

The song is essentially a disyllabic coo, 'coo-uh', repeated in sequence; sometimes the first syllable is so heavily inflected it becomes almost disyllabic itself. A full song sequence begins a little hesitantly but picks up timing and pitch to a sustained peak and brief fade, over the course of anything up to around a dozen repetitions. Birds generally sing from high perches and the song can pick up quite a colouring resonance from the immediate surrounds.

WOOD PIGEON

COMMON WOOD PIGEON, COLUMBA PALUMBUS

AUDIO: CD 1:58, 3:07

J F M A M J J A S O N D

Wood Pigeon song is one of the most familiar sounds of the countryside, and now through much of our urban areas too, in fact anywhere where there are some trees or bushes. Though they feed on open ground, sometimes in large gatherings, song is only given from a perch, generally at a discrete distance from others. A good chorus on a calm morning or evening can spread a soft, pervasive murmur across a whole landscape.

The usual advertising call, or song, is a repeated cooing to the rhythm of 'a proud wood pigeon' or 'take two doo's, Taffy' if you prefer (where did that come from?), at slow to deliberate pace. Voicing, in terms of huskiness, tone and pitch, and the actual pattern of the phrase differs a little between individuals.

You also sometimes hear a faster cooing phrase, in a chuckling rhythm, referred to in BWP (2004) as a display call and thought to be associated with the male's 'bowing-display'. Possibly more frequently heard is the nest call of a male – a low, drawn-out, husky crooning note, descending in pitch.

Birds often give a short series of wing-claps rising into a downward glide, sometimes repeated, in a kind of display flight; and the clatter of their wings when flushed is a general alarm signal to all.

COLLARED DOVE

EURASIAN COLLARED DOVE, STREPTOPELIA DECAOCTO
AUDIO: CD 1:03, 3:07

With a repeated, rather pure-toned cooing for a song, Collared Dove has become something of an optimist's Cuckoo. So the fact that they sing all year round brings a hint of spring to any season!

Song is usually a trisyllabic phrase, repeated in series: emphasis is on the middle syllable, with the last syllable abrupt (long-long-short). But individual voicing varies and there are aberrant patterns. Voice is higher-pitched and purer in tone than Wood Pigeon. Birds also often call in flight with a distinctive, wheezing 'ffew', usually repeated a few times, and the rapid whistling of their wings on takeoff is characteristic.

Ten Cate (1992) has studied the coos of Collared Doves and recognises three different types, perch-coo, bow-coo and nest-coo, each with its own modulation characteristics. Nevertheless differences between individuals were greater in perch-coos and bow-coos, which are concerned with territorial defence and mate attraction.

TURTLE DOVE

EUROPEAN TURTLE DOVE, STREPTOPELIA TURTUR

AUDIO: CD 2:44

Donald Watson writing of his childhood in Kent in the 1920s remembered 'No sound is more evocative of childhood summers than the ceaseless purring of turtle doves'; sadly this is only true of a much more restricted area of Britain now. For me it's also a sound evocative of warm sunshine, but in my case from time spent in Mediterranean areas, where the birds are still common.

The male's song is based on cycling round a rhythmic series of purring notes in sequences of up to around 15 seconds. When close by, a lower gulping note can be heard accompanying each sequence. BWP (2004) reports several other calls that sound like short variants of song phrases, used by both male and female. It's not clear to what extent females 'sing'. Turtle Doves have no connection with turtles; the name derives from the specific *turtur*, describing the bird's voice.

RING-NECKED PARAKEET

ROSE-RINGED PARAKEET, PSITTACULA KRAMER

A fairly recent addition to our fauna, Ring-necked Parakeets can be very noisy, particularly in gatherings at roosts; otherwise when birds call they tend to draw attention because of their loudness. The main call is a rather falcon-like 'keea-keea-keea ...', possibly most similar to Hobby, but with a slightly trilled thickness sometimes creeping in. Otherwise, various trilled chirping is heard and a raspy call like Jay is reported in BWP (2004).

CUCKOO

COMMON CUCKOO, CUCULUS CANORUS

AUDIO: CD 2:08, 3:08

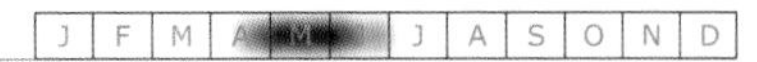

Males are very vocal during the breeding season, females less so; apart from juveniles, migrants are mostly silent. The advertising call (BWP, 2004), let's call it song, of the male is one of the most iconic bird sounds, traditionally heralding spring, though the birds have become rather scarce in many areas in recent decades and Collared Dove's song often provides a substitute!

Males sing with their disyllabic 'ku-koo', first syllable around a third higher than second, from arrival on the breeding grounds in April through to June, when song wanes as the peak of sexual activity passes. Towards the end of the song period the male's voice can sound rather hoarse. Song can be heard at any time of day, though output is at a peak in the early morning and evening. Excited males often add a third syllable for a few phrases and in encounters give out 'gowking' calls, a low chuckle in a wheezy voice.

Females call just occasionally at longish intervals with a hard bubbling, rather like a brief whinny from Little Grebe. Juvenile hunger calls are a rather wheezy 'shri-shri-shri …'; recent research has been examining to what extent these calls mimic those of their hosts.

OWLS – TYTONIDAE AND STRIGIDAE

Sound plays an important part in the lives of these mainly nocturnal birds, and not only for their communicative interactions: both families have excellent hearing, important for hunting in the dark. Their facial discs help to gather sound into their ears, which face forwards, and (at least in the case of Barn Owl) their ears are not quite symmetrical, which helps in localising a sound source. The only member of the Tytonidae here is Barn Owl, a classic 'screech owl'. The Strigidae have a tendency for hooting songs, more strident calls and, in the case of the *Asio* owls, barks and wing-clapping.

BARN OWL

BARN OWL, TYTO ALBA
AUDIO: CD 1:38

Not a particularly vocal species, though adults on territory give an occasional series of their 'screeching' calls most evenings. Young in the nest can be noisy, giving a hissy rendition of the adult call, often described as 'snoring', though apparently such calls are also given by adults (BWP, 2004).

The adult's call is a drawn-out, hissy screech, usually rising slightly in pitch to an abrupt ending, though this may vary with circumstances; some birds have a marked ringing tone in the voicing. Generally the call is given singly at longish intervals, sometimes several in series at shorter intervals, and I've come across one instance of a bird repeating the call at short intervals for a while. Various different voicings of the basic screech are recognised in BWP (2004), given in mobbing or distress; and bill-snapping is also given in threat and alarm. There are other calls, associated with paired birds and generally only heard around the nest site.

EAGLE OWL

EURASIAN EAGLE OWL, BUBO BUBO

Opinions differ over whether this species was ever part of the indigenous fauna of Britain, but we now have pairs breeding in the wild and it is common in bird of prey collections, as well as individuals' private aviaries. So it is not so outlandish to come across some of the intriguing vocalisations of this species, even in unusual places. Across the Channel in continental Europe, the species is fairly widespread.

The advertising call is a deep hoot, disyllabic and descending in pitch – 'hoo-uh', repeated at intervals, typically around 10 seconds; although rather soft, it carries well. Females have a similar call, slightly higher-pitched. When excited, both sexes give a rapidly repeated hoot – 'huhuhuhu …'. Various softer clucking sounds are also heard from paired birds. Alarm calls include a loud, croaking bark and high-pitched piping. Bill-snapping and hissing are produced in threat; and a repeated yelp ('yeeheehee') from the young.

LITTLE OWL

LITTLE OWL, ATHENE NOCTUA

AUDIO: CD 1:39

J	F	M	A	M	J	J	A	S	O	N	D

Often described as very vocal and noisy, isolated pairs can be quite discrete, only giving vocal clues to their presence at the start of the breeding season and when alarmed with young in the nest or nearby. Often birds disturbed at the nest site will exit the area silently with their low, unobtrusive flight, though they may give a few alarm calls at a distance.

The male's song is an even, short hoot, ending with an upward inflexion and a slight creaking in the voice, repeated at intervals of around 5–10 seconds. It's quite low-pitched for such a small bird and is fairly easy to imitate with your deepest whistle. The female has a similar song, a little higher-pitched and in a slightly hoarser voice. Dusk and just before dawn are probably the most reliable times to hear song; output seems to be highest in the late winter and early spring, even among birds at the northern limit of their range in Northumberland.

The most frequently heard vocalisation, used for contact and mild alarm, is a mewing call, which rises to a loud, sharp yelp in excitement. Outright alarm is marked by a short, penetrating 'kik', usually rapidly repeated in short bursts; I only hear this occasionally from my local birds. Young call with throaty or hissy 'schrrr'; I suspect that a similar call from an adult may be the female soliciting food from the male, but have yet to be sure of this.

SNOWY OWL

SNOWY OWL, NYCTEA SCANDIACA

Voice plays little part in the identification of such a distinctive bird; nor is it of much importance in drawing your attention to the bird's presence, since they are rarely vocal away from a breeding site. The advertising call is a 'loud, hollow, booming hoot' mostly heard from the male (BWP, 2004). Alarm calls consist of a rather hoarse croak from the male, quite Raven-like and usually repeated in a short series, and a hoarse squeal from the female (noted from recordings of the Fetlar birds from 1967). Cackling calls and guttural clucking often accompany routine activity round the nest, although rarely heard. Both adults and young hiss and bill-snap when threatened.

TAWNY OWL

TAWNY OWL, STRIX ALUCO

AUDIO: CD 1:66

This resident woodland species is probably our most widespread owl, though absent from Ireland. It is the source of the almost legendary owl call 'tuwit-tuwoo', which I believe originated with Shakespeare. Like most legends, it's based on an element of truth, though not factually quite accurate: it's probably a conflation of two distinct vocalisations, the hooting song and the sharp 'kewick' call. Furthermore both sexes hoot and give the 'kewick' call. It's a vocal species all year round, particularly from late winter into spring and at times in the autumn, with a wide variety of calls.

The male's song is typically a rather pure, resonant double hoot, 'hooo', pause for 3–4 seconds, then 'hu, hu-hu-hooo'; but frequently birds give single hoots and, when excited, variations with a more wailing, mewing or rasping quality.

Females give similar songs, but with a more husky voice.

The tremulous hooting call (or 'bubbling-call' in BWP, 2004), a rapidly-trilled and drawn-out soft hoot given by both sexes, is much quieter than the full song and appears to be used to summon the mate, then given by both birds alternately or together. I've heard this from a single bird in an aviary, so the function may be rather more subtle (or perhaps its human keeper was a mate-substitute). I've also recorded very soft, short cooing hoots given by paired birds close together in March, the different pitches creating a lovely intimate duet.

The main contact and alarm call is typically a sharp 'kewick'; but often just sounds like 'wick' and sometimes 'wick-wick-wick', when it becomes difficult to distinguish between this and similar calls from Long-eared Owl. Calls of recently fledged young are a kind of baby version of the call, rather coarse and hissy ('chu-ssee').

LONG-EARED OWL

LONG-EARED OWL, ASIO OTUS

AUDIO: CD 2:12

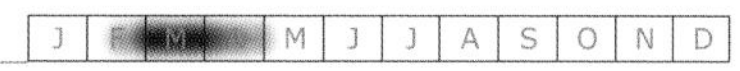

An elusive and to a certain extent nomadic species. Communal winter roosts appear to be silent affairs and I've never heard a bird call outside the breeding season (once a possible) and rarely away from a breeding site.

Birds settling on a breeding territory become vocal in the late winter, with apparently some song in late autumn. Calm, dry nights in February and March are probably the best time to hear them. All of the singles and pairs I've listened to have been vocal and displayed at nightfall for around half an hour. A pair observed between 7pm and 1am on 9 April were quite vocal between 7.40 and 8.20pm, then were only briefly vocal when the male returned to the wood about once every hour. Both male and females are said to 'sing'.

The male gives a longish series (typically 15 seconds to 1 minute) of short, low-pitched hoots, usually gradually rising a little in pitch and loudness. It is rather soft and, despite what many guides say (BWP, 2004, give several references for audible up to 1 kilometre/two-thirds of a mile or more), does not carry far. On the basis of listening to around eight different males (often on multiple occasions), I've never been able to hear the song beyond around 150 metres (500 feet) distance, and usually much less. The female gives single hoots (nest-call in BWP, 2004), rather higher-pitched than the male, slightly drawn-out, with a distinctive, reedy, nasal timbre (like blowing through tissue paper over a comb), delivered at long intervals (typically 5–20 seconds apart). This carries a little further than the male song and may be audible at around 250 metres (820 feet) in calm conditions.

Both sexes give short display flights with slow wing-beats and wing-clapping (a short series of individual claps compared to Short-eared's rapid series). This is probably the loudest indication of their presence. Typically the male will give a song series perched in a tree, while the female sings/calls nearby; then he will display with wing-claps in a short flight round the area, landing on the ground nearby, where he will give another song series. The female will launch into a display flight, coming in to land by the male where mating takes place with soft staccato hoots.

Adults appear to go quieter once settled into breeding, though a range of softer vocalisations can be heard when adults visit the nest site, especially when the male brings food, including soft chittering and tremulous hooting similar to that of Tawny Owl or Short-eared Owl song.

Females, and occasionally males, call in alarm with a slightly nasal, husky 'kwek', often given as a double. But the Long-eared Owl sound most familiar to birders is probably the hunger calls of fledged young: a creaky squeaking, like a rusty hinge on a gate opened slowly (heard from June to August).

SHORT-EARED OWL

SHORT-EARED OWL, ASIO FLAMMEUS
AUDIO: CD 2:15

Sound does not play much of a role for birders in identifying this rather diurnal species, but it can be useful for drawing your attention to their presence on an open moor or saltmarsh at some distance. They aren't particularly vocal birds, but when several are hunting the same area, birds often call when in proximity, and occasionally confrontations occur with excited calling. They tend to be rather unobtrusive in the breeding season and the male's song is rarely heard, so much so that one wildlife recordist I know claims that males do not sing in Britain. (His recording, which has appeared on many audio guides, was made in Scandinavia.)

Male song is a steady rhythmic series of short hoots, typically about 16 lasting 4 seconds. The song is given in flight, usually at some height – possibly 30–50 metres (100–160 feet), and is repeated at intervals; it may be that the hoots are synchronised with the bird's wing-beats. The first time I heard this song, on the Moray moors in Scotland, I paid it little attention, having it down as a Lapwing's wing-beats in the distance.

The usual contact and alarm call is a muffled, coughing bark, which may be in a series of short and sharp notes or a single more drawn-out one. It swells rather to an abrupt ending. Birds call readily in alarm, either near the nest site or coming across a person unexpectedly when hunting. Alarm calls may be accompanied by wing-clapping – a short rapid series, unlike Long-eared Owl. Other calls include a rasping squeal, given in distraction displays, and a trilling in greeting a bird arriving at a winter roost (BWP, 2004).

NIGHTJAR

EUROPEAN NIGHTJAR, CAPRIMULGUS EUROPAEUS, CAPRIMULGIDAE
AUDIO: CD 1:69 CALLS, CD 1:75 SONG

J	F	M	A	M	J	J	A	S	O	N	D

As with most nocturnal birds, sound is our main medium for connecting with them and Nightjars are as much known by their sound as the creepy superstitions they have unfairly been lumbered with. Nightjar, night-churr, fern-owl, goatsucker, etc. is crepuscular and mainly heard at dusk and dawn, just occasionally by day.

Usually perched on the branch of a tree while churring, the song carries well, maybe even up to 1 kilometre (about two-thirds of a mile) in calm conditions and can be heard from the bird's arrival in late spring through to midsummer, though it can also be heard in winter quarters.

The male's song is a continuous churring sound, 'like a Harley-Davidson in the distance' (anonymous Northumberland farmer). It consists of a pulse of sound repeated in quick series, a rattle, holding a higher pitch for longer periods, every so often dropping to a lower pitch (around a third) briefly; the pulse rate actually speeds up at the lower pitch. In full display, a song session ends with the male taking off, the song churr falling away in a decrescendo sequence, like a diesel motor petering out, and the bird flighting around briefly with individual wing-claps (above back – BWP, 2004), giving a dry crack.

A similar, lower-pitched and softer, more bubbling trilled sequence is sometimes given in shorter bursts from the ground, possibly also by females (BWP, 2004), so this ground vocalisation may be behind suggestions of something like song from females. But in their 15-year study of Nightjar, the Stour Ringing Group in Dorset (Cresswell, 1996) never had any experience of a radio-tagged female churring, so all such churring vocalisation generally may be limited to males.

Margaret Rebbeck (1998) made a fascinating study of a small population of Nightjars in Yorkshire, involving recording and analysing the males' songs. She charted parameters like pulse-rate and phrase lengths, recorded within considered territories, to identify individual males and followed the group over three years. Spacing is territorial, but males can sing at a good distance from the nest site. Breeding males tended to cease song at fledging. The fact that a male will sing at several places (up to 1 kilometre or about two-thirds of a mile from the nest) within what can be quite a large territory, coupled with their moving quickly in the darkness, means it's easy to overestimate the number of males singing in an area.

The main contact call is a brief 'cu-ik', slightly nasal in tone. BWP (2004) reports a female using a shortened version of this call 'wik'; and in alarm both sexes use a 'chuk' call, similar to Blackbird alarm calls.

SWIFT

COMMON SWIFT, APUS APUS, APODIDAE
AUDIO: CD 1:23

Intermittently very vocal around breeding sites, but less so elsewhere (BWP, 2004). Birds call in high-speed flights past the nest site, in group flight 'chases' and in larger social gatherings above the breeding area, which become a chorus of screaming. Birds nesting in my neighbour's eaves cling briefly to the wall outside the nest in the latter part of breeding, calling as if to entice the young out. Calling seems to be most frequent in the morning and evening, but can be heard at any time of day, given suitable conditions.

The main call, and the only one normally heard, is a high-pitched trilling, sounding more or less like a thin, slightly rasping scream, usually repeated several times. Pitch and voicing vary a little, but most full calls slow down and fall a little at the end; sometimes short staccato versions are heard, or one or two shorter notes precede the full drawn-out call. BWP (2004) reports several other, rather different, calls related to particular situations (e.g. on the nest, pre-copulation, mobbing a predator), but these are not often heard.

KINGFISHER

COMMON KINGFISHER, ALCEDO ATTHIS, ALCEDINIDAE
AUDIO: CD 1:76

Frequently calls at some point during a flight, particularly around takeoff and alighting, though may be rather quieter outside the breeding season. The main contact and alarm call is a thin, rather pure whistle, very like the 'seep' call of Dunnock, though possibly more sibilant ('tsüü'). In relaxed flight it may give several well-spaced calls, but often when alarmed gives a short burst of several quickly repeated calls.

In display, birds sing with excited variations on the basic call (i.e. piping whistles) and maybe some warbling (BWP, 2004). There are other occasional calls: I've once heard one of two birds together repeatedly calling with a brief 'tsuk', which is probably the 'excitement call' in BWP.

BEE-EATER

EUROPEAN BEE-EATER, MEROPS APIASTER, MEROPIDAE
AUDIO: CD 3:14

A vocal species at all times, birds call around the nesting area, on the move, while hunting insects and when perched. Calls carry well and are often the first sign of their presence in the vicinity, so are very useful for finding this spectacular bird. The main call is a rather brief, liquid 'quip', quite distinctive and loud. Voicing varies with context and there are other calls, but generally recognisably similar to the basic call.

HOOPOE

EURASIAN HOOPOE, UPUPA EPOPS, UPUPIDAE
AUDIO: CD 3:08

Male song is frequent in the breeding season, particularly during the morning. It is considered rather silent at other times of year (BWP, 2004).

Song is a persistent sequence of two- or three-note phrases, 'hoop-hoop', with a similar purity of tone to Cuckoo or Collared Dove, though Hoopoe's notes are pretty much of the same pitch. It carries well and can be heard from nearly 1 kilometre (half a mile or so) away in calm conditions. Calls are rather harsh, ranging from a brief grating squawk to a more drawn-out, hollow rasp.

WOODPECKERS – PICIDAE

The family may be named after their habit of tapping away at wood to dig out insects and nest holes, but not all drum very often; by far the most commonly heard drummer is Great Spotted Woodpecker. Lesser Spotted drums occasionally and other species found in continental Europe, but not Britain, are more regular drummers. Vocally they have a tendency for giving series of a repeated, often rather strident, note – the advertising calls of Wryneck, Green Woodpecker and Lesser Spotted Woodpecker are all of this form.

WRYNECK

EURASIAN WRYNECK, JYNX TORQUILLA
AUDIO: CD 3:12

Birds taking up breeding territory are vocal and quite loud, though go quieter once nesting is under way (BWP, 2004); but birds on migration are generally silent.

The advertising call or song is a rather shrill rising note, 'kew-kew-kew …', repeated insistently in bursts of about 3–5 seconds at intervals of about 10–12 seconds. It's very similar to calls of the small falcons, Hobby and Kestrel, as well as the advertising call of Lesser Spotted Woodpecker. Both male and female sing, often in a loose duet. Birds alarmed on the nest are reputed to hiss like a snake.

GREEN WOODPECKER

EUROPEAN GREEN WOODPECKER, PICUS VIRIDIS
AUDIO: CD 1:53, 3:11

J F M A M J J A S O N D

Both sexes are rather vocal throughout the year, especially in spring with the onset of the breeding season. Drumming is rarely heard, but occasional. They call readily in alarm and recently fledged young can be noticeably vocal. The usual advertising call is a loud, distinctive, 'laughing' yaffle (giving the bird its old colloquial name), 'kyu-kyu-kyu …', with up to 30 syllables, normally given in single bursts at quite long intervals, with a slight decrescendo to the sequence.

In alarm or excitement and in flight it gives a similar call, but shorter (maybe only 3 syllables) and repeated at short intervals. In greater alarm, for example at an intruder near the nest site, it may repeat monosyllabic, shriller yelps 'kyew'. With variations in voicing (such as calls of young), may be confused with Goshawk calls or even Jackdaw occasionally. In courtship, birds may call repeatedly with subdued, rather hoarse and reedy calls (though pleasant) 'kree-kree-kree …', varying pitch and rhythm quite musically, while pursuing and soliciting prospective mate.

GREAT SPOTTED WOODPECKER

GREAT SPOTTED WOODPECKER, DENDROCOPOS MAJOR

AUDIO: CD 1:55 DRUMMING, CD 3:13 CALLS

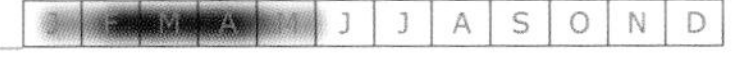

A vocal species, readily calling in alarm when disturbed, and the woodpecker species of our area most frequently heard drumming. Vocal throughout year, both sexes drum, mainly through the spring, but females less frequently (BWP, 2004).

Drumming typically has around a dozen strikes – 5–20 per burst (BWP, 2004), generally at quite long intervals, typically in early spring around three per minute, and may end abruptly or have a hint of a fade. The quality of sound is not always a good indicator of species, since the nature of the substrate is largely the determining factor; as well as tree branches, birds are regularly observed using metal poles. It is also frequently heard tapping, but is not always digging out food.

The usual contact and alarm call is a sharp, rather thick 'tchik', often also rendered 'pip'; in full alarm it's repeated insistently at short intervals. When agitated or excited, it gives a spluttered, chattering burst of this call. Other calls include various subdued, hissy squeals, rather similar to some Mistle Thrush calls (BWP, 2004). Young in the nest often maintain a continuous piping for long periods.

LESSER SPOTTED WOODPECKER

LESSER SPOTTED WOODPECKER, DENDROCOPOS MINOR
AUDIO: CD 3:12, 3:13

It's mainly vocal during the breeding season, but in general less demonstrative with both calls and drumming than Great Spotted. It can remain quiet for long periods, even in the spring; I once followed a bird for around two hours in the Wyre forest and recorded a single call, repeated several times as it flew off.

Drumming is in longer bursts than Great Spotted, typically around 25 strikes per burst, often given several times in succession, and tends to have a more lightweight, even sound, depending on the substrate; the rate of the strikes is similar in both species.

More often heard is the advertising call, a rather shrill repeated note, 'kee-kee-kee …', typically in a series of 8–20 (BWP, 2004), which may be given at a slower, deliberate pace, when it can sound like Wryneck (though pitch of notes less slurred), or rattled off more rapidly, when it can sound like an agitated Kestrel. It also has a 'chik' call for contact and alarm, similar to Great Spotted, but thinner and higher-pitched.

LARKS – ALAUDIDAE

All three lark species treated here belong to different genera and have rather different songs. Woodlark and Skylark share a tendency to sing in flight, repeat syllables in a song phrase and give multi-syllabic calls; Shore Lark rather less so.

WOODLARK

WOODLARK, LULLULA ARBOREA

AUDIO: CD 1:69 SONG, CD 3:46 CALL

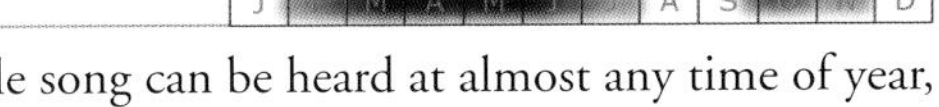

A rather vocal species in which male song can be heard at almost any time of year, though most frequent through spring into summer. It is much admired, and many people's favourite, because of the melodic quality of the song and the clear tone of voice; calls also tend to be in short melodic phrases. Song, usually given in flight, can be heard at any time of day or night, though birds regularly sing before dawn, when they may be the only passerines singing.

Song is in varied sequences of repeated notes, each sequence tending to fall in pitch and accelerate slightly in tempo. It's more or less continuous, sequences following each other after a very short interval. Tone is usually described as fluty and the tempo is quite leisurely; it typically includes phrases like 'lu-lu-lu …', hence its generic name.

Calls are usually of several syllables, typically 'to-li-wee' or 'de-lui' in alarm. When flushed, a party gives similar but rather subdued twittering calls. I've also heard a more trilled or rattling 't-wi-t-wi-t-wi' from a disturbed bird.

SKYLARK

SKYLARK, ALAUDA ARVENSIS

AUDIO: CD 1:25 SONG, CD 3:46 CALL

A vocal species throughout the year. Though song can be heard occasionally in bright spells through autumn and winter, output increases as spring approaches and remains high through to summer. Males can be heard at any time of day and are often the first to be heard before dawn in open grassland ('up with the larks'); song remains frequent through sunny mornings. Sometimes birds sing while perched, but usually a bird takes off and begins singing, while gradually rising almost vertically on fluttering wings to become a speck in the sky.

The song is fluid, continuous and 'chirping', with a cheerful impression, and may be sustained unbroken for long periods, often over 10 minutes and exceptionally up to 30 minutes; mimicry of other species is quite common (particularly Curlew, where they share habitat). There's a tendency to repeat syllables several times, making a distinct phrase (similar in style to Woodlark). Perched song is probably at a slightly more leisurely pace, just slightly less continuous and separate in phrasing.

Calls are given intermittently by birds in flight, whether singles or a flock on the move, and sound like a brief snatch of song with varied 'chirrupy' motifs.

SHORE LARK

HORNED LARK, EREMOPHILA ALPESTRIS
AUDIO: CD 3:44 CALL

Most vocal with song during the early part of the breeding season, becoming quieter as breeding progresses (BWP, 2004). Usually calls when flushed, though the calls are rather quiet and indistinct.

Song may be given perched or in flight, sometimes in a continuous stream of chirpy phrases, when it is rather similar to Skylark, but with a more tinkling quality; more often in brief verses to a stereotyped pattern, when it sounds rather bunting-like (or maybe even Stonechat as in the recordings in Roché & Chevereau, 2002). In a recording by John Gordon from Turkey, the similarity to buntings (particularly Ortolan Bunting) is marked and the timbre has a soft 'burr'. The bunting-like quality is rather interesting and potentially confusing, since birds may breed in similar habitat to Snow and Lapland Buntings.

The main call is a pipit-like, brief 'tseet', or extended to a slightly more distinctive 'tsee-du', and there is also a rather buzzy or wheezy 'tseer'. All are in a thin, fine voice, with a soft metallic ring.

MARTINS & SWALLOWS – HIRUNDINIDAE

All the hirundine species treated here are very vocal birds, calling frequently in flight with constant variation on their basic calls, often giving the impression of vigorous chatter; they also call readily in alarm at any disturbance or predator flying over. Song, though rambling rather than stereotyped, tends to be a more formal elaboration of calling with a few recurring motifs. House Martins can rise to some lovely lilting passages and the voice does become sweeter in song. Swallows clearly spend time singing, though it's also difficult to detect any structure to their songs.

SAND MARTIN

SAND MARTIN, RIPARIA RIPARIA
AUDIO: CD 1:78

Although a vocal bird thoughout the year, it's rather quieter in poor weather. Birds call frequently around the nesting colony and while foraging elsewhere in company, while single birds (rare in such a gregarious species) may be quiet.

The main call is a short dry trill, often repeated as a double 'trrp-trrp'. In alarm, it is a higher-pitched 'tcheur', lightly trilled. There does not appear to be any song as distinct from rhythmic and varied sequences of the buzzy calling phrases.

HOUSE MARTIN

COMMON HOUSE MARTIN, DELICHON URBICA
AUDIO: CD 1:24 SONG & CALL

As a very sociable and vocal species, the air can be filled with their chirpy calls around breeding sites, and this is particularly noticeable in high summer when there is less general bird song to be heard.

Vocally similar to Sand Martin, the calls are slightly harder, with a clearer timbre, so can give more of the impression of a rattle (as opposed to buzz); it possibly calls in quicker rhythms than Sand Martin, other than the latter's song style, and with more varied melodic phrasing. A frequent phrase is in the form 'drrp, drip-a', with the final syllable at a lower pitch. In alarm, it is a higher-pitched, descending 'tseur', again rather similar to Sand Martin.

Song is a pleasantly musical, soft twittering, incorporating short, bubbling trills, and delivered at a hurried tempo, sometimes given in snatches on the wing, but usually more prolonged in the vicinity of the nest, often actually in or perched beside it.

SWALLOW

BARN SWALLOW, HIRUNDO RUSTICA

AUDIO: CD 1:20 SONG, CD 1:24 CALL

Generally a very vocal bird, Swallows can be heard throughout the day, though song is especially notable on fine mornings in spring and summer. Song is given in snatches on the wing, but is more prolonged and continuous from a perch. Autumn gatherings around migration time can be garrulous.

Song is a stream of twittering at a brisk, even tempo, every so often including a distinctive, drawn-out, raspy (or fast clicking) note, like sucking in air through pursed lips, followed by a brief whistle ('prrrr-te-weeo'). Overall the twittering notes have a rather squeaky and slightly wheezing timbre.

The main call is a brief 'vit', usually repeated; in alarm, birds call with a staccato 'ti-da', the second syllable at a lower pitch, usually given on the wing, vaguely similar to Pied Wagtail 'chissik', but more sudden and exclamatory.

PIPITS AND WAGTAILS – MOTACILLIDAE

All our pipit species give their longest and most elaborate songs in parachuting song-flight, where they flutter up almost vertically, then float down slowly with out-spread wings, singing all the way. Meadow Pipit and Rock Pipit give rudimentary versions of their songs when perched, a series of repeated cheeping syllables, which also serves as the introduction to the full song, given on the ascent. Tree Pipit has a more elaborate perched song, with a varied series of phrases. The wagtails, at least those in our region, are slightly unusual in that, despite being closely related to pipits, they only have rudimentary songs and rather erratic singing behaviour. For Yellow and Grey Wagtails song is a simple, rather high-pitched trill; with Pied Wagtail it's not clear what its song is, though all species sometimes can be heard delivering a rather subdued, twittering kind of subsong.

TREE PIPIT

TREE PIPIT, ANTHUS TRIVIALIS

AUDIO: CD 1:70 SONG, CD 3:18

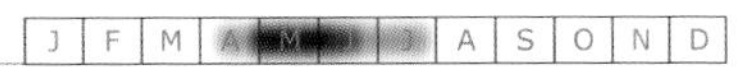

Fairly vocal during the breeding season, particularly the male with song; birds readily call in alarm on their nesting territory with an insistent cheeping. Apparently rather quiet in winter (BWP, 2004).

Male song is in very pleasant, rather languid verses, often maintained throughout the day. Birds deliver a series of shorter verses from a high perch, then launch into a song-flight with parachuting descent (like Meadow Pipit) and a much extended verse, before continuing from, usually, another perch. Each verse is made up of a series of repeated notes, the opening phrase having a similarity to both Chaffinch and Redstart (often its neighbours); the tempo is moderate and steady, but most verses include a distinctive series of more drawn-out, fine, slurred notes that slow the flow, typically 'seea-seea-seea …' or 'wuuy-wuuy-wuuy…'. Interestingly in Thorpe's experiments with Chaffinches in the 1950s, Tree Pipit was the only other species (of those he tried), from which young Chaffinches would learn songs.

The usual call heard on breeding grounds is a monotonously repeated 'chi', given anxiously. Migrants call with a more distinctive, wheezy 'speez', usually given in flight. Apparently this is also given in the breeding areas, particularly by males during the incubation period (BWP, 2004), but I've rarely heard this call in spring.

MEADOW PIPIT

MEADOW PIPIT, ANTHUS PRATENSIS

AUDIO: CD 2:14, 3.:18 SONG, CD 3:43 CALL

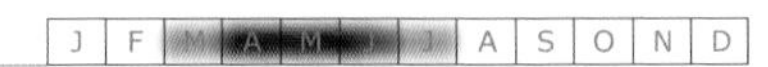

Particularly vocal in breeding areas, with male song frequent throughout the day, birds can also often be heard calling at other times and rarely fly any distance without giving a few calls. Males tend to sing from a much lower perch than Tree Pipit, rarely above human head height.

Like Tree Pipit, the male's song is only given in its fullest version in song-flight; but the perched song is far simpler, just a series of repeated, piped notes, which tend to differ between individuals, typically 'chit' or 'sweep'. When rising into the song-flight, birds continue with this note and at their zenith accelerate into a series of twittering trills, with some slowing of the tempo, as they parachute down.

The usual contact call, generally given in flight, is a thin, rather squeaky 'tseek', with maybe several in series. In alarm, it's an insistent 'chit', barely distinguishable from Tree Pipit, although often doubled to 'chitit' – a rather insect-like chirp (orthopteran). In antagonistic encounters, they often give a rippling repetition of something like a cross between the previous two calls.

ROCK PIPIT

EURASIAN ROCK PIPIT, ANTHUS PETROSUS

AUDIO: CD 2:90 SONG

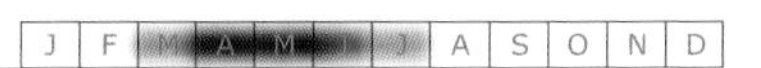

Rather a vocal species, with song quite frequent in the breeding season and calls usually given when flushed or in social interactions. The vocabulary and song structure are broadly similar in form to Meadow Pipit, though the voice tends to be a little fuller and harder, perhaps as a result of higher background noise levels in their habitat.

Song, like Meadow Pipit, is a sequence of repeated notes when perched, usually rather hard, with a slight metallic ring and a hint of a trill (though short); in flight, the repetition is accelerated into a sequence of seeping notes, light buzzes and trills on the parachuting descent.

The usual contact call is a rising 'tseek' like Meadow Pipit, but rather hissy or wheezing. In full alarm, a repeated, cheeping 'tsük', again with that hint of metallic timbre differentiating it from Meadow Pipit.

Water Pipit *Anthus spinoletta* calls and song are very close to Rock Pipit, though with familiarity song can be recognised by distinctive motifs (Mullarney et al., 1999). Calls in my recordings are a slightly wheezy 'tweep', rather fuller and lower-pitched in general than Meadow Pipit.

YELLOW WAGTAIL

YELLOW WAGTAIL, MOTACILLA FLAVA
AUDIO: CD 1:28 SONG, CD 3:30 CALL

The species is vocal during the breeding season, but less so at other times. Song has occasionally been heard in a quiet form at autumn roosts, but not in winter quarters (BWP, 2004). Birds on the move tend to call intermittently in flight.

The usual form of song heard in Britain (*flavissima*) is in verses of two sibilant, trilled notes, 'sriee, sriee', given from a low but prominent perch. Occasionally a more continuous, softly twittering song, possibly subsong, is heard, usually breaking out of repeated call notes and incorporating the main song notes.

The usual call heard in Britain is a rising 'tsweep', often after a bird has just taken off, and repeated a few times at intervals. Calls, and maybe song too, vary between the different races, and blue-headed birds recorded in Poland tend to call with a descending 'tsli-e', and sometimes a simple 'sli'.

GREY WAGTAIL

GREY WAGTAIL, MOTACILLA CINEREA
AUDIO: CD 1:79 SONG, CD 3:30 CALL

Grey Wagtail can be rather vocal during the breeding season, otherwise it tends to call in flight. Male song can be frequent in the early part of breeding and birds call readily in alarm at intruders into the nest area and when with dependent young.

Male song is in verses, repeated at short intervals, of a slightly shrill, sibilant note, repeated several times; often birds vary subsequent verses with several slightly differing notes, such as 'tsu-tsu-tsu', then 'si-si-si-si'.

It might be mistaken for part of a Blue Tit song, though rather more powerful and tending to ring out under riverside trees and banks, and is still easily missed as the sound blends with other sibilant passerine song and the general susurration of running water.

Occasionally, a softer twittering subsong is heard, usually from birds foraging at the waterside.

The usual flight call is a brief 'chi', usually given as a double 'chi-chi', where it is more distinctly two separate notes, compared to Pied Wagtail's disyllabic 'chis-sik', and rather harder or more percussive. In alarm, birds intersperse this call with a rising, slightly trilled 'tsirr'.

PIED WAGTAIL

PIED WAGTAIL. MOTACILLA ALBA YARRELLII
AUDIO: CD 1:06 SONG. CD 3:30 CALL

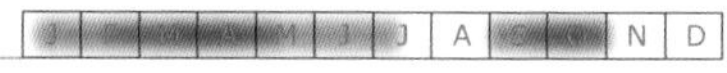

A fairly vocal species throughout the year, and perhaps more so in the breeding season, yet males do not appear to have a formal song. It usually calls when on the move, particularly after takeoff. Communal roosts can give off a dense twittering and apparently sometimes a chorus of bill-snapping, 'sounding like small twigs catching fire' (BWP, 2004). No one has pointed to any consistent differences in the song and calls of White Wagtail *Motacilla alba alba* compared to Pied Wagtail.

The usual call for contact and mild alarm is a 'chis-sik', often given in flight. Perched birds may repeat variations of this call at short intervals in a casual kind of song (typically 'chirrie', 'chissi', 'chichichi'). In a more excited moment birds break into a sustained, twittering warble, still recognisably Pied Wagtail from the voicing.

In alarm around the nest site, or from birds with dependent young, the main call is quickly repeated, in a terse form, and interspersed with another call, a slightly burred, descending 'chreea'.

WAXWING

BOHEMIAN WAXWING. BOMBYCILLA GARRULUS. BOMBYCILLIDAE
AUDIO: CD 3:25

Generally, at least in winter, a rather vocal and gregarious bird, flocks are rarely silent for any length of time and singles in flight tend to call quite frequently; reported as rather quieter on their breeding grounds (BWP, 2004).

The main call is a distinctive, sibilant, bell-like trilling, 'tsir-r-r-r', very useful for latching onto the presence of a flock feeding nearby or a fly-over. Certain phrases in Greenfinch song or the trilling part of some Blue Tit songs can sound similar – a false alarm for the arrival of the star of the winter garden. Other occasional calls are less distinctive. Song is said to be a mix of variations on the calling phrase and other harsher sounds (Mullarney et al., 1999).

DIPPER

WHITE-THROATED DIPPER, CINCLUS CINCLUS, CINCLIDAE
AUDIO: CD 1:83 SONG, CD 1:82 CALL

J	F	M	A	M	J	J	A	S	O	N	D

About the only period when I don't hear dippers singing is when all the other songbirds are singing – from the height of spring through into summer. From the first hint of autumn, they come back into song and continue right through the winter to the early spring, dusk and dawn being the most reliable times to hear them, irrespective of temperature. On the other hand, birds call regularly throughout the year.

The form of the song is a stream of fast, varied chattering at a steady pace, with a range of notes from short trilled whistles, ringing clicks to squelchy churrs, each note usually repeated a few times. It's fairly loud, but because the birds often sing from beneath an overhanging bank and beside tumbling waters, it's often not audible at any great distance. Which is a pity, since it's a rather pleasantly varied and cheerful song, and a true expression of the resilience of this bird, sometimes perched on midwinter ice for his or her delivery.

The bird I worked on for my best recordings used to sing regularly at dusk under the bridge where I assumed he and his partner roosted. He would sing for short periods then fly off, but be back again after a brief interval; when his mate (I assume) arrived, his singing would go up a notch and usually they would soon head off on a fly around at treetop height (the stream was bordered by scattered trees), the male still singing the while. On the sessions in late February I could hear the excitement build, eventually a plop in the water and fast rattling sequences where I assumed the pair were mating. This might happen several times as night gradually came on. Moorhens coming in to roost, Tawny Owls beginning to call, freezing toes, time to go home. They were great sessions, just a few hundred metres from my home at the time.

The usual call given in flight and alarm is a very terse 'zit', generally repeated several times; in excitement and on nest visits, a short rippling churr.

WREN

WINTER WREN, TROGLODYTES TROGLODYTES, TROGLODYTIDAE

AUDIO: CD 1:10, 3:05 SONG, CD 3:33 CALL

J F M A M J J A S O N D

The ubiquitous and vociferous Wren can be heard singing in virtually any habitat at any time of the year. The powerful delivery, with body and wings quivering, is possibly the loudest of any of our species, relative to its size. At certain times of the day in the latter half of the year, Wrens may be the only passerine singing in a woodland; then they sound like the real owners of the wood. Birds call readily in alarm at intruders.

The song is quite stereotyped in 4- to 5-second verses, each consisting in a series of high-pitched trills and rapidly repeated notes, often with a marked sibilance. Sometimes birds only sing the first part of their song and omit the ending phrases, particularly when singing outside the breeding season. On the other hand, a male may also sing an exceptionally long verse by stringing two together (as do Blackbirds). Autumn song, especially in August and September, can be rather formless, perhaps from young birds, and sound very like Dunnock.

The usual contact and alarm call is a sharp 'tak', irregularly repeated, but run together into a hard rattle in full alarm. Juveniles call with a thin, hissy 'tsee'. Thicker hissy calls and song in a similar voice, often heard in the autumn, may also be from young birds; occasionally other odd calls are heard.

DUNNOCK

HEDGE ACCENTOR, PRUNELLA MODULARIS, PRUNELLIDAE

AUDIO: CD 1:14, 3:05 SONG, CD 3:33 CALL

A fairly vocal species throughout the year, and its song can be heard at any time, except during the summer moult, though output is highest and the songs fullest during the breeding season. Birds call frequently in contact and alarm and a kind of subsong can often be heard in courtship in the spring.

Full male song is in 2- to 3-second verses of a hurried warble at an even tempo and loudness, mostly in fairly clear-toned, brief whistles, interspersed with slightly longer, trilled or burred notes. It's quite tuneful, at a fairly even pitch, though at the jaunty pace it may be difficult to grasp the phrasing. It appears stereotyped in structure, though verses may be varied slightly; each male has a repertoire of up to eight songs, retained year to year usually with only minor changes (BWP, 2004). The subsong in spring is rather quieter, more sustained, and with a lovely fluid rippling quality.

The usual alarm and contact call is a very pure, whistled 'tsoo', with a light sibilance; there is also a tremulous brief trill in a similar voice, outside the breeding season and given particularly at dawn and dusk.

In March 2000 I witnessed an event that raised questions about bird song that are still not quite answered. I heard some snatches of Dunnock song outside our sitting room and looked out to see two Dunnocks engaged in a fight. Over the next 15 minutes I watched (recorded and videoed), as the dominant bird mercilessly and triumphantly pulverised its combatant, every now and then delivering a loose verse of song, with the other bird grasped by bill and neck. And it was merciless (though of course this is an anthropomorphic description); several times the subordinate bird escaped its assailant's clutches, but before it had gone a few metres the dominant bird had caught it again and continued, until I approached too close and the poor thing was left barely alive, with its face a bloody mess. I was shocked at such raw violence in a bird that for most of the time appears so unassuming and rather timid. And so are the songs (that generally serve to defer physical combat) a war-cry, songs of triumph, or just the sheer expression of territoriality?

CHATS & THRUSHES – TURDIDAE

This family includes some of our finest singers, with many species noted for their clear tones and varied phrasing. They mostly have large, dark eyes and are active early and late. They tend to provide the first wave of the dawn chorus. In almost all species full song is semi-stereotyped: it's given in fairly regular verses at even intervals, each verse generally conforming to an overall pattern, but made up of varying phrases. The chats of more open habitats tend to sing from lower song-posts and frequently make short, more or less vertical song-flights. The rest are mainly birds of open woodland and the woodland edge, where trees and scrub offer relative security, and they tend to sing from more or less prominent perches.

Calls of most species tend to include both whistles and chaks, considered at root to be stealth calls and mobbing calls respectively. The chats are so named because of the hard pebble-hit calls some of them have. Some also have a propensity for 'noise' (crackling, rustling, rattling), particularly Black Redstart song and some Wheatear song.

There are two distinct inclinations in the songs of our thrush species: fluty, whistled notes and twittering. This is fairly clear in the songs of Blackbird, Song Thrush, Mistle Thrush and Ring Ouzel. Fieldfare and Redwing are rather different. Both certainly have a propensity for varied twittering; but whereas Redwing does have a formal phrasing in the full song that, although not flute-like in tone, is a strong clear whistled motif, Fieldfare on the other hand does not appear to have any formal song, or any whistled phrasing of this type.

ROBIN

EUROPEAN ROBIN, ERITHACUS RUBECULA

AUDIO: CD 1:15, 3:05 SONG, CD 3:33 CALL

J F M A M J J A S O N D

A vocal species throughout the year, although song is rarely heard for a brief period in summer during the moult from around mid-July to mid-August. In the autumn, females take up winter territories, in which they sing. It is one of the first birds to begin singing in the morning and often the last at dusk, although it can often be heard singing in towns at night.

Full male song is in verses of a melodic, whistling warble, rather high-pitched, though covering quite a wide frequency range, giving an overall wistful or bitter-sweet impression. Tempo is varied with languidly drawn-out notes interspersed with fast, rippling runs; some of the higher whistles can sound quite wheezy, almost squeezed out, and some of the lower runs almost chattering. Phrases (or motifs) tend to alternate in pitch above and below 4 kHz and this is apparently an important factor in the birds' own species recognition (BWP, 2004). Individuals may have a large repertoire of motifs – 275 in one bird (BWP, 2004), although these are continually modified; no evidence of individuals sharing motifs has been found. Each subsequent verse varies.

Mimicry is included in songs to some degree, although it is not always easy to pick out in the swift phrasing. One bird I recorded often opened a bout of song with mimicry of Common Gull; I also have recordings with mimicry of Blackbird calls, Chaffinch and a wolf whistle so accurate and full it surely must have been copied from a person (as opposed to a Starling). I've also heard occasional Robin songs that sound just like a snatch of Blackcap song, where it's difficult to say whether the bird is producing an exact copy (mimicry) or assimilating the style of Blackcap. Or possibly it's just an accidental similarity of phrasing.

Autumn song is often said to be weaker; it may be rather quieter, with less pure whistles and more rambling phrasing (if that's possible!). My impression is that verses tend to be shorter too, though this conflicts with an opinion conveyed in BWP (2004). But then I wonder how much our impression of autumn song is coloured by particular characteristics of female song, or even by young birds singing for the first time.

The main contact and alarm call, frequently heard in winter at dawn and dusk, is a sharp, clear 'tic', often repeated in a short series. Sometimes one hears slightly thicker versions of the call and almost chattering runs; whether these are different calls from the first, just individual variation or have some other significance I don't know. Another common call is a brief descending 'tse'; and during autumn and winter, something I note as a trickle call, like a quick descending arpeggio, often repeated several times. There's still so much to learn about Robins.

NIGHTINGALE

COMMON NIGHTINGALE, LUSCINIA MEGARHYNCHOS

AUDIO: CD 1:40, 3:20 SONG, CD 3:34 CALL

J	F	M	A	M	J	J	A	S	O	N	D

So long celebrated in mythology and literature, the Nightingale has acquired almost legendary status as a singer, yet males only sing for a relatively short period from late April, when they arrive, to early June, and in Britain only in the south where their numbers are declining.

Usually singing from within the cover of shrubbery, they do perform during the day, but at night they have the stage largely to themselves, all adding further mystique to the powerful exuberance of their song. Beware that other species sometimes sing at night: several warblers, including Sedge, Reed and Marsh, as well as Robins occasionally.

Male song is in verses around 2–4 seconds long at intervals of about the same length; often opening slightly hesitantly with a repeated note, building in volume or a stumbling phrase, and the power kicks in with one or more phrases of loud, quickly repeated notes, at a fast tempo with precision timing (often like a machine gun), then an abrupt end. Syllables range from pure and clear to buzzy or scratchy, all marked by crisp enunciation. Typical phrases include an opening series of building clear, 'sobbing' whistles, 'wee-wee-wee-wee …', a rather deep 'jug-jug-jug …' or 'chooc-chooc-chooc …' and a sharp 'tu-tu-tu …'.

Catchpole and Slater (1995) quote Todt's figures of 100–300 song types as the repertoire size for Nightingale and the song is frequently described as varied. Nevertheless, striking though Nightingale song is, for me it leaves an impression of repetitiveness and mechanical timing; it's more the song of a vocal athlete than a skilled musician. It blasts rather like an operatic diva or the lead guitar in a heavy metal band. Still, it's a very impressive voice from a rather dull brown bird that you rarely see.

The main contact and alarm calls are a sweet, brief whistle 'weet', a rather deep, hollow churr, almost a croaking sound, and a thick 'tuk' in a similar voice. Recently fledged young call with scratchy churrs, similar to Sand Martin, interspersed with 'tuk's, more similar to the adults'.

BLUETHROAT

BLUETHROAT, LUSCINIA SVECICA

While mainly vocal in the breeding season, snatches of Bluethroat song can also sometimes be heard in winter (BWP, 2004). Calls are heard all year round. They also sing in the darkness; in a male recorded in Poland, song output was highest just after nightfall. No vocal differences have been recognised between the two subspecies, *svecica* and *cyanecula*.

Song is in rather long verses (typically about 8–21 seconds), which open on a repeated note, sometimes of several syllables, gradually increasing a little in tempo, before moving into a brisk, more varied passage of whistles interspersed with crackling sounds. Many of the notes, other than the crackling sounds, are imitations of other species.

The main contact and alarm calls are a dry throaty 'trak' and a brief whistle 'üt', similar to the other chats; Mullarney et al. (1999) also refer to a hoarse, cracked 'brzü', heard in the autumn.

BLACK REDSTART

BLACK REDSTART, PHOENICURUS OCHRUROS
AUDIO: CD 1:21 SONG, CD 3:34 CALL

Quite vocal all year round, their song is heard sometimes in autumn and occasionally in winter (BWP, 2004). They can be heard at any time of day, sometimes at night, but output is highest at dawn. They generally sing from a high perch, often a rooftop in towns.

Song is in two-part verses. The first part opens with a whistle before a repeated note, sometimes similar to Common Redstart, sometimes more of a trill or rattle; then a pause, before a phrase with a bristling sound leading to a whistled ending, usually comprising a few repeated notes again, similar to the opening. It is marked by the broken, stumbling rhythm and odd bristling sound.

The usual contact and alarm calls are a hard, very brief clicking 'tak' and a short, slightly sibilant, rising whistle 'swi'; often in alarm the two calls are interspersed.

REDSTART

COMMON REDSTART, PHOENICURUS PHOENICURUS
AUDIO: CD 1:47, 3:17 SONG, CD 3:34 CALL

J	F	M	A	M	J	J	A	S	O	N	D

Redstarts are a personal favourite of mine; this stems from before my recording days, hearing a bird singing a bit like a Chaffinch by Loch Maree and realising that the song was rather different. And there was a gorgeous male Redstart in the top of a birch tree; I think it was the first time I'd had the chance to watch one at leisure after previously only tantalising and fleeting glimpses. They are quite common in my area of Northumberland (including the garden of my previous house – the best reason for living there!); but many birdwatchers aren't aware of them because they aren't tuned in to the male's song.

While rather vocal during the breeding season, song is also occasionally heard from migrants in Africa (BWP, 2004). It calls readily in alarm at intruders in breeding areas. Males are often the first birds singing, well before dawn, but can be heard at any time of day, particularly during the early part of the breeding season in sunny periods. It tends to sing from a high perch in a tree, but often not right at the top, just below, so can be difficult to spot.

The full male song is in rather short verses, each opening with the same phrase, a brief high whistle (like the call), followed by a repeated lower note (typically 2–4 times), almost a rattle. This opening does not vary between verses, but leads into a short, sweet variable warble, which may include liquid whistles, fine clicks, metallic scratchy rattles and often mimicry. Every so often the singer inserts a slightly longer warbled verse without the opening, frequently before flitting to a new perch. The warbled part does not carry well, but when heard clearly from a good singer it can be some of the finest bird song to be heard, with crisp and precise enunciation to match a Nightingale, though rather more understated. One day I'd like to get a close recording of a male singing in courtship of a female, having once heard this (it was a sustained passage of the warbling mode of song and absolutely beautiful).

The main contact and alarm calls are a rising whistle, slightly disyllabic 'hwee' like Willow Warbler, but briefer, and a hard, clear clicking 'tic', like Robin; both calls are interspersed in alarm. In antagonistic and courtship situations various fine scratchy and buzzy calls are heard; the young also call with a rougher, scratchy buzz.

WHINCHAT

WHINCHAT, SAXICOLA RUBETRA

AUDIO: CD 2:16, 3:21 SONG, CD 3:35 CALL

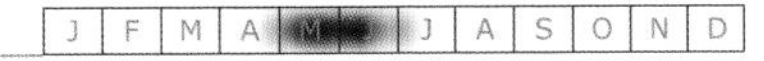

Whinchat is vocal during the breeding season, with male song frequent in the early part, but rather quieter at other times, though apparently song is occasionally heard in winter areas (BWP, 2004). It calls in alarm at intruders into the nesting area, but is heard calling rather less frequently than Stonechat or Wheatear. Male song is in brief verses, just 1–2 seconds long, and when in full song at short intervals, and is usually given from a low perch. Each verse includes both clear whistles and scratchy churred syllables, with no other apparent regular structure, and usually some mimicry. The overall impression is pleasantly chirpy and jaunty. Mimicry of Grey Partridge, Corn Bunting and Sand Martin is rather common (at least in my area of northern Britain), all these species having a grating or buzzy quality to their voices, which blends well with the similar timbre in Whinchat's voice.

The usual contact and alarm call is a brief descending whistle and a short slightly thick 'tchk', generally given as a pair: 'phew-tchk'.

STONECHAT

EURASIAN STONECHAT, SAXICOLA TORQUATA

AUDIO: CD 1:67, 3:21 SONG, CD 3.35 CALL

J	F	M	A	M	J	J	A	S	O	N	D

Vocal during the breeding season, though song sessions may be a little unpredictable, dawn being the best time. It sings from slightly higher perches than Whinchat, such as the top of a gorse bush or even a telephone wire, and occasionally in a vertical, bouncing song-flight. It calls readily in alarm at intruders to the breeding area or otherwise when disturbed, although rather quiet in winter.

Song is in brief, hurried verses of a warbled mixture of whistles and lightly churred syllables, tending to open on a higher-pitched note and end lower. Altogether it is rather quicker-paced, more whistling and with less variation between verses than Whinchat. Mimicry is only occasional. Overall the song bears some similarity to both Dunnock and Whitethroat.

The main calls are a fast, thick, rattling 'trrk', quickly repeated in alarm, interspersed occasionally with a brief rising whistle 'wiss'.

WHEATEAR

NORTHERN WHEATEAR, OENANTHE OENANTHE

AUDIO: CD 2:20 SONG, CD 3:35 CALL

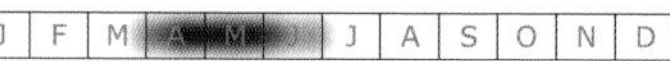

Generally, they are rather vocal birds on their breeding grounds, singing well through the spring into summer, depending on marital status and phase of breeding. At peak of display, fluttering song-flights are frequent. Passage birds call occasionally, particularly if flushed, but are rather quiet and often solitary for much of the time.

Male song is a strange affair with excited brief outbursts of a hurried and garbled chatter. A closer listen reveals a mix of chakking phrases and whistled phrases, generally opening with chatter and finishing with a whistled flourish. Often one gets an impression of repetitiveness, though it's difficult to grasp a formal structure to the song. At times birds seem to trail off into meandering subsong, playing with odd noises and soft, though deceptively accurate, mimicry: I have recordings with Golden Plover and Wheatear present and cannot say for certain whether some sequences of calls are from the Plover in the distance or soft imitations from the Wheatear close by (I suspect the latter). Sometimes it includes whirring or bristling noises, probably vocal rather than feather rustling.

The usual alarm and contact calls are a thick 'chak' and a short whistle 'sü', given together in alarm, but with more chakking. Also heard, at least during the breeding season, is a buzzing call on an even pitch 'zzzu', probably the 'bree' call mentioned in BWP (2004), and rattled 'chak's in antagonistic encounters.

RING OUZEL

RING OUZEL, TURDUS TORQUATUS

AUDIO: CD 2:17 SONG, CD 3:31 CALL

Like the other thrushes, Ring Ouzels are generally quite vocal birds, calling readily when disturbed. But I have sometimes found the males' singing periods a little unpredictable; quite often I've found no birds singing on sunny spring mornings (late April to early May) in sites where I know there are birds present. At other times I've found one or more birds singing insistently for much of the morning. Presumably this variability has been related to the social context (number of males and females) and the particular phase of the breeding cycle at the time. I've often found males singing well in the evening in northern Scotland.

The basic form of the male's song is a simple, loud, whistled syllable, repeated usually 2–4 times; this phrase carries well and at a distance is all that can be heard.

But when males are in full song mode, they follow this phrase with a sequence of explosive twittering of variable length; you need to be reasonably close to a bird to hear this part of the song, and usually a bird will be put off from singing by the time you are close enough to hear the full sequence.

The main call is a hard, full 'chak', building to a rapidly rattled series in alarm. BWP (2004) reports a 'dcherr' and a 'zrrp' as given in flight, including on migration – possibly two renditions of the same call and perhaps equivalent to the higher-pitched whistles and squeals of the other thrushes.

BLACKBIRD

COMMON BLACKBIRD, TURDUS MERULA
AUDIO: CD 1:09, 3:04 SONG, CD 1:08, 3:31 CALL

Generally, this is a very vocal species and one of the great entertainers of the garden for me (the other being Robin). Song season is slightly shorter than Song Thrush; it's thought that, whereas Song Thrush responds to the changing light, Blackbirds are more tuned to temperature and it's usually February before the first males are singing, often even March here in inland Northumberland. They are justly admired for their song, but they are also characteristic of winter dusk soundscapes, with their choruses of chinking as they go to roost. And in the garden they are always quick to respond to anyone or thing they feel is intruding.

The male's song is in well-defined verses, notable for the full, flute-like voicing and melodic lilt of the main phrase; the ending accelerates into higher-pitched, twittering phrases, of less immediate grasp to our ears. Not only does the main phrase have something that strikes us as a recognisable melody, birds vary it from verse to verse, generally with something that conveys a hint of thematic development for us. Most of the birds I hear sing very varied songs, where the link from verse to verse, other than overall structure, is tenuous. But then I regularly come across birds that sing simpler main phrases and often repeat the same motif in subsequent verses with slight variations, almost playing on the theme. I'm not sure what the underlying differences are between the different singers or if it is random individual variation; but I seem to encounter the simple-theme singers in more isolated sites, and conversely all the birds in the denser populations of village gardens seem to be busy singers.

During the autumn and winter months, particularly September–October and January–March, sometimes males can be heard singing very quietly, hidden away in a bush; this subsong is usually a rather loose continuous twittering, but you can pick out motifs of full Blackbird phrases. In early spring, with a female near, the sounds and structure become more refined, as he slips into courtship mode, but all still only audible within a few metres. Consequently it's difficult to know how regularly males spend time in subsong. In October 2008 I found an adult male in subsong almost every day for over a week at the same spot in the garden, under a cotoneaster bush (from which he would take a few berries every so often). Which also goes to show that it's not only immature birds coming into their first breeding season that sing in this way: this was an adult male in October, who almost certainly had held territory and probably bred the foregoing summer.

In a subdued response to an intruder, birds give a low 'pook' or 'tuk' alarm call; this does not necessarily signify low level of danger, since a female may give this call softly when someone approaches her nest, but rather that the caller does not want to give the full game away. These calls can be intensified to a thicker, harder 'chuk' when a bird becomes more alarmed, then change to the full mobbing 'chink's at a higher pitch for outright scolding. There's often a chorus of such calls when birds are going to roost in winter, perhaps signifying a nervousness or conflicting motivations, or a reluctance to enter cover in darkness.

When birds break cover, if flushed for instance, they often give a rattling sequence of these calls in flight. These vary from simple rattles to more developed phrases, sometimes almost a nervous chuckle, which seem to be individually distinctive, or can be.

The main contact call is a rather thin, trilled, sibilant 'tssee', yet a little fuller and less high-pitched than similar calls from smaller passerines, and not so shrill as Redwing. At times this can be the commonest call given during the winter months and is often heard from migrants moving in. A similar call, usually less trilled, is often heard from a pair around nesting time.

SONG THRUSH

SONG THRUSH, TURDUS PHILOMELOS

AUDIO: CD 1:16, 3.04 SONG, CD 3:31 CALL

J	F	M	A	M	J	J	A	S	O	N	D

Males become very vocal for periods during the breeding season and birds call readily in alarm when disturbed around the nest site or when mobbing a predator. Otherwise they are rather quiet and the usual, rather lightweight, calls when flushed are easily missed. Birds begin singing quite early in the year, depending on conditions, responding more to the increasing daylight, where Blackbirds respond to rising temperature. I once heard a bird in full song in mid-December at 11pm in Edinburgh, singing under the castle lights. Song can be heard at any time of the day, though frequently early and late.

Song is loud, varied and with a distinct tendency for rhythmic repetition of phrases; often notes are short, clear and powerful, but include passages of high-pitched, wheezy warblings, which may be prolonged and almost continuous, especially as summer comes on. Though maybe not obvious to a listener, there is a tendency to sing in rather broken verses, typically about 4–8 seconds long, each beginning with a series of loud phrases and finishing with a twittering or chattering flourish.

Mimicry is often present and expert, some birds being more prone to it than others; in my area I've noted copies of Tawny Owl and Nuthatch calls quite frequently, as well as Quail song, Nightjar calls and the opening of Redstart song. I've a recording from northern Scotland where a bird clearly mimics the calls of juvenile Golden Eagle; this is also noted in Captain Knight's *Book of the Golden Eagle* (1927), where the listeners were fooled into thinking there was another eyrie nearby.

Repetition has long been a noted feature of Song Thrush song, encapsulated in a poem by Robert Browning:

That's the wise thrush: he sings each song twice over,
lest you should think he never could recapture
the first fine careless rapture.

The idea is updated in the Collins guide (Mullarney et al., 1999) to 'sounds "cocksure" and "dogmatic"' – in other words, repetition drives the point home.

The usual alarm and contact call is a rather soft, thin, brief 'tsip', often given by flushed birds and normally repeated a few times at intervals. Full alarm is a lower, repeated 'chuk', breaking into a loud, rapid rattling 'tschig-ig-ig …' at a higher pitch, also heard sometimes from birds going to roost.

FIELDFARE

FIELDFARE, TURDUS PILARIS
AUDIO: CD 3:31 CALL

Migrants and wintering birds are quite vocal, regularly calling when on the move, gathered in a flock or when disturbed. As spring approaches, flocks become very vocal, or even noisy, when perched up in a gathering, often with Redwings, and subsong becomes more frequent.

The usual call is a short sequence of thick 'shuk' notes in a brief phrase; the note is variable in intensity with mood and can be inflected and wet, where the phrase is a chuckle, or harder voicings in agitation when the phrase becomes more of a rattle.

Sometimes perched birds call with single notes. Birds also give an occasional short, strained, squealing call, particularly when on the move.

Subsong is a continuous stream of twittering, full of soft squealing notes, interspersed occasionally with chakking phrases, quite attractive for all that. It's difficult to recognise anything that could be described as full song, as distinct from this subsong which is also given on the breeding grounds, but birds do perform in song-flight in their breeding areas.

REDWING

REDWING, TURDUS ILIACUS
AUDIO: CD 3:31 CALL

Rather vocal birds, migrants and settled wintering birds are frequently heard calling when on the move or perched up and call readily when disturbed or nervous. Full song is generally only heard in breeding areas, but also sometimes from migrants in spring. The high sibilant flight calls are a classic seasonal characteristic in Britain on October evenings as birds move into the country.

Structurally, the full song is similar to that of a Blackbird: a full-voiced, 'tuneful' sequence leading into a twittered ending. In Redwing the first section is stereotyped and different geographical groups have their own dialect type; they may also have distinct elements or styles for the twittered second sequence, but it's so complex and rapidly delivered that it would take a full study to recognise. Depending on the mood of the bird, and perhaps the phase of breeding, the second twittering part may be very brief or prolonged for a good few seconds. Migrant gatherings in the spring can produce a dense chorus of this kind of twittering in subsong; as spring progresses a few birds start adding the opening part occasionally.

The usual call given in flight is a high-pitched, sibilant 'tsüü', often slightly trilled, with an electric 'zing' timbre, drawn-out and slurred down at the end; the full call can sometimes sound like Treecreeper, though often shorter versions are given. Nervous birds, generally perched or when flushed, give single 'gak' calls, in a slightly nasal tone. Full alarm (also heard around roosting) is a rapid, rattling 'tuk-uk-uk …', harder and less thick than Song Thrush.

MISTLE THRUSH

MISTLE THRUSH, TURDUS VISCIVORUS
AUDIO: CD 2:03, 3:04 SONG, CD 3:31 CALL

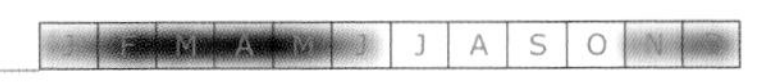

A fairly vocal and rather aggressive species: the birds call readily in alarm at intruders when breeding and when scolding competitors for their food resources. Song begins early in the year and sometimes sounds full from birds singing in November. The 'stormcock' is noted for singing lustily high up on some treetop on wild, windy days in the early spring, though usually in the brighter periods on such days.

Male song is much closer to Blackbird than Song Thrush, but generally in shorter verses and more hurried, with less deliberate phrasing and a slight burr to the voice. Verses open with a loud, fluty motif, rather more warbled and indistinctly phrased than Blackbird, and tend to peter out in a thin, brief twitter. Verse timing varies from a very regular stream to seemingly hesitant and random; phrasing in the verses also varies from strikingly repetitive to constantly varied. Occasionally the twittering mode of song can be in more prolonged passages. The appeal of Mistle Thrush song for us is also highly variable: it can be dull, uninspiring and repetitive, but at times can provide some of the most cheerfully pleasant, musical variations on a theme to be heard in bird song, all in a full, clear-toned voice (a highly personal impression!).

The main call is a distinctive, dry, slightly clicking rattle, varying according to mood from rather subdued in contact to higher-pitched, harder and quickly repeated in alarm. Oddly for the thrushes, this seems to be the only loud call generally used, other than the hard-to-locate 'seep' call shared with many species, though BWP (2004) has references to a few other calls.

WARBLERS – SYLVIIDAE

This family is best considered by genus, since there are more vocal characteristics shared within genera than within the family overall. Living in fairly dense vegetation as many warbler species do, there is a limit to the effectiveness of visual signalling for medium-distance communication. As an adaptation to this constraint on visual communication, many have developed song to a high degree, rather than plumage (the classic 'little brown jobs'). Those species that sing from relative security within vegetation are able to sing fairly continuous songs. Some of the more open habitat species indulge in little song-flights, often vertically from a perch, to get noticed (typically Sedge Warbler, Dartford Warbler and Common Whitethroat). It's considered that song functions more for mate attraction than territorial maintenance in many species, where the males sing much less (or cease entirely) once they have a mate.

Cetti's Warbler is the sole representative in our region of the swamp-warblers (BWP, 2004) or bush warblers (Baker, 1997), although there are more species in eastern Asia. Cetti's calls have a similarity to *Locustella* species calls (pitch inflection), though song behaviour is singular. The *Locustella* genus also has more species in eastern Asia, but the European species all have insect-like songs, which has given the name to the genus.

The *Acrocephalus* warblers, reed-warblers (BWP, 2004) or marsh warblers (Baker, 1997), have songs of far more elaborate structure, with an almost improvisatory organisation, and delivery is in more or less continuous passages. Mimicry may constitute a large part of the song, as with Marsh Warbler. Males tend to remain at a song-post for the duration of a song session. The song period is quite short, though unmated birds may sing persistently through to summer, and paired males may resume song to a lesser degree after breeding. Calls include thick 'tak's and scratchy 'churr's.

Hippolais, tree warblers, have much in common with the *Acrocephalus* warblers, and there has been some reconsideration of the taxonomy of these groups recently. Song tends to be fast, more or less continuous, includes mimicry and is prone to cycle round a phrase or sequence. Calls are sharp 'tak's and thicker chattering notes.

Sylvia, scrub warblers, include some of the best-known and admired singers: Blackcap, Garden Warbler and Whitethroat in Britain, the Mediterranean hot-heads and Orphean Warblers in Europe. Males sing both from fixed song-posts and while on the move, interspersed with foraging.

Phylloscopus, leaf warblers, are represented in Britain by Willow Warbler, Chiffchaff and Wood Warbler as breeders, and by a range of fascinating vagrants, more or less regular, at times of passage. Their songs are rather simpler, more or less stereotyped, but distinctive and sweet on the ear. They tend to sing while foraging through tree foliage. Calls are neat whistles.

The *Regulus* species, 'crests', are tiny, with very high-pitched voices. Their songs share some structural similarities with the *Phylloscopus* species, rather stereotyped and cyclical.

CETTI'S WARBLER

CETTI'S WARBLER, CETTIA CETTI

AUDIO: CD 2:49 SONG, CD 3:36 CALL

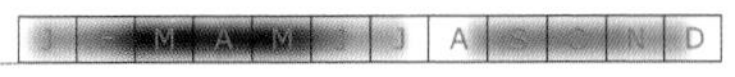

A fairly vocal bird that can be heard all year round, although its song output is highest in the breeding season. In my experience, calls are mostly given in alarm, and readily at any intruder to the nesting area.

Male song is in explosively loud verses at long intervals (typically 20–60 seconds or more), during which the bird tends to move unseen through cover; each verse tends to be given from a different spot. Output tends to be highest early on spring mornings. Notes are fairly clear-toned, though with some chirpiness to the voice, which is sometimes compared to Nightingale.

Verses begin with an exclamatory opening note or two and continue after the slightest pause with an introductory phrase leading into a repeated phrase, though some song types only have the repeated phrase without an introduction (for example, birds in Britain and Lesvos, Greece). A typical song for Britain might be 'chip, chuwee-chuwee-chuwee'. The song is stereotyped and each male has a distinct song type, which he keeps for life. Each geographical region has a basic theme and, within a region, individuals' song types vary in length, structure and timbre (BWP, 2004).

The usual alarm and contact call is a very terse 'chip', perhaps more accurately transcribed as 'pwit', with some similarity to *Locustella* calls; occasionally rattles and churrs are also given in alarm and excitement.

SAVI'S WARBLER

SAVI'S WARBLER, LOCUSTELLA LUSCINIOIDES

AUDIO: CD 3:16 SONG

Male song is quite frequent in the breeding season, though BWP (2004) describes the species as not very vocal on the breeding grounds. Song has been noted in winter. Output is highest in the morning and again at dusk. It is not heard calling often, but is possibly more prone to call in alarm at intruders into the nesting area than Grasshopper Warbler.

Male song is a reeling very similar to Grasshopper Warbler, but with a duller, more wooden tone compared to gropper's slightly metallic ring. Though the rate of the pulsed syllables is faster (50 per second), producing a buzzy smear, the pitch is rather lower than gropper. Reeling sequences begin with several stuttering, lower-pitched notes (like the call), where groppers begin their reel more smoothly, and this is a good diagnostic feature of Savi's.

The main call is similar to other *Locustella* warblers, a brief, slightly thick 'tsuk', and rather fuller than Grasshopper Warbler.

GRASSHOPPER WARBLER

COMMON GRASSHOPPER WARBLER, LOCUSTELLA NAEVIA

AUDIO: CD 2:40, 3:16 SONG, CD 3:36 CALL

Male song is frequent during the breeding season, otherwise a rather quiet species. It is not heard calling very often; I've only heard calls once, out of many encounters, but that bird called almost continuously for over 20 minutes, for no apparent reason. Song can be heard at any time of day, but mainly at dusk and into the night, sometimes during the night, and from dawn to mid-morning; it's usually given from near the top of a plant stem or a lower branch of a bush.

The male song is a distinctive continuous pulsed note (actually a pair of elements at about 25 per second), with a slightly dull metallic ring, often likened to the sound of stripping line from a fly-fishing reel, hence the frequent use of the term reeling. Although named for the similarity of the song to grasshoppers, it's actually closer to that of some bush-crickets (such as Great Green Bush-cricket), though much louder and fuller-voiced, and only really confusable with its close relatives Savi's Warbler and, further east, Lanceolated Warbler.

Individuals may sing for long periods (several hours), with only short breaks between songs; the sound carries well, audible to 500 metres (550 yards) or occasionally further in good conditions, but appears to drift as the singer turns his head from side to side, also generating a ventriloquial effect. Gilbert White (1788) comments: 'Nothing can be more amusing than the whisper of this little bird, which seems to be close by though at a hundred yards distance; and when close at your ear, is scarce any louder than when a great way off'.

The main contact and alarm call is a sharp 'plik', with a similar metallic ring to song syllables, though voicing is variable and may be a thicker 'tchik'.

SEDGE WARBLER

SEDGE WARBLER, ACROCEPHALUS SCHOENOBAENUS

AUDIO: CD 2:47, 3:22 SONG, CD 3:37 CALL

The birds are vocal on the breeding grounds and apparently throughout the year (BWP, 2004). Passage birds call fairly freely and birds always call readily in alarm when disturbed. Song output is high when they first arrive in breeding areas, but Catchpole (1973) found song to cease after pairing; unpaired birds maintain a high output. This implies that song in this species is more concerned with mate attraction than territorial advertisement. Birds are occasionally heard singing at night.

Male song is in rather long verses, typically around 20 seconds, but up to one minute, beginning hesitantly, gradually picking up momentum to a peak of intensity, before fading rather quickly. Erratic, stuttering rhythms and short scratchy or buzzy syllables are characteristic of the species. The amount of mimicry varies between individuals, much of it based on higher-pitched whistled calls (i.e. rather different and standing out from the other syllables in the song), typically including such species as Willow Warbler, Swallow, House Martin and Reed Bunting. Note the matching of elements between the singer in the recording and his neighbour in the background. Birds usually sing from near the top of some herbage or a low bush and intermittently rise in a fluttering song-flight.

The usual alarm and contact calls are a short, rather deep and hard 'tuk' and a quite deep, grating churr; also heard is a higher-pitched, more scratchy churr, probably from young birds. Occasionally in alarm a brief burst of hard 'tak's is given, in a kind of spluttering call, similar to Wren.

MARSH WARBLER

MARSH WARBLER, ACROCEPHALUS PALUSTRIS

AUDIO: CD 2:45, 3:22 SONG, CD 3:37 CALL

J	F	M	A	M	J	J	A	S	O	N	D

Fairly vocal throughout the year, with song as well as calls heard in winter. Males sing on passage (usually from within cover) and output is high until pairing, when it drops to a low level. Calls seem to be given sparingly in the early part of breeding, but may be more frequent with dependent young.

It is one of the outstanding singers of our region (though sadly rather rare in Britain now) and a real pleasure to listen to. It can be difficult to assess what full song is in the case of such a varied and effusive singer, but having listened to many birds singing on passage through Lesvos, where they don't breed, I think I have a feel for it. The passage birds seem to meander in terms of tempo and dynamic structure; the birds I've listened to in Poland and Britain (on potential and actual breeding sites) have tended to a certain overall structure to their songs. Singing is in loose, quite long verses (structurally like Sedge Warbler), which begin hesitantly, or maybe sparingly, and build to a frenzied intensity, before falling away again.

Mimicry is prolific and accurate, making up most of the song; the sounds of House Sparrow, Swallow, Linnet, Goldfinch and Blue Tit have often featured in the songs I've listened to. A bird I recorded in Northumberland, after a Blackbird gave its alarm rattle some way off, immediately began its next verse with mimicry of Blackbird 'tsuk' alarm calls, leading into several renditions of a Blackbird rattle, then Song Thrush alarm calls. It's not simply a matter of including copies, since birds often thematise their mimicry in a kind of caricature of another species (as do shrikes).

Marsh Warbler mimicry was the subject of a kind of forensic investigation by Dowsett-Lemaire (1979), who studied the species imitated in the repertoires of 30 birds (mainly from Belgium) and identified mimicry of 113 African species, some with a restricted range; she was then able to suggest the probable autumn and winter areas in east Africa for the birds studied. Individual repertoires included an average of 76 imitations, with more African species than European.

Fast, rippling, liquid trills and hissy, nasal notes ('tchay') are characteristic and may be diagnostic in Marsh Warbler song. I'll pass you over to John Walpole-Bond for the definitive description of the song. It consists of 'a mass of mimicry rattled off, some of it in tones low, rolling, blurred, and gurgling; some of it, again, in a key high-pitched, liquid, trilling, and very clear: the rest in pants, sighs, wheezes, and even nasal phonetics … It is a song which at one time somewhat slow, subdued, laboured, and even snatchy, suddenly flashes into quick, smooth, sustained, effortless rhythm – a hurried flow of tune loudly effusive, brilliant, and intensely passionate even to the verge of delirium.' Wow! Nevertheless their voice isn't loud, nor can it be described as full – rather high-pitched and a little thin – but with superb articulation.

The usual contact and alarm calls are a sharp, tongue-clicking 'tak' and a slightly harsh, scratchy churr, not easily separated from that of Reed Warbler.

REED WARBLER

EURASIAN REED WARBLER, ACROCEPHALUS SCIRPACEUS

AUDIO: CD 2:42, 3:22 SONG, CD 3:37 CALL

J	F	M	A	M	J	J	A	S	O	N	D

This is a vocal species throughout the year, particularly so in the breeding season, and a little song as well as calls can be heard in the winter areas too. Output is highest in the early morning, but can be quite high in the afternoon in unpaired birds. Later in the breeding season, groups of paired males sing at dawn and a little at dusk, which Catchpole termed 'social song', but rarely during the day (Catchpole, 1973). Sometimes birds are heard singing during the night.

Song is in a continuous stream at a steady, medium-paced tempo, unlike either Marsh or Sedge Warblers, with their wide variations. It's a mixture of chirpy and squeaky syllables, generally rather lower-pitched and fuller-voiced than the other two species, and though there is quite a wide frequency range to the syllables, the overall impression of the song is that it stays around the same pitch.

Some individuals include a fair amount of mimicry, including occasionally of Marsh Warbler, which can be deceptive.

The usual alarm and contact call is a low, often rather quiet churr, a little scratchy, but not as harsh as Marsh Warbler, and may become more squealing in alarm or antagonism.

ICTERINE WARBLER

ICTERINE WARBLER, HIPPOLAIS ICTERINA

It is very vocal early in the breeding season, with song frequent, less so after pair formation (BWP, 2004), and calls quite readily in alarm. It mostly breeds in continental Europe but there have been several breeding records in Britain recently. It's a fine singer and rather more loud, strident and explosive than similar warblers of our region.

Male song is rich and varied, often with much mimicry, and broadly comparable to Marsh Warbler. In structure it's more broken than Marsh Warbler, without recognisable verses with the regular build to ecstatic passages of that species, more repetitive and in a fuller, louder voice. Most syllables or phrases are repeated several times, then often after a pause repeated again and on to a different phrase. Occasionally it breaks into a faster, more continuous passage. Squeaky and harder, harsh notes soon become diagnostic with a little experience.

The main calls are a thick 'chuk', often doubled, and may be followed by a rising whistle, in a characteristic phrase 'tch-tch-whee', which has been referred to as 'dideroid'.

DARTFORD WARBLER

DARTFORD WARBLER, SYLVIA UNDATA

AUDIO: CD 1:68 SONG, CD 3:38 CALL

While vocal with song early on spring mornings, it is also occasionally heard in the autumn, and is described as 'not a persistent singer' (Walpole-Bond in BWP, 2004). It calls readily in alarm at intruders into nesting areas, when roving with young or if generally irritated at your presence.

Song is in short verses of a fast, high-octane blend of chattering and whistles, usually incorporating the sound of its call here and there. It's similar to some of the other Mediterranean *Sylvia* warblers, but fairly distinctive in the northern part of its range and only really comparable with Stonechat or Whitethroat. The rhythm is a hurried mix of fluid and stuttering, and the overall impression is of the churring voice. Song is generally given from the edge or top of a low shrub, typically gorse, and in a fluttering, vertical song-flight, sometimes in transit to another perch.

The main call is a thick churr, sometimes rather drawn-out and falling slightly in pitch, not unlike that of Whitethroat, but with a distinctive nasal whine. Often one or two sharper syllables are added at the end 'dürrr-da-da'.

LESSER WHITETHROAT

LESSER WHITETHROAT, SYLVIA CURRUCA

AUDIO: CD 1:30 SONG, CD 3:39 CALL

J	F	M	A	M	J	J	A	S	O	N	D

Quite vocal, calling readily when disturbed, though the song period can be short. Output is high early in the breeding period but declines sharply, and males are rather quiet during their mate's fertile period (Klit, 1999). Subsong is heard in autumn and winter.

The male's song has two modes, termed by Klit 'twitter' and 'trill'; the twitter is a warbled sequence, rather similar to ecstatic song from Common Whitethroat, and the trill is a repeated louder syllable, producing a rattle, similar to a prolonged phrase of Chaffinch song. In its most usual form, at the start of the breeding season, song is in verses opening with a brief warble emerging into the rattle. The rattle is louder than the warble and may be the only part audible at any distance; Klit has suggested that the warble serves more for mate attraction and the rattle for territorial male-male communication. This is reinforced by more emphasis on the warble early in the season and the dominance of the rattle later; I've heard at least one bird giving verses of warbling with little evidence of the rattle.

The main contact and alarm call is a sharp 'tsuk', similar to Blackcap but just distinguishable with experience. Other calls include a low churr, similar to Common Whitethroat, from nervous birds, and churring squeals and yikkering from excited birds. Also, accompanying early song, males may intersperse a few very high-pitched whistles (barely audible to ageing ears!).

WHITETHROAT

WHITETHROAT, SYLVIA COMMUNIS
AUDIO: CD 1:45, 3:21 SONG, CD 3:38 CALL

A very vocal species, with song frequent, particularly early in the breeding season, but often heard into summer, and its alarm calls are a common sound on a summer walk along a hedgerow.

Male song is given in two styles. The usual perched song is in brief verses, often repeated at short intervals, comprising a melodic jingle, descending in pitch through the verse, at a rather jaunty pace, in a slightly grating voice. The second style is a continuous stream of sweet warbling, with clear, fine whistles and often some mimicry interspersing motifs of the first style, richly varied and overall comparable with Blackcap song. The second style, sometimes referred to as 'ecstatic' song, is given in fluttering song-flight, when moving from one song-post to another, and when courting a female. Occasionally one comes across birds singing in a kind of intermediate way. Output of song falls appreciably on pairing, and males singing persistently later in the season are usually unpaired birds (Balsby, 2000).

The main contact and alarm calls are a rising, wheezy 'dweep, dweep' or possibly 'vüid, vüid', generally repeated quickly, and a low, buzzy, slightly nasal churr, usually given singly at intervals from within cover. Occasionally it also gives thick scratchy 'tchk' calls, particularly after the breeding season (BWP, 2004).

GARDEN WARBLER

GARDEN WARBLER, SYLVIA BORIN

AUDIO: CD 1:42, 3:19 SONG, CD 3:39 CALL

The species is vocal throughout the year, particularly during the breeding season, with song often persistent even through July (possibly unpaired males); song is also occasional in autumn and winter. Males sing from a prominent perch for periods, but frequently from within cover while foraging. They are heard calling less often than Blackcap, but call readily in alarm at an intruder near the nest area. Distinguishing between Garden Warbler and Blackcap song is something many, even experienced, birders find difficult. However, with practice, the difference is clear. Occasionally birds of either species sing a little like the other, particularly early in the season when a bird may be singing more loosely, warming up (plastic song). It's worth listening for a longer period in these situations.

Full song is usually given in verses of around 3 to 5 seconds' length, occasionally extended into a more continuous warble. It's marked by the even, hurried tempo and rather even overall pitch, generally lower than Blackcap. There are few sustained notes and it's hard to pick out clear phrasing: it fair bubbles along. There is a slight burr to the voice and a general lack of the clear whistles that permeate Blackcap song. Mimicry can be quite common and accurate, but easily missed in the speed of delivery. Excited birds move into sustained passages of a kind of higher-pitched falsetto wheezing, still warbling at a brisk tempo.

The main call is a coarse 'chuf', lower in pitch and given singly in contact, rising in pitch and intensity when alarmed, and repeated insistently in series. It's a slightly longer note than the tongue-clicking call of many of its congeners; the length, coarse timbre and rapid, regular repetition are fairly diagnostic. They also sometimes give an odd, subdued bubbling churr in alarm. BWP (2004) reports various rasping, churring and rattling calls given in situations of dispute and sexual excitement.

BLACKCAP

EURASIAN BLACKCAP, SYLVIA ATRICAPILLA
AUDIO: CD 1:41, 3:19 SONG, CD 3:39 CALL

J	F	M	A	M	J	J	A	S	O	N	D

A fairly vocal species, particularly notable for the male's song in the early part of the breeding season, though birds can be rather quiet and unobtrusive for much of the time. Subsong is occasional in autumn and may become quite common and fuller as winter progresses, particularly in southern parts of the range. Birds call readily in alarm at intruders into breeding area, and often when disturbed at other times (including migrants).

Blackcap is a popular singer and a favourite for many. With a varied and melodically phrased song it provides a welcome lead-line in a woodland or scrubland chorus. I find Blackcap's voice a little shrill sometimes – apparently birds in the south of the species' range are deeper-voiced (BWP, 2004) – and generally prefer the more mellow sound of Garden Warbler, though a good singer is worth listening to for a long while. Nevertheless, I often hear long passages of birds singing rather tightly structured verses with no real sparkle in the phrasing.

Typically, birds sing for shortish periods, then move on and take it up again somewhere nearby; but they do have favourite song-posts, prominent if not conspicuous, often at mid-height, usually higher on average than Garden Warbler, and frequently even in treetops. They will also sing low down from within cover, usually a less structured, more continuous song (subsong/plastic song), especially early in the breeding season. Song output is at a peak early in the breeding season during territory establishment and pair formation, when they can often be heard throughout the day. There's a resurgence of song before a second brood, otherwise late singers are thought to be unpaired birds (Simms, 1985).

Full song is in verses with short intervals, that build from a hesitant jumble of thin and scratchy notes into more fluent phrasing in a clear, fluting whistle, ending with a distinct motif. The fluted phrases towards the end reach full volume and tend to be more stereotyped than the first part; individuals have a few favourite endings which they use regularly. Shirihai et al. (2001) quote Svensson that birds of an area share the same endings, which thus form recognisable local dialects. Mimicry can be more or less frequent and very accurate.

Compared with Garden Warbler, Blackcap song has more articulated and varied phrasing, with variations in pace and more broken rhythms. Verses end in a flourish, usually a recognisable motif. In the syllables of Blackcap song, purer tones and slightly shrill whistles predominate in comparison to Garden Warbler's bubbling 'burr'.

The main contact and alarm call is a classic *Sylvia* tongue-clicking 'tak', quickly repeated in alarm or excitement. Also given in alarm is a variable, rasping or squeaky 'zeur' or 'sweer' (BWP, 2004). Other calls heard occasionally include wheezy whistles (which may be variants of previous), mewing and churring sounds.

WOOD WARBLER

WOOD WARBLER, PHYLLOSCOPUS SIBILATRIX

AUDIO: CD 1:63 SONG, CD 3:29 CALL

J	F	M	A	M	J	J	A	S	O	N	D

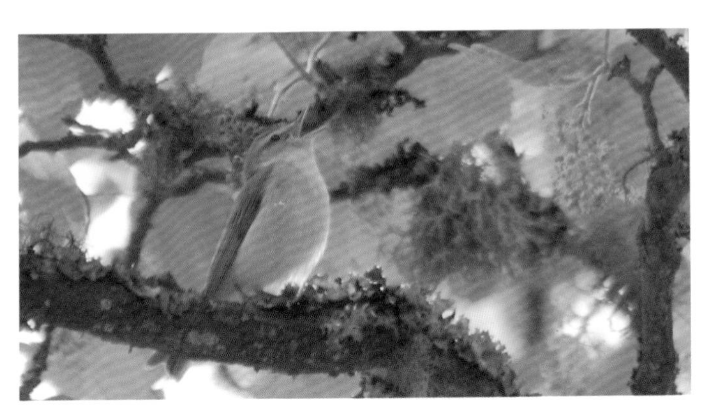

Male song is frequent in the early part of the breeding season, often heard throughout the day, and becomes intermittent on pairing, though males often try to attract a second female; song may also be given during spring migration, but rarely in winter. It calls readily in alarm at intruders in the nesting area and in aggressive encounters, otherwise it's reported as rather quiet on autumn migration and in winter (BWP, 2004).

The male's song is in verses based on repeated thin silvery 'tsit' notes, opening slightly hesitantly, before accelerating into a quick tempo, falling a little in pitch and ending in a sibilant trill. He repeats this verse at intervals for much of a spring day, every so often (typically about once for every dozen trills) inserting a series of plaintive notes between verses, like the contact and alarm call (usually described as alternative song and could be the relic of an interstrophic call – cf. Willow Warbler and Chiffchaff).

Birds sing from medium to high perches, usually well beneath the tree canopy; verses are usually given in pauses while foraging, with occasionally several given from the same spot, and every so often in horizontal song-flight with shivering wings. After pairing, often only an abbreviated trill song is given when in the vicinity of the female.

The syllables of the song cover a rather wide band of higher frequencies, and, when heard in a forest community, Wood Warbler songs fill a large slice of the available frequency spectrum. They can be heard at up to 400 metres (450 yards), ringing out in the sub-canopy acoustic. At peak output birds sing about seven verses per minute.

The main alarm and contact call is similar to the 'düü' or 'pew' notes of the alternative song, with a timbre reminiscent of Bullfinch; voicing varies slightly. Other calls heard occasionally include a shrill 'see-see-see' from excited males, repeated 'chk' or 'wit' notes around the nest and hissing sounds in various contexts.

CHIFFCHAFF

COMMON CHIFFCHAFF, PHYLLOSCOPUS COLLYBITA

AUDIO: CD 1:49, 3:02 SONG, CD 3:29 CALL

J	F	M	A	M	J	J	A	S	O	N	D

A vocal species throughout the year, with song frequent during the breeding season, from their early arrival and again into autumn; females are also reported to sing in autumn (BWP, 2004). Song is also heard occasionally during the winter months in southern England. Calls are readily given in alarm at intruders during the breeding season and migrants are usually fairly vocal with calls. It has quite a repertoire of calls mainly associated with breeding, but is mostly rarely heard except for the main contact and alarm call.

Song is in verses of a slow and steady series of 'chiff'-like syllables, sometimes the onomatopoeic 'chiff-chaff', but often with a three-note lilt, occasionally more varied. Verses are normally between two and five seconds long, sometimes occasionally longer. Singing birds may repeat a short, dry 'tret' call between song verses ('interstrophic call'), heard more often early in the breeding season, though sometimes through to July. Song is usually given from within the canopy of trees or scrub, occasionally from a more exposed perch in the outer foliage; birds tend to sing a verse, move on foraging, then stop to sing the next verse.

Song types with more articulated phrasing, a more broken rhythm, typically accelerating a little, or with a short trilled ending, may indicate an Iberian Chiffchaff *P. brehmii*. A little care is needed, since these are not easily separated from unusual songs of Common Chiffchaff.

The main contact and alarm call is a short, rising whistle 'weep', not so disyllabic as Willow Warbler, although occasionally it can be rather similar. Then the other characteristic becomes important: Chiffchaff calls have something of the timbre of a squeaky toy, with sometimes a hint of sibilant wheeziness. Willow Warbler calls in a more rounded whistle. It can also be confused with Chaffinch 'weet' calls. In late summer and autumn, variations on this main call are heard, often an inflected 'sweeoo' or just plain 'swee'; usually these are from young birds drifting south, but I've heard such from an adult female in spring.

The latter calls are sometimes optimistically taken for Siberian Chiffchaff *P. collybita tristis*: but their diagnostic call is a rather featureless, whistled 'see', sometimes dropping in pitch slightly at the end; it's been described as like the distress call of a young chicken or a high-pitched Bullfinch. The calls of Iberian Chiffchaff are more distinctive, a descending 'tsew', rather like Reed Bunting.

GOLDCREST

GOLDCREST, REGULUS REGULUS
AUDIO: CD 2:06, 3:26 SONG, CD 3:27 CALL

A very vocal species throughout the year, with calling frequent and often varied from parties on the move and foraging. Calls are rather softer and simpler from solitary migrants and birds in mixed winter flocks, but they are rarely silent for long. Male song is frequent from early spring through the breeding season and again in autumn. They have quite a vocabulary of calls, though all rather similar in sound to us, since all their vocalisations are very high-pitched; excited song often includes some lower-pitched, chattering phrases (song endings). In human hearing the ageing process affects our perception of higher frequencies first, and sadly the voice of Goldcrest, and presumably Firecrest, usually becomes inaudible in later years.

Song is in verses of around 3 seconds (usually 2.5–4), which build on cycling a rhythmical phrase at a very high pitch, reaching a crescendo usually with a fuller terminal flourish; sometimes the terminal flourish may be omitted, a verse may be run straight into the next and occasionally the cyclical phrase may be extended, exceptionally to over 20 seconds (BWP, 2004). Overall it's a rather stereotyped warble, with a varied ending, in a sweet, slightly sibilant, high-pitched whistle. At peak singing times, intervals between verses are short.

Individual males have a repertoire of endings (minimum 18), some of which are shared with all the males in a local population, others with few; an individual's repertoire remains very constant from year to year. Song endings often include mimicry, particularly the final note. In excited singing (such as fights or with female present), males string together song endings in a continuous twittering: I have a recording of this featuring mimicry of Chaffinch, Long-tailed Tit and various Paridae calls, including at least Coal Tit.

Males usually sing while foraging in the foliage at a tree's mid-height, but often lower; occasionally they will fly to the top or some other prominent perch to deliver a few verses in succession. In the spring, males establish large pre-territories with song and calls but once paired maintain smaller nesting territories; neighbouring males regularly (several times a day) meet at their borders for long 'song-duels' (Haftorn in BWP, 2004).

The calls are mostly high-pitched, sibilant whistles, varying from soft, short contact notes to loud, more drawn-out and repeated notes, often signifying excitement or intention to fly; birds call readily and the various kinds of call and patterns of calling encompass a functionally complex vocabulary. One parameter of variation in the calls is frequency modulation; the longer calls may be given in a tonally pure form or with fast frequency modulation to sound something like a sibilant trill (and very like Treecreeper). It can be difficult to separate such calls from those of Long-tailed Tit or Treecreeper; the short contact calls are also very similar to those of Paridae species and it's worth noting that all these species readily band together in autumn and winter to forage as a loose flock.

WILLOW WARBLER

WILLOW WARBLER, PHYLLOSCOPUS TROCHILUS

AUDIO: CD 1:43, 3:03 SONG, CD 3:29 CALL

J	F	M	A	M	J	J	A	S	O	N	D

A vocal species all year round, with song frequent throughout the breeding season for much of the day, waning in July and with a good resumption into autumn. It is also heard in winter a little, becoming more frequent into spring. Birds call freely through the year, including on migration and during winter. Although hardly a virtuoso performer, they are a very popular and welcome singer: their voice and song patterns are so easy on the ears and, in a well-populated habitat, their interspersed songs provide a lovely rippling, almost arpeggiated theme that echoes into the distance. They are highly territorial when breeding and male chases are common especially at the start of the breeding season.

Song is normally in verses of about 3 seconds, each a cascading, melodic sequence of slurred whistles, slightly sibilant, usually descending in pitch through the sequence. The first few notes build in volume to a peak, later declining again and slowing slightly towards the end. Often you can make out distinct phrases of repeated syllables, similar to Chaffinch with which they often share their territories, and some find it difficult to separate the two species – persevere. Though some syllables approach the clipped notes of Chaffinch song and the whistled voice can be quite strident, there are no harsh or percussive elements.

Although verses appear similar and some birds can sound repetitive, normally each verse is varied a little and a good singer finds a nice balance in thematic variation.

Excited males often repeat a short, raspy or wheezy note in the intervals between verses of song, presumably homologous with the interstrophic call of Chiffchaff. This call is very similar to the calls of recently fledged young. At the peak of the breeding season birds tend to sing from favourite song-posts on their territories, a prominent perch at the top or side of a shrub or small tree. Otherwise song is often given more casually, pausing from foraging to deliver a verse. Song in flight is rare, other than in antagonistic chases.

The main contact and alarm call is a short whistled 'hooeet', typically with a fuller tone, more drawn-out and disyllabic than the equivalent call of Chiffchaff. The 'hoo' is held for a fraction of a second before rising in pitch more abruptly on the 'eet', where typically the whole Chiffchaff call rises in pitch. In alarm the calls may become sharper and shorter, more like Chiffchaff, and variations are heard from juveniles in the autumn. Other calls are sometimes heard in specific contexts, including a rattle or drawn-out trill from males in chases and a softly yikkering Cuckoo alarm call.

FIRECREST

FIRECREST, REGULUS IGNICAPILLUS
AUDIO: CD 3:26 SONG

In my (rather limited) experience this is not as vocal a species as Goldcrest, although songs and calls associated with breeding can be frequent. Songs and calls are broadly similar to Goldcrest and all high-pitched, though marginally lower than Goldcrest.

Its song is very similar in form to Goldcrest, but lacking a terminal flourish. Where Goldcrest's cyclical phrase has some pitch variation within it, Firecrest's equivalent is little more than a rhythmically repeated note at a constant pitch; and Firecrest's song increases in tempo through the sequence, until it runs away with itself at the end, whereas Goldcrest's is at a more or less steady pace, though increasing in power. The overall pitch of the song syllables often drops fractionally during the sequence, while Goldcrest's may rise in pitch, at least up to the terminal flourish.

The main calls are similar high-pitched whistles to Goldcrest, including short contact notes, 'zit' or 'sisisi', longer, drawn-out notes in series and shrill trilling in excitement and courtship. Firecrest's calls tend to be slightly lower-pitched, less sibilant, often with a sharper metallic ring and more percussive voicing than Goldcrest, but these differences may not be consistent. Both species have a tendency to give the main contact and flight call in groups of four (BWP, 2004). Mullarney et al. (1999) suggest a tendency to open with a longer note, followed by two to three shorter notes rising in pitch and accelerating.

FLYCATCHERS – MUSCICAPIDAE

The two species treated here belong to different genera and their vocal behaviour is very different: nevertheless both have a similar sharp 'tak' call. In general flycatchers' voices tend towards fine, rather high-pitched whistles. The *Ficedula* species have rather melodic songs.

SPOTTED FLYCATCHER

SPOTTED FLYCATCHER, MUSCICAPA STRIATA
AUDIO: CD 1:57 SONG, CD 3:28 CALL

Very vocal during the breeding season, with calling frequent, often seemingly all day long. This persistent calling seems to take the place of full song, though a rather quiet, twittering subsong, not easily audible at any distance, is frequent until egg-laying (BWP, 2004).

The main call is a thin, high-pitched, rather sibilant 'tsee', very like similar calls from Robin, though slightly longer and often lightly trilled; in persistent calling, notes may be given in a regular stream at a rate of more than one per second, often just slightly varied. In alarm, birds call with a sharp, clicking 'chik', often accompanied by the 'tsee' call, so typically 'tsee, chik'.

When calling intensely in the earlier part of the breeding season, occasional trilled phrases may be inserted, in a kind of halfway stage to the quieter subsong. Subsong given in courtship is an intense but quiet stream of twittering, with many brief, sibilant trills and can include mimicry; the bird in the recording included mimicry of Swallow, Starling and Blue Tit (or possibly Great Tit).

PIED FLYCATCHER

EURASIAN PIED FLYCATCHER, FICEDULA HYPOLEUCA
AUDIO: CD 1:64 SONG

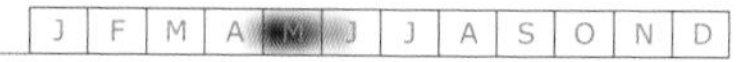

A rather vocal species, but although the song output is high when males arrive in their breeding areas, the song period can be quite short and males cease singing fairly abruptly once they acquire a mate (Espmark & Lampe, 1993). Unpaired males may continue to sing through to June. On first arriving, birds tend to sing from high perches, then, when attracting a female, song tends to be focused on the male's choice of nest site. They call readily in alarm at intruders into breeding area; migrants can be quite vocal with calls on passage.

Song is in verses, generally about 2.5–4 seconds in length, at short intervals when output is high. Each consists of a series of notes at a regular moderate pace, with clear phrasing, often repeating a figure, and giving a pleasantly melodic impression, almost 'sweet'. There is a tendency to alternate high and low notes, so typically something like 'swee-chu-chu, swee-chu-chu, swee'; some males have far more complex motifs in their repertoire and a bird I recorded in Poland gave a very tuneful descending arpeggio of six notes. Lampe and Saetre (1995) found that females preferred males with larger song figure repertoires and more versatile song, given a choice.

The main contact and alarm calls are a sharp, whistled 'plik' and a clicking 'tak', the latter more often heard from migrants. When calling in alarm often both are given.

BEARDED TIT

BEARDED REEDLING, PANURUS BIARMICUS, TIMALIIDAE
AUDIO: CD 2:43

Bearded tits are one of those species for which it pays to learn the sound of their voice; spending much of their time hidden in dense reeds, their calls are the best clue to their presence. A rather sociable and fairly vocal species, calling is sporadic as birds call briefly to keep in touch, then go quiet for a while. The birds are said to be most active and vocal in the spring as breeding gets under way, then again in the early autumn as family parties are roving through the reeds and excitement builds prior to dispersal to wintering sites.

The main call is a distinctive 'ptew' note, often described as ringing and sometimes referred to as a 'ping'; certainly it's quite audible even with a stiff breeze rustling the stands of phragmites and can usually be heard up to around 50 metres (160 feet) away. Heard at close range, a slightly wheezy timbre becomes apparent. The actual voicing of the note can vary, ranging from just a brief percussive 'pit' to a purer, more drawn-out 'tee', which may be a categorically different call. Excited birds may give bursts of fast repetition, such as when a party rises from the reeds for a short flight. Flocks are said to rise above the reeds in a towering flight when preparing to move out in autumn, but I've never witnessed this.

LONG-TAILED TIT

LONG-TAILED BUSHTIT, AEGITHALOS CAUDATUS, AEGITHALIDAE
AUDIO: CD 1:44, 3:27

A very vocal species throughout the year, but mainly with calls and appears not to have any territorial song (BWP, 2004). Birds foraging in a flock call frequently to maintain contact and give alarm calls readily if confronted with an intruder nearby. Their contact calls are often the best indicator of a mixed passerine flock moving through woodland in autumn and winter, Long-tailed seeming to act as the convenors of the flock.

The usual contact call is high-pitched sibilant 'tsee', which is typically given in a short run of 3–4, descending slightly in pitch. A short, thick 'tchup', interspersed occasionally, may signify slight nervousness; in alarm or excitement, birds give a bubbling rattle or trill 'trrrr', often quickly repeated, which may also be interspersed with 'tchup' calls.

BWP (2004) describes song as a quiet twittering or trilling given in aggressive encounters and a 'distinctly different' bubbling given by both sexes around the nest site.

TITS – PARIDAE

The members of this family have recently been reclassified and, where the species used to be considered to belong to a single genus *Parus*, they have been organised now into several genera; I've given the old scientific names in brackets. Bearded Tits and Long-tailed Tits belong to different families and have rather different vocal behaviours from the Paridae: neither has a formal song. Crested Tit, which is still considered to belong to the Paridae, is rather similar. Otherwise the members of this family have wide vocabularies and stereotyped songs, where individuals tend to have a repertoire of several song-types. The range of the vocalisations of Coal, Blue and Great Tits is very wide and calls can be rather similar. Distinguishing between them is often a matter of voice: Coal thin, slightly sibilant and high-pitched, Great Tit lowest-pitched and fullest and Blue Tit somewhere between in terms of calls, though the song is high-pitched. Marsh Tits and Willow Tits are rather different, but broadly similar to each other.

BLUE TIT

BLUE TIT, CYANISTES CAERULEUS (PARUS CAERULEUS)
AUDIO: CD 1:11, 3:02 SONG, CD 3:24 CALL

J F M A M J J A S O N D

Vocal all year round, with both song and calls, though song output is highest from late winter through the spring and rather rare during the summer moult and as autumn turns to winter.

The commonest song-types differ in style from the other species of the family in that they are often a stereotyped verse, rather than a cycled motif. Typically opening with two or three high-pitched thin whistles, a verse moves into a repeated note or trill at a slightly lower pitch, the whole with a pure, silvery sound ('see-see-te-chü-chü-chü-chü'), usually repeated at short intervals. But other song-types, which cycle round a motif, such as 'seetehühü-seetehühü-seetehühü …', are fairly common too. Males have repertoires of three to eight different song types (BWP, 2004), and female song, similar to males, is reported to be fairly frequent in antagonistic situations and alarm around the nest site. A prolonged, rhythmic, high-pitched and sibilant trilling is given in courtship, generally leading up to mating 'swee-swee-swee …'.

The usual alarm and contact call is a rattly churr, rising slightly in pitch and often introduced by a brief whistle like the song. A tetchy sharp repeated note is also frequent 'tch-tch-tch …', though like so many of the calls in its wide vocabulary it's often not easily distinguished from similar calls of Great Tit and Coal Tit; and, like the other members of the family, it intermittently calls with soft 'tsip's in contact while foraging.

GREAT TIT

GREAT TIT, PARUS MAJOR
AUDIO: CD 1:12, 3:02 SONG, CD 3:24 CALL

J F M A M J J A S O N D

A vocal species all year round with a wide vocabulary and much individual variation, though BWP (2004) reports females to be considerably less vocal than males. Song begins early in the year, fades in the summer, with a fair resumption in the autumn. The species has been well studied, both in the wild, such as in Wytham woods over a long period by various Oxford University researchers, and more informally through tame birds living freely, e.g. Jellis (1977) and Howard (1952).

Song is in verses of a repeated motif, of usually two or three notes, often with a slightly buzzy or churring timbre, though also frequently described as chiming and metallic (BWP, 2004). Typically rather tuneful with crisp enunciation, one of the commonest song-types is a two-note see-saw, often rendered 'tea-cher', the pitch interval approximating to a third. It's been found that songs from birds of denser woodland tend to have a lower maximum frequency, narrower frequency range, and fewer units per motif, than the songs of birds in more open habitats (Hunter amd Krebs reported in BWP, 2004). More recent research has found that birds in cities sing more loudly and with higher-pitched songs than birds in quieter habitats and that they respond more to the particular songs appropriate to their habitat (Mockford & Marshall, 2009). A chattery, repetitive (a cycled motif) subsong can also be heard in the spring.

It's difficult to know where to begin with Great Tit calls since there is so much variety: experienced birders quip that if you hear an unusual call in woodland, the chances are it's a Great Tit. In alarm the most general call is a rather hollow, rattling churr, often introduced by a couple of sharp whistles; a sharp repeated 'tch-tch' is frequent and a Chaffinch-like 'spink'. As well as a variety of short, bright whistles, birds also have various call motifs, not always clearly distinct from song; possibly the commonest in my area is 'see-huee', the 'huee' very like a Willow Warbler call.

CRESTED TIT

EUROPEAN CRESTED TIT, LOPHOPHANES CRISTATUS (PARUS CRISTATUS)
AUDIO: CD 2:10

Rather a vocal species, with calls given intermittently all year round, but their vocabulary is less varied than the other family members of our region and they lack a distinct song.

The diagnostic call is a purring trill, slightly stuttered and even squeaky. Birds also call with a thin, sibilant whistle, often with a slight trilling modulation, very similar to the contact calls of Long-tailed Tits and often given in similar rhythms. Both calls are often given together, heard all year round, and serve as both alarm calls and song, when they tend to be repeated in combination excitedly.

COAL TIT

COAL TIT, PERIPARUS ATER (PARUS ATER)
AUDIO: CD 2:04, 3:02 SONG, CD 3:24 CALL

J	F	M	A	M	J	J	A	S	O	N	D

A vocal species, with a wide vocabulary of calls; their song is heard almost all year round, though output is highest in spring.

Their song is in verses of a stereotyped figure, usually two notes alternating, occasionally three, cycled round and broadly similar to Great Tit, typically 'wheetü-wheetü-wheetü …'. Delivery is at a lively pace, brisker than Great Tit, higher-pitched and often with an emphatic pitch inflection. There tends to be a slightly sibilant, metallic ring to the voice.

Possibly the commonest call is 'teut-ti' or just 'teuy'; in alarm or scolding it is a hard 'tchi-tchi-tchi', similar to Blue Tit and Great Tit. There is an inclination to very fast repetitions (trills) 'tsi-tsi-tsi …' and 'sisisi …' in excitement, as well as slurred sibilance 'te-tseur-tsi' and typical soft 'tsip's in close contact, like the rest of the family. Overall it's just as varied in its vocalisation as Great Tit, though less distinctive and with a less varied range of song types.

WILLOW TIT

WILLOW TIT, POECILE MONTANA (PARUS MONTANUS)

AUDIO: CD 1:61, 3:23 SONG, CD 3:23 CALL

J F M A M J J A S O N D

The species is vocal throughout the year, though its song is possibly even less common than that of Marsh Tit. Even when a male is singing there can be quite long intervals between verses. A marked difference between the songs of birds in the Alps and the rest of Europe has been noted (BWP, 2004).

Male song is typical for the family, a stereotyped repetition, normally for lowland Europe, a single, down-slurred rather pure whistle 'tsew-tsew-tsew …', with a similarity to Wood Warbler's inter-verse calls. Apparently individuals may have up to three different song-types in their repertoires, but they are 'not very easily distinguishable' (BWP, 2004). The pace of delivery is rather deliberate, sometimes almost jaunty, but not as brisk as Marsh Tit. Birds (males?) also have a different mode of singing with a continuous, sibilant trilling, interspersed with warbled phrases. It is labelled as 'aggressive' song in BWP (2004), but when I recorded this from a bird near its nest site in Poland (during nest-building phase), there was no evidence of aggression in the context.

The main distinctive contact and alarm call is a buzzy, slightly nasal 'tchay' note, usually repeated several times, and sometimes preceded by a few short, thin whistles, so typically 'zi-zi-tchay-tchay-tchay'. Although the timbre is roughly similar to calls of Marsh Tit, the pace of the repetitions is slow and the notes are quite drawn-out. Other calls include soft, brief whistles similar to other Paridae species, a rather thickly slurred 'tseur' from a family party in summer and terse 'chit's from a single bird in winter.

MARSH TIT

MARSH TIT, POECILE PALUSTRIS (PARUS PALUSTRIS)
AUDIO: CD 1:50, 3:23 SONG, CD 3:23 CALL

J F M A M J J A S O N D

A very vocal species, perhaps more so on the whole than Willow Tit, though song may be more sporadic than the better-known species of this family. Paired birds tend to remain together all year and frequently call in contact. It has a varied vocabulary of calls.

Male song conforms to the family trait, a stereotyped figure that is cycled round in short verses, each male having a few different types. The most basic type is a single, explosive syllable, typically 'tchew-tchew-tchew …', but others can be slightly more elaborate, such as 'ti-wheeoo'. Delivery is brisk and loud, always at a faster pace than Willow Tit.

The main distinctive contact and alarm call is a combination of a sharp whistle and a churred syllable, 'pi-tchew', which may be extended into a 'pi-tchewuwuwu' or 'pi-tchaweeu'; often birds call with just the explosive whistle 'pit', which is quite distinctive with experience, softer contact whistles less so. Both songs and calls are livelier than Willow Tit, with a brisker delivery of syllables, though structurally rather similar.

NUTHATCH

EURASIAN NUTHATCH, SITTA EUROPAEA, SITTIDAE
AUDIO: CD 1:48, 3:12 SONG, CD 3:27 CALL

J F M A M J J A S O N D

A vocal bird throughout the year, its song and loud calls are associated with year-round territory maintenance. Song output is highest from late winter through the spring, with some resumption in the autumn, otherwise it's mostly heard calling.

Male song has two forms, both rather loud and in verses around two to three seconds long, based on a repeated note, but differing in the kind of note and the tempo of delivery. The trilled song is a quickly repeated short, clear whistle 'pee-pee-pee-pee …', each sequence rising slightly in pitch and falling towards the end; the other form has a more drawn-out note, usually rising in pitch 'twee, twee, twee …', but some types fall, often slightly shrill, and repeated at a more deliberate slower rate than the trill. But since the tempo range is continuously variable between the two extremes, it could be questioned whether these two forms of song are categorically distinct.

The main call is a sharp, clear 'twoit', like a pebble hitting ice, given singly or often in pairs, even in runs of three or four, and repeated rapidly in excitement. Also quite distinctive is a thin, high-pitched 'zeet', quieter than the previous call but with a sharp electric timbre.

TREECREEPER

EURASIAN TREECREEPER, CERTHIA FAMILIARIS, CERTHIIDAE

AUDIO: CD 1:56, 3:03 SONG, CD 3:27 CALL

J	F	M	A	M	J	J	A	S	O	N	D

A rather vocal species, with calls heard throughout year and song frequent in spring, a little more casual in early summer and again in autumn. Loud calls are intermittent, though frequently calls with soft 'tsip's while foraging and, though not especially distinctive, these calls are useful in drawing your attention to a bird's presence nearby (often on the far side of a tree trunk!). The voice is high-pitched, thin and sibilant.

Song is in rather short, stereotyped verses, distinctly phrased, descending in pitch and accelerating towards the end (structurally similar to Chaffinch but much higher-pitched). It's easily missed because of the high pitch, which is masked by other woodland passerines singing in the same frequency range, such as Blue Tit and Wren.

Loud calls are drawn-out, high-pitched, sibilant whistles, often given in an evenly spaced series, each note holding its pitch or maybe falling just slightly ('tseüü, tseüü, tseüü'). One kind has a shivering timbre, from rapid frequency modulation, but in excitement is pure and almost hissing. Listen out for the soft 'tsip' contact calls.

GOLDEN ORIOLE

EURASIAN GOLDEN ORIOLE, ORIOLUS ORIOLUS, ORIOLIDAE

AUDIO: CD 1:62 SONG

This species is vocal during the breeding season, with song frequent and calls distinctive when given.

Its song is in lightly varied, brief verses in a melodious, fluty voice, comparable to the opening phrase of Blackbird song, with distinctive pitch inflections, particularly a pitch jump as in a human yodel, typically 'weela-weeyu'. It usually gives the impression of two parts and is very distinctive and charming once heard. A more continuous subsong, with similar phrases, though slightly clanky, is often heard from migrants and early in the breeding season.

The commonest call is a slightly drawn-out, rising squawk (not a word I like to use, but the best description), 'vraaak' – rather hoarse and shrill (with a hint of Jay). In alarm a falcon-like 'gigigi …' is reported by other authors.

SHRIKES – LANIIDAE

Shrikes, though silent for long periods, can be quite vocal birds. Calls tend to be slightly harsh chatterings and explosive chaks, with a scratchy tone of voice; song tends to be an understated warble, sometimes regarded as subsong, finely articulated and laced with superb mimicry, including a mixture of harsh and sweeter sounds.

RED-BACKED SHRIKE

RED-BACKED SHRIKE, LANIUS COLLURIO
AUDIO: CD 1:74 SONGS AND CALLS

Like the other shrikes, it's very unpredictable when a bird might sing; for much of the time males remain silent or, particularly in breeding areas, give intermittent series of contact/alarm calls that carry an air of irritation and petulance. But when one does come across a singing male, they will often sing on and off for long periods. On the whole, migrants rarely call.

The main call is a rather buzzy 'jow', usually repeated and quite like similar calls of House Sparrow; a series of these calls may begin with, and end with, a more excited, slightly squeakier 'jewi', repeated more rapidly than the previous call. Male song is a rather thin, high-pitched warble, with crisp enunciation and full of mimicry. There's a similarity to Marsh Warbler song or even Blackcap plastic song in the fast rhythms, precise voicings and intermittent clear notes. House Sparrow mimicry tends to be frequent.

GREAT GREY SHRIKE

GREAT GREY SHRIKE, LANIUS EXCUBITOR

Though hunting birds perched on the lookout may appear silent for long periods, especially midwinter, the Grey Shrikes can be quite vocal, possibly more so than is at first apparent, since much of their vocalisation is rather quiet. There's a grey area, particularly marked in this species, where it's difficult to say whether a bird is calling or singing.

The male's primary song is a continuous low chattering warble, including fluid melodious phrases, harsher sounds and mimicry. It can be heard for most of the year, but is normally given in the presence of a female, and BWP (2004) suggests that females and young may sing in this way at the end of the breeding season. More often what one hears is the secondary song: a simple phrase of two or three call-like notes repeated at short intervals (1–3 seconds), typically a liquid 'clik-clik'. It may be a characteristic of the northern Great Grey, compared to the Southern Grey, that they elaborate on this slightly with a different quieter note. The simplicity and repetition give the impression of a calling bird, though there are also aspects of song: some behaviour just doesn't fit the categories.

Atkinson (1997), in a research paper ghoulishly titled 'Singing for your supper: acoustical luring of avian prey by Northern Shrikes', found that winter singing by both sexes served to attract potential prey, in the form of small passerines, to the singing bird.

Calls in alarm and confrontation include a variety of rasping screeches, rather like Starling or a small Jay.

CROWS – CORVIDAE

The crow family are a fairly vocal lot, as they are also to various degrees very sociable. Their voices tend to be 'guttural', croaking and rattling: hence the name 'crow' or 'craa'; but this undermines the subtlety of their vocalisations and they do produce some strange sounds. Their subsongs can be fascinating, if only one can get a chance to hear them. And they can be great mimics.

JAY

EURASIAN JAY. GARRULUS GLANDARIUS
AUDIO: CD 1:52

Jays are rather vocal and social birds, often going around in pairs or small groups. Aside from their loud alarm calls, they can frequently be heard producing a range of quieter calls, some with a similar buzzy timbre to the alarms, but including some very odd sounds that hardly sound like a bird at all, such as squeaking tree branches. Beware also of their mimicry, particularly of Buzzard and Tawny Owl calls.

Their most characteristic and frequently heard call is a buzzy screech, given in alarm at an intruder (often oneself) and in other situations. There are two types: the full-on noisy screech and a more stylised (more musical?) mewing rasp. In contact between individuals, softer variations of these calls are given.

Birds are also heard singing softly with call notes, clucking, whistles, Golden Oriole-like fluty notes and mimicry (Moorhen seems to be frequently copied). Some have suggested that the Golden Oriole type of phrases is a particular type of song of Jays: given the species' propensity for mimicry, it's difficult to say for sure.

As well as mimicry included in song, they are prone to give single renditions mimicking the calls of Buzzard and sometimes Tawny Owl 'kewick'. This is rather interesting and unusual, since most mimicry in the passerines occurs as part of the male's song; there could well be a different function to this kind of Jay mimicry – I've wondered about distraction or deliberate deception. There may be potential benefits in making an intruder or even other small passerines think there is a predator about. Or is it a kind of disguise? I've also several times heard them producing sounds like water droplets or trickles. A fascinating species vocally, but, because of continued persecution in Northumberland, local birds are very wary and difficult to record beyond the alarm calls.

MAGPIE

EURASIAN MAGPIE, PICA PICA

AUDIO: CD 1:07

Vocal throughout the year, though there's little information on seasonal rhythm of song. A wide repertoire is described by BWP (2004), but I'm not very familiar with the species, since they are very scarce in north Northumberland due to persecution.

They are best known for the rattle call, a distinctive rhythmic 'chak-ak-ak ...' frequently used in film to suggest unease and menace. This appears to be their most formal vocalisation, but they have various other chacking and more squealing calls. When moving into song, they become rather quieter (subsong) and chatter softly with clucks, squeaks and mewing sounds. Captive birds are known to be good mimics, particularly of the human voice, but mimicry is rarely heard from wild birds.

CHOUGH

RED-BILLED CHOUGH, PYRRHOCORAX PYRRHOCORAX

AUDIO: CD 3:15

The species is vocal and obvious throughout the year, typically with variations on the eponymous 'chough' call. The call bears some similarity in voice to Jackdaw in the explosive opening, but is generally more prolonged, descending in pitch and with a distinctive zing in the timbre. There is considerable variation in voicing and expression. It is reported to have a quiet chattering and warbling song, in common with other corvids (BWP, 2004). In alarm, it voices a short, harsh repeated 'ker'.

JACKDAW

WESTERN JACKDAW, CORVUS MONEDULA

AUDIO: CD 1:22, 3:15

A very vocal species, often breeding in loose colonies, spending much of their time in family parties or small flocks, or often in winter as part of a larger mixed flock with rooks. It has a wide range of calls that all inter-grade to a certain extent.

The main contact call is an explosive 'choc', or 'jack' as in the name; in interactions, repeated variations on 'huc's are given, often in phrased motifs, and a drawn-out 'jarrr'. In alarm, typically scolding an intruder into the nest area, it is a hoarse, churring low 'chaarrr', sounding closer to Carrion Crow than the other calls. For song BWP (2004) reports 'ceaseless chatter' and 'quiet soliloquy'; though chatter is frequent, I've never heard anything like the subsong of the other corvids. Although mimicry is reported from captive birds, this has not been recorded from wild birds.

ROOK

ROOK, CORVUS FRUGILEGUS

AUDIO: CD 1:34 (AND MANY OTHER PLACES IN THE BACKGROUND)

Rook must vie with Starling and Jackdaw as the most vocal bird of our area. They are rarely silent and constantly express themselves with their voice. This has been both a blessing and a pain to me. The quietest place I've lived was the hub of much Rook activity with a scattered rookery and, believe me, they are never silent. I've been out at 4am in late March (well before dawn) trying to record Tawny Owls, and the Rooks kept calling intermittently in the darkness. Birds frequently give soft moaning calls in flight, barely audible even to a close observer; in fact the range of odd soft calls they give is astonishing.

The main call is very similar to Carrion Crow, although usually sounding less harsh, with a slightly softer timbre (though still hoarse) and generally slightly more drawn-out to a less abrupt ending. Calling rhythms are generally different with sequences often less formal and evenly spaced than Carrion Crow. That said, Rook calls are very variable in their voicing and birds produce all manner of strange sounds at times, from popping clucks, moans and sighs through to coughs, rattles and outright yelps. A common and distinctive call is a kind of yodelling 'chow-da', with the second syllable at a much higher pitch. They also give rattles, similar to Carrion Crow, when mobbing a predator. A varied subsong is sometimes heard from solitary birds perched up, usually with the characteristic head-bobbing and tail-fanning.

CARRION CROW

CARRION CROW, CORVUS CORONE
AUDIO: CD 1:05, 1:36

Vocal throughout the year, but its calling is more intermittent than Rook. Crowing calls are often given in a more formal and even series than Rook, typically three to four in quick succession.

The main call is a rough 'craa' repeated several times in an evenly spaced sequence, normally with a hard rattle in the voice. Sometimes you hear odd honky or nasal-toned variations, though whether these are versions of the primary call particular to certain individuals or are a more general variation occasionally delivered by all birds, I don't know.

Occasionally you hear birds produce a series of odd softer sounds, such as hollow hoops 'howk-howk-howk' or throaty clicks, and this may be a kind of song. They do give a more continuous song of croaking and bubbling sounds, and maybe some mimicry (BWP, 2004), often around the nest site. When mobbing a predator, such as a Buzzard, birds often give a drawn-out rattle, in a similar voice to their main call, though more strained and higher-pitched.

HOODED CROW

HOODED CROW, CORVUS CORNIX

Hooded is similar to Carrion Crow in voice and vocabulary. Mullarney et al. (1999) consider Carrion Crow to 'sound a bit harder and more malevolent in tone', but others have often described Hooded as the one with the harder voice.

My impression is that Hooded often has a more emphatic rattle to the main crowing calls, but, given the wide variation that occurs in just the main calls and the clear plumage difference, it's largely unnecessary to look for a consistent difference in voice.

STARLING

COMMON STARLING, STURNUS VULGARIS, STURNIDAE
AUDIO: CD 1:04 SONG, CD 1:63 CALL

J F M A M J J A S O N D

A very vocal species all year round, with song possibly at its lowest level in summer. It has a wide vocabulary with a range of intermediate vocalisations somewhere between call and full song. As well as solitary individuals, birds often sing in duets, from prominent perches (TV aerials and chimney pots being very popular), and communally, when gathered in a flock. When foraging in a flock, birds often maintain a loose chattering song and, gathered at a roost, produce a mass of warbling.

Full song is in long verses usually opening hesitantly with a few copies, then maybe a few louder whistles lead into precise imitations of the calls of a range of species, as highlights in a constant, rhythmic flow of soft chattering whistles, some runs of bill-clicking and churrs, ending with a few shrill whistles; the vigour of the performance is marked by an erect posture, throat hackles bristling and drooping, quivering wings, often occasionally waved. The mimicry is expert; but, as seems to be the case in much mimicry, the calls are imitated as they are heard –

that's to say the imitation of a Pheasant call sounds like a Pheasant call in the distance rather than the sound of a Pheasant calling where the Starling is perched. Birds will also copy electronic noises, car alarms and human whistles; one bird I recorded mimicked the shrieks of children playing in the schoolyard down the road.

Individuals are thought to have repertoires from around 20 to 60 song-types and birds continue to learn new phrases through their lives. The whistled songs show local dialect groupings and birds at roosts tend to gather with those of the same dialect group.

The first song [CD 1:04] opens with mimicry of calls of a gull species, possibly Common Gull; the alarm calls of Song Thrush move quickly on to a phrase with Chaffinch calls, a loud 'chiff' and a bill ripple, then a stream of mimicry embellished with occasional other sounds (mainly short churrs) in counterpoint. Blackbird alarm calls, Rook clucking, Jackdaws, Dunnock 'tremble' calls, Greenfinch trills mixed with Chaffinch 'spink's, and into bill chattering rhythms (with a hint of Long-tailed Tit 'see-see' calls creeping in). Even the two loud 'tchirr's at the end are embellished with Jackdaw calls. It's a 40-second masterpiece, characterising its sonic environment – a rural garden near the coast.

Calls include a subdued, rippling 'churr' on taking flight and odd ticking sounds; in alarm a harsh 'jarr', a little like Jay, and a sharp, shrill 'jit' often in a fast, brief jibbering sequence. Juveniles call with trilled, buzzing churrs, often given as an almost constant stream from a foraging group.

RAVEN

NORTHERN RAVEN, CORVUS CORAX

AUDIO: CD 2:19, 2:30

A vocal species throughout the year, birds call regularly in flight and can be heard from a fair distance. Their voice is similar to Carrion Crow and Rook, but deeper and more powerful; although it's been described as rougher in voice, it's also in some ways more musical (perhaps more tonal).

The basic call, often given in alarm at intruders, is a croaking 'krra-krra-krra', similar to Carrion Crow, but lower-pitched and fuller. Birds keeping in contact in flight often give a more abrupt, deep 'kronk' or a rather higher-pitched 'pruk'; the latter is quite easily imitated and can often draw a bird in. There's much variation in voicing round these basic calls.

Displaying birds produce a range of strange sounds, particularly a kind of guttural 'y-gung'. Birds will also sing softly, and a recording I've heard included notes like water droplets, which may have been mimicry (Jays also produce water-like notes).

I've also recorded a bird in its first spring (rescued in poor health, then released) producing streams of varied soft sounds, as if practising, especially on early mornings in January; by February the sequences were becoming more dominated by variations on the main adult calls.

Young birds, recently fledged, call with a kind of howl; by the autumn they are giving adult-like calls, but often higher-pitched and less rich, or possibly harmonically simpler.

HOUSE SPARROW

HOUSE SPARROW, PASSER DOMESTICUS, PASSERIDAE
AUDIO: CD 1:02

A very vocal and sociable species, heard all year round and almost all day long! Its wide vocabulary of calls ranges from chattering chirps to churrs and more tonal liquid sounds.

Male song is rather basic, with little rhythmic or melodic elaboration to warrant the title song, being a fairly regular stream of notes with slight variation, including chirps and higher silvery squeals; in excited interactions, more liquid twittering and chattering phrases.

Calls include a regularly repeated 'chow', often doubled, and in alarm rattling churrs. The vocabulary and social interactions of House Sparrows are so complex and interwoven, they are not easily deciphered; I can only sketch out an overview here.

TREE SPARROW

EURASIAN TREE SPARROW, PASSER MONTANUS, PASSERIDAE
AUDIO: CD 1:33 SONG, CD 3:46 CALL

Tree Sparrow is vocally very similar in sound and vocabulary to House Sparrow and is generally just as garrulous. Overall the voice gives an impression of slightly more refinement (less rough).

Some of the notes in song are quite distinctive, with a more liquid tone, and occasionally almost melodious warbling phrases are heard, never quite matched in House Sparrow. But the most distinctive call is the hard 'tek, tek', usually given in flight.

FINCHES – FRINGILLIDAE

In territorial behaviour the finches fall into two groups and this is reflected to a large extent in vocal behaviour. The fringilline finches, Chaffinch and Brambling, while forming flocks in winter, spend the spring and summer in pairs with mutually exclusive feeding and breeding territories; males can be territorially aggressive and sing loud stereotyped songs. The cardueline finches tend to be more sociable throughout the year and breed in loose colonies (or at least show a clumped distribution). Birds within a party or flock frequently call with such a variety of motifs that it sounds like singing. And the male's full song tends to be a more intense, varied and rather more formal elaboration of such calling; the songs of these finches tend to be less loud and far-carrying than that of Chaffinch. Crossbill vocal behaviour is broadly similar to the other cardueline finches; but Bullfinches sing only softly (including occasionally females) and Hawfinch very softly. All species tend to call intermittently in flight, typically with monosyllabic chip calls; and most carduelines have a slurred whistle call, typically 'tooey' or suchlike.

BRAMBLING

BRAMBLING, FRINGILLA MONTIFRINGILLA
AUDIO: CD 3:40 CALL

Occasionally Brambling are rather vocal, though calls can be quite intermittent and rather soft at times. Their song is only rarely heard in Britain, and then generally in the north from males lingering in spring or the occasional breeder. But it's worth bearing in mind if you're in the Scottish Highlands in spring or summer that I came across a singing male in a Sutherland birch wood one June. Brambling call readily in flight, especially new arrivals in the autumn, and can often be picked up in a wintering finch flock from their 'tchway' call.

Though closely related to Chaffinch, Brambling song is very different, more akin to the wheezing trill of a Greenfinch; it is possibly harder and more nasal than that of Greenfinch, and each burst is around one second in length.

The flight and contact call is 'chuk', but rather thicker and less tonal than a typical finch chip, and comparable more with that of Twite. Very distinctive is their drawn-out 'tchway', with a rather nasal twang to it.

CHAFFINCH

CHAFFINCH, FRINGILLA COELEBS

AUDIO: CD 1:17, 3:03 SONG, CD 3:40 CALL

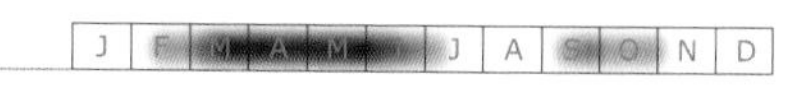

Chaffinch is rather vocal all year round, though its song is only given from late winter to early summer, with a slight resumption in the autumn. It has a number of different calls, some of which are restricted to the breeding season.

Male song is in stereotyped verses, typically a descending series of short trills, usually accelerating slightly in tempo, in distinct phrases, with a terminal flourish, the whole lasting two to three seconds; delivery is at regular intervals, at a rate of between five and nine per minute, often for long periods. Individuals have a repertoire of usually between one and six song-types: normally one type is repeated for a while, then the bird changes to a different type from his repertoire, sometimes in response to a neighbouring male's singing. Full song is loud and carries well; a softer, more continuous warbling subsong is often heard in

February, gradually becoming louder, with clearer phrasing (plastic song), and half-hearted versions of the full song are common later in the summer.

The usual flight and contact call is a rather soft, brief 'chu' or 'chiff', often repeated several times, but not in rhythmic series. In alarm, it is a sharp 'chink', rather like the 'spink' of Great Tit. A chirpy rattle is often heard from males in the breeding season. Territorial males also have a call they give during the breeding season, often for long periods, almost as shorthand for song. It's come to be referred to as the 'rain call', since it used to be thought that it foretold rain; maybe it's heard more often in poor weather, when birds are trying to conserve energy, but I haven't noticed any weather-related pattern. It's rather variable in form from a rising 'weet' to a more even churr, though males of any locality tend to have the same version (see page 43 for further discussion of this call).

SERIN

EUROPEAN SERIN, SERINUS SERINUS

Generally a rather vocal species, with song frequent in the breeding season, though continued throughout the year (BWP, 2004), and calling regular in flight.

Their song is in bursts, sometimes lengthy, of a very fast, high-pitched jingle, with a metallic silvery quality similar to Corn Bunting. There's a hint of a fine harshness: Mullarney et al. (1999) quote the comparison to the sound of crushing glass. It's very distinctive once heard and is given both perched and in a slow wing-beat song-flight, like Greenfinch. It's difficult to pick out any verse or phrase structure.

The main call is a short trill, rather clear and slightly tinkling, 'trit-it-it', often given in flight; the timbre of the song voice is just discernible. In alarm, it is a disyllabic 'tzü-ey', rising in pitch and with a wheezing timbre.

GREENFINCH

EUROPEAN GREENFINCH, CARDUELIS CHLORIS, FRINGILLIDAE

AUDIO: CD 1:18, 3:06 SONG, CD 3:41 CALL

Quite a vocal species with song intermittent throughout the day in spring and summer. When not singing, calls are frequent, marked by short runs of notes or trills – called 'tremolos' in BWP (2004).

The main contact call is a brief 'chiff', fuller and slightly harder than Chaffinch, but not always easily distinguished, sometimes slightly longer, sounding like 'chewe', but often repeated or trilled. In alarm, or from more excited birds, it is a repeated, drawn-out, full 'tooey', often with a rather wheezy timbre.

Male song in its fuller, more elaborate mode is a continuous stream of phrases at a relaxed pace, mainly based on trilled variations of the contact call, interspersed with wheezes, sweeter 'teu-teu-teu' motifs and whistles, and thin, tinkling trills (often like Waxwing), with maybe the occasional hint of mimicry. It is very reminiscent of captive Canaries. Song is given perched or in a slow wing-beat, zig-zag song-flight, often tracing a wide circle. Birds also have a much simpler, secondary song style, often heard through summer from perched birds: a buzzy, drawn-out wheeze repeated at intervals, similar to Brambling song, but not quite so nasal in timbre, usually with descending pitch, but not always.

GOLDFINCH

EUROPEAN GOLDFINCH, CARDUELIS CARDUELIS

AUDIO: CD 1:19, 3:06 SONG, CD 3:42 CALL

J	F	M	A	M	J	J	A	S	O	N	D

Vocal birds throughout the year, with song frequent, at its most formal through spring into summer, and almost always calling at intervals in flight. Voice is marked by the fluent, liquid quality of the notes and the rhythmic lilt in the phrasing.

The usual contact call, given perched or in flight, is a short rhythmic phrase, 'whit-a-whit', with a clear bright tone to the notes; this is occasionally interspersed with a thinner, higher-pitched phrase 'swi-ti' or just 'stic'. Actual phrasing is variable, and birds frequently play with the phrases, in a stream of variations merging with song. Other calls include a very slightly wheezy, drawn-out, rising 'deu-ey' or falling 'dzwee-eu'; short, buzzy trills are repeated in threat and aggression (often heard around feeders).

Their song is a lovely, varied stream of phrases, with calls, trills, whistles and wheezes, most phrases repeated once or twice, all at a rather fast pace, in a loose verse structure with rather sudden pauses. The overall impression is of a turbo-charged Greenfinch that has been listening to a Linnet; generally rather higher-pitched than either of these species, and with a tinkling ring to many of the notes. Birds tend to sing vigorously for a minute or two from a perch, then suddenly take flight.

SISKIN

EURASIAN SISKIN, CARDUELIS SPINUS

AUDIO: CD 2:05 SONG, CD 3:47 CALL

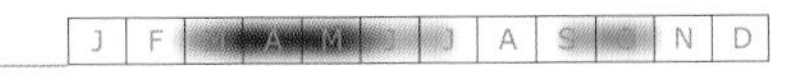

Siskin is one of the most vocal species of finch and the birds are rarely silent for long except when feeding. They have quite a vocabulary of calls and there appears to be wide variation on some of those calls – whether this is down to individual variation, geographic variation or related to different population groups, is uncertain.

Calls are varied, but commonly a disyllabic 'teu-li' and rising 'teuy', both in a slightly wheezy voice, and a higher-pitched, purer 'tee' or slightly descending 'teu'. More subdued, thicker chattering calls (almost sparrow-like, but lighter weight) are also frequent from birds in a flock or in flight, particularly when taking flight, and given in a short run 'tch-tch-tch'. Birds may mix up these calls, seemingly randomly.

Male song in breeding areas is frequent in a fluttering song-flight throughout the season and at any time of day; during winter, communal song can build up to quite an intensity in a flock. By late winter and early spring, males spend more time singing perched alone; song is then an intense stream of varied call notes, in repetitive phrases typical of the cardueline finches, and much mimicry; bursts usually last around 10 to 20 seconds, sometimes longer, and are interspersed with a few call notes. Here and there it includes a characteristic drawn-out buzz on an even pitch. By summer and with the increase in fluttering song-flights, the song perhaps has less mimicry, a more formal structure and is more rhythmic.

LINNET

COMMON LINNET, CARDUELIS CANNABINA

AUDIO: CD 1:32 SONG, CD 3:41 CALL

J F M A M J J A S O N D

A vocal species all year round, the male is rarely silent through spring and summer, and calls are regular from winter flocks, except when in an intensity of feeding. Communal song is also quite frequent from perched flocks in winter or more sparsely when feeding. During the breeding season, as well as odd song whistles and short snatches of song, birds may call repetitively for long periods.

The main call and the one used in flight is a slightly squeaky and hard 'chuc', given singly or in rhythmic phrasing, 'chuc-a' and 'chuc-a-chic' cropping up frequently. Various sweeter, drawn-out whistles, as used in song, are also used as calls, typically 'piü', 'fee' and 'chew-ee', often slightly burred and with an emphatic pitch inflection.

Song is in varied sequences of repeated call notes, sweet whistles, trills and buzzes, with a very pleasant wistful melodic quality, much of it moderately paced, but with some quicker bursts. It gives a very tuneful impression, compared to much bird song. Singing birds can often give long, excited sequences rattling a single call note, perhaps better described as tittering. It's difficult to say to what extend females sing, but BWP (2004) makes reference to antiphonal duets of calls and motifs between male and female.

TWITE

TWITE, CARDUELIS FLAVIROSTRIS
AUDIO: CD 3:42 CALL

Twite are fairly vocal all year round and rather similar to Linnet in general vocal behaviour. Full song, as opposed to informal snatches of song motifs, appears rather rare, but it may just be that I haven't been in the right place (breeding areas, presumably) at the right time. Winter flocks can be very vocal, even noisy at times. Calls are frequent in flight.

The main flight call is a typical finch 'chuc', but rather thick and with a characteristic twang somewhat like Brambling; it is often given in rhythmic motifs like Linnet. More distinctive is the contact and alarm 'twite' call, a rising, wheezy 'tveeut', also often given in flight.

Very characteristic is the alternation of two motifs at short intervals, typically with a higher and lower ending, like 'chee-te-waa, tee-tu-teweeü'. Whether this is singing or calling is debatable; fuller song is a more varied mix, rather like Linnet, including trills, rattles and wheezing whistles. The slightly nasal, wheezing timbre in the voice distinguishes it from Linnet, as well as characteristic motifs.

LESSER REDPOLL

LESSER REDPOLL, CARDUELIS CABARET
AUDIO: CD 1:80 SONG, CD 3:47 CALL

Redpoll species are slightly unusual among the finches in that they are rarely heard singing an obvious song: display is mainly in an undulating flight accompanied by series of repeated notes and trills. Occasionally birds are heard delivering meandering passages of twittering, but this is more in the character of subsong and is usually from a bird loafing with a small party in the spring. Nevertheless, this sociable species, often encountered in small parties or mixed with Siskin in a flock, is fairly vocal throughout the year. Opinion is divided as to whether and how the calls of Common Redpoll differ from Lesser.

The usual contact call, often given in flight, is a short sequence of a fairly typical finch chip, 'tchi-tchi-tchi', with a slight scratchiness, more or less metallic, sometimes with more of a 'tsü' sound. In alarm, and other contexts, it is a slightly hissy, rising 'teuee'.

In display flight, song comprises the usual flight calls interspersed with stereotyped buzzy or purring trills, 'tsrrrrr', sometimes more brittle and rattling. This is frequently heard during the breeding season, when both parts may also by given by perched birds. There is also a more continuous song given by perched birds, consisting in a leisurely stream of varied chatter calls, trills and twittering, with some semblance to Siskin song, but not so fast, more hesitant and with distinctively Redpoll motifs.

CROSSBILL SPECIES

RED CROSSBILL, LOXIA CURVIROSTRA
AUDIO: CD 2:11 SONG, CD 3:47 CALL

A very vocal group, frequently calling in flight, though song, while heard particularly from autumn through to early spring, is sporadic, and calls while feeding are quiet.

There has been much interest in crossbill vocalisation in the last few decades, particularly with reference to Scottish Crossbill, its taxonomic status and identification. This has largely focused on calls rather than song. Following work by Jeff Groth in North America, Magnus Robb recorded and studied crossbill calls in Europe leading to a long and incredibly detailed article in Dutch Birding (Robb, 2000), in which he recognised six different classes of Common Crossbill based on call differences, as well as Scottish and Parrot Crossbills. This system is further discussed and developed in Constantine et al. (2006). Meanwhile Ron Summers and others were investigating the crossbills of northern Scotland, trapping birds, taking bill and wing measurements and recording calls from them; their work is reported in Summers et al. (2002), where they recognise four types of flight call and five types of excitement call. Summers had already reported the presence of significant numbers of Parrot Crossbills breeding in Abernethy Forest.

This work is incredibly detailed and complex, and far beyond my scope here. I also find it rather difficult to equate some aspects with my understanding of vocal behaviour in birds, where calls are variable in voicing according to 'emotional' state, and in some cases the ecology underlying putative taxonomic status. I've had trouble matching many of my own crossbill recordings to any of the type classes of the published recordings and sonograms. The mud has been stirred up and I'm waiting for the water to clear. So in this account I'm going to cop out and lump them together, in the interests of providing a simple summary. Despite the divergence mapped for the various calls, there's generally something distinctively crossbill about them.

The most frequent call we tend to hear is the flight call, a fairly typical, though distinctive, finch 'chip', rather clipped, varying from a clear, full 'jip' to a thinner 'tswip' with more transient sibilance, and with a wide variation in fundamental pitch.

The excitement calls tend to be fuller, slightly longer and less clipped, with something of a nasal timbre, 'choop' or 'tüüp', generally repeated for a while by a perched bird watching what's going on.

Their song is a varied stream of variations of twittering, squeaky notes and whistles in rhythmic motifs around the call notes, usually including some lovely rippling trills, maybe with a drift in pitch. Their song is generally given from the top of a conifer, while the rest of the party feed nearby.

SCOTTISH CROSSBILL

SCOTTISH CROSSBILL, LOXIA SCOTICA
AUDIO: CD 2:11 CALL

The flight calls reported for Scottish Crossbill are not easily distinguished by ear from some of the Common Crossbill flight call types; the most distinctive vocalisation identified by Summers et al. (2002) appears to be the excitement call, rather deep, brief and slightly churred, 'trüp'. Parrot Crossbill *Loxia pytyopsittacus* flight calls are a clean, full 'chup', lower-pitched than other crossbill species. Excitement calls are rather lightweight by comparison, a brief 'teep'. Both descriptions are based on examples given by Constantine et al. (2006).

SCARLET ROSEFINCH

COMMON ROSEFINCH, CARPODACUS ERYTHRINUS

Though this species can hardly be called a regular breeder in western Europe, singing males have cropped up in Britain most years recently. Documented breeding is slightly intermittent, but given the remote locations of some of the sites, it may be a little more frequent than proved.

Although taxonomically classified with the cardueline finches, the song style, in simple stereotyped verses, is really much closer to the buntings. Each verse comprises a cadence of around five sweet whistles, with a slight rhythmic lilt, generally falling in pitch over the sequence.

The usual call is a slightly hoarse, Greenfinch-like, rising 'tüw-eh', with a hint of the nasal timbre of Brambling 'tchway' calls.

BULLFINCH

EURASIAN BULLFINCH, PYRRHULA PYRRHULA
AUDIO: CD 1:60 SONG, CD 3:41 CALL

Bullfinches are, on the whole, quite vocal, though not very vociferous. Pairs and small parties generally keep in touch with each other with soft calls; and males can be heard courting females with their soft song seemingly at any time of year. Though not particularly noted among birders for their song, Bullfinches were valued as caged birds as much for their voice as their looks and were known as good pupils in learning tunes from their keepers, even quite complex sequences. Both sexes sing, though the male more frequently and the female's song is usually rather simpler.

The usual contact and alarm call is a brief, full tonal 'tew', usually descending in pitch, sometimes almost disyllabic, but with various voicings can be an even 'tee' or a rather Greenfinch-like 'chup'. Odd harmonic content in the call (so-called 'trumpet call') may indicate a Northern Bullfinch. In close contact, various softer whistles and sometimes lightly churred calls are used, bordering on song.

Its song is usually so soft that it's rarely heard: a hesitant sequence of call-like piping notes, squeaky buzzes and tonal churrs, without much apparent rhythm – very pleasant for all that. Sometimes it sings with a repeated short cadence of notes, though BWP (2004) differentiates this from song, referring to it as a 'sequence-call'.

HAWFINCH

HAWFINCH, COCCOTHRAUSTES COCCOTHRAUSTES
AUDIO: CD 3:33

Hawfinch is one of those species for which it really pays to have a grasp of the main call, though it is very similar to the alarm call of Robin. They are quite vocal birds, calling rather frequently. There is no distinct loud song, though the call-song and a softer subsong, rather like Bullfinch, is quite frequent in the early spring. The latter is so quiet that, without a parabolic reflector focused on the singing bird, it's unlikely to be heard.

The main contact and alarm call is an explosive 'tzic', with a sibilant emphasis in the 'z' distinguishing it from Robin alarm calls; voicing varies slightly and the call can be given loudly in alarm or softly in close contact. Often it's accompanied by their other frequent call, a drawn-out sibilant 'zee' or 'tseü'. BWP (2004) describe full song as a mix of these calls, given in a well-spaced series with constant subtle variation, 'thus difficult to recognize as song'.

The softer, more varied song given in courtship is a steady stream of thin whistles, piped churrs, squeaks and clicks, with no apparent rhythm and all sounding rather conversational. It's usually accompanied by ritualised movements and posturing. How I'd like to observe this from a good vantage point!

BUNTINGS – EMBERIZIDAE

Buntings, generally birds of open habitats, are highly territorial (at least the males) in their breeding, but flock together in the winter. All species are rather vocal with generally small repertoires of stereotyped songs, which show interesting patterns of sharing between neighbours. Their voices are rather fine in enunciation; songs vary from the melodic tunes with sweet whistles in Lapland and Snow Bunting to the sharp syllables of Yellowhammer and Corn Bunting. There's a tendency to repeat notes or phrases. Birds tend to call readily, though can be quiet at times. Although their songs may be repetitive, simple ditties, they are a very interesting family vocally.

LAPLAND BUNTING

LAPLAND LONGSPUR, CALCARIUS LAPPONICUS
AUDIO: CD 3:44 CALL

The species is vocal throughout the year (BWP, 2004), although wintering birds can remain quiet and elusive. Usually calls are when taking flight. Song is rarely given in Britain and only likely to be heard in the Scottish Highlands, where the species has bred. The usual flight call is a rather quick, light chatter ('tik-a-tik'), quite similar to both Yellowhammer and Snow Bunting, but recognisable with familiarity. Birds also often call in flight with monosyllabic 'teu' or 'tchi' notes, at a distance confusingly similar to Snow Bunting calls but heard a little more clearly; they have a slightly wheezy timbre, not so pure as Snow Bunting.

Male song is in stereotyped verses, sometimes with phrases shortened or omitted – quite complex and lengthy for a bunting, and, though whistled and tuneful, marked by a slight grating burr in the voice.

SNOW BUNTING

SNOW BUNTING, PLECTROPHENAX NIVALIS
AUDIO: CD 2:23 SONG, CD 3:44 CALL

Fairly vocal, more so in the breeding season, though wintering birds can be rather quiet. Birds call in flight intermittently. Song seems to be most frequent in the early morning, although verses can be at long intervals, and are said to be given in flight as well as perched. There is a wide repertoire of calls in the breeding season (BWP, 2004).

Song is in stereotyped verses with distinct phrases, usually with some alternation of motifs, delivered at an even, unhurried pace, with lilting rhythm; rather tuneful and cheerfully melodious, with some pitch slurring. At a distance the notes sound like clean whistles, heard closer a very slightly raspy burr is apparent. Individual males have several song-types (BWP, 2004); two birds heard in the same Cairngorms corrie on the same morning had different song-types.

The main contact and alarm call is a rather soft rippling chirrup, often compared to Crested Tit; it tends to be the commonest call from a group of birds in winter, but is also heard on breeding grounds. A clear, descending 'tyew' is often heard from lone birds in flight in winter, as well as during the breeding season. Other calls include a slightly buzzy 'chee'.

YELLOWHAMMER

YELLOWHAMMER, EMBERIZA CITRINELLA
AUDIO: CD 1:29, 3:03 SONG, CD 3:44 CALL

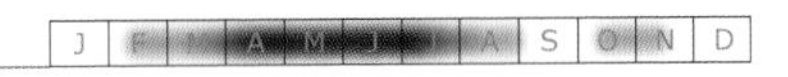

Generally this is quite a vocal species, especially the males during the breeding season, while females are rather quieter. Male song is particularly noticeable in summer as other species go quiet, and can be heard at any time of day. Males also call frequently when perched up and not singing with very terse, precise calls. Wintering birds usually call when taking flight.

Song is in stereotyped verses, 2 to 3 seconds long, each male usually having several song-types. The song builds on a quickly repeated syllable, normally accelerating and rising slightly to a crescendo and breaking into two (occasionally one) high, thin, hissy whistles like 'see-saw'. The first part could almost pass for the stridulation of a grasshopper, though much louder. Many song types have a slightly metallic ring to the syllable (though usually slightly grating), some a more churred syllable. The traditional mnemonic is 'a little bit o' bread and no chee-eese'. It's a very lovely, simple song, with an understated elegance, oozing summer warmth from fields with traditional hedges and a good one for beginners to learn.

The main contact and alarm call is a short 'zit' often alternating with 'chee', frequently heard from birds watching you like a sentinel. A brief rippling 'trrilip' is sometimes heard from perched birds, but most often as birds take flight.

CIRL BUNTING

CIRL BUNTING, EMBERIZA CIRLUS
AUDIO: CD 1:72 SONG

Quite a vocal species, with song fairly frequent during the breeding season, including through the summer like Yellowhammer. Male song is basically a drawn-out rattle or trill, slow enough for the individual syllables to be heard, given at fair intervals, generally with a rather clear timbre and slightly metallic ring, sometimes sounding like a shuffle between two notes. The calls I've heard are both thin, high-pitched whistles – a brief 'tsip' and a more drawn-out, descending 'tsew'; but Mullarney et al. (1999) report a sharp, clicking 'zitt'.

REED BUNTING

COMMON REED BUNTING, EMBERIZA SCHOENICLUS
AUDIO: CD 2:41 SONG, CD 3:45 CALL

Rather vocal throughout the year, with a fairly long song season; quite prone to giving its main call, particularly when nervous at the approach of an intruder, otherwise winter birds can be quite unobtrusive and certainly the other calls are rather nondescript.

Male song is in fairly stereotyped verses of three to four drawn-out syllables, usually including a trill, typically something like 'tzee, tzee, cher, tur-r-r'. It's been described as feeble (for example in the British Library CDs), but it actually carries well and is usually easily picked up even in a sonically dense community. Although described above as stereotyped, I have just been listening to recordings in my collection and though verses in a sequence are very similar, no two adjacent verses are exactly the same, which is unusual for a bunting. Researchers recognise two singing styles based on the tempo (intra-song intervals) and Erwin Nemeth linked this with mating status. So even in the 'feeble' song of Reed Bunting there is far more going on than is initially apparent.

The main contact and alarm call is a drawn-out, heavily inflected descending whistle 'tsyew', heard all year round. The other call most often heard is a short, slightly burred or buzzy syllable, 'chee' or 'tzü' (possibly a different call, but I suspect just a different voicing); it is most frequent in autumn, from juveniles (BWP, 2004), and in early spring.

CORN BUNTING

CORN BUNTING, MILIARIA CALANDRA

AUDIO: CD 1:26 SONG, CD 3:45 CALL

J	F	M	A	M	J	J	A	S	O	N	D

A vocal species throughout the year, especially during the breeding season; male song is persistent in spring and summer, and occasional in winter flocks (BWP, 2004). Its repertoire, song-type sharing and relation to breeding ecology has been well researched by Peter McGregor and others (for example McGregor et al., 1988).

Their song is in stereotyped verses, each male usually having two to three song-types, with neighbourhood groups sharing the same repertoire, producing a local dialect system. Verses are rather short (2–3 seconds), based on a sharp, rather metallic 'pik' syllable, opening hesitantly, but quickly accelerating into a fast jangling, with a slight drift in pitch. It is often compared to rattling a set of keys, but as the verse accelerates, syllables merge into a distinctive kind of shrill scraping noise. Birds sing in a characteristic upright, 'called-to-attention' posture with bill open wide.

Calls include a sharp 'tik' or 'plik', rather like the opening syllables of song, and an even terser 'bt', often given in flight or when taking flight (particularly from winter flocks) and, when repeated from several birds, producing an electrical crackling effect. In alarm the 'plik' call may be interspersed with a churred, slightly descending 'chrrü'.

REFERENCES

Amrhein, V. & Erne, N. (2006) 'Dawn singing reflects past territorial challenges in the winter wren', *Animal Behaviour* vol. 71: 5, 1075–1080.
Armstrong, E. A. (1963) *A Study of Bird Song*, Oxford University Press.
Atkinson, E. C. (1997) 'Singing for your supper: acoustical luring of avian prey by Northern Shrikes, *Condor* 99: 203–206.
Baker, K. (1997) *Warblers of Europe, Asia and North Africa*, Helm.
Balsby, T. J. S. (2000) 'The function of song in Whitethroats *Sylvia communis*', *Bioacoustics* 11: 17–30.
Bircham, P. (2007) *A History of Ornithology*, HarperCollins.
BWP (2004) *Birds of the Western Palearctic interactive*, BirdGuides Ltd and Oxford University Press.
Catchpole, C. K. (1973) 'The functions of advertising song in the sedge warbler (*Acrocephalus schoenobaenus*) and the reed warbler (*Acrocephalus scirpaceus*)', *Behaviour* 46: 300–320.
Catchpole, C. K. (1976) 'Temporal and sequential organisation of song in the sedge warbler (*Acrocephalus schoenobaenus*)', *Behaviour* 59: 226–47.
Catchpole, C. K. & Slater, P. J. B. (1995) *Bird Song – Biological themes and variations*, Cambridge University Press.
Ten Cate, C. (1992) 'Coo types in the collared dove *Streptopelia decaocto*; one theme, distinctive variations', *Bioacoustics* 4(3): 161–183.
Crane, K. & Nellist, K. (1999) *Island Eagles*, Cartwheeling Press.
Cresswell, B. (1996) 'Nightjars – some aspects of their behaviour and conservation', *British Wildlife* vol. 7: 5.
Dabelsteen, T., McGregor, P. K., Lampe, H. M., Langmore, N. E. & Holland, J. (1998) 'Quiet song in song birds: an overlooked phenomenon', *Bioacoustics* 9, 89–105.
Dowsett-Lemaire, F. (1979) 'The imitative range of the song of the Marsh Warbler *Acrocephalus palustris*, with special reference to imitations of African birds', *Ibis* 121 (4) 453–468.
Espmark, Y. O. & Lampe, H. M. (1993) 'Variations in the song of the pied flycatcher within and between breeding seasons', *Bioacoustics* vol. 5, 33–65.
Gellinek-Schellekens, J. E. (1984) *The voice of the Nightingale in Middle English Poems and Bird Debates*, Peter Lang.
Flegg, J. (1981) *A Notebook of Birds 1907–1980*, Macmillan.
Hartshorne, C. (1973) *Born to Sing – An Interpretation and World Survey of Bird Song*, Indiana University Press.

Howard, L. (1952) *Birds as Individuals*, Collins.
Jackson, K. H. (1971) *A Celtic Miscellany*, Penguin.
Jellis, R. (1977) *Bird Sounds and their Meaning*, BBC.
Kearton, R. (1900) *Our Bird Friends*, Cassell.
Klit, I. (1999) 'The function of song forms in the Lesser Whitethroat *Sylvia curruca*', *Bioacoustics* 10: 31–45.
Koch, L. (1955) *Memoirs of a Birdman*, Phoenix House.
Lampe, H. M. & Saetre, G.-P. (1995) 'Female Pied Flycatchers Prefer Males with Larger Song Repertoires', Proc. R. Soc. Lond. B. 262, 163–167.
Mabey, R. (1997) *The Book of Nightingales*, Sinclair-Stevenson.
Mann, N. I., Dingess K. A., Barker K. F., Graves J. A., & Slater P. J. B (2009) 'A comparative study of song form and duetting in neotropical *Thryothorus wrens*' *Behaviour* 146: 1–43.
McGregor, P. K., Walford, V. R. & Harper, D. G. C. (1988) 'Song inheritance and mating in a songbird with local dialects', *Bioacoustics* 1(2-3): 107–129.
Mitchell, W. R. (1973) *Highland Winter*, Robert Hale & Co.
Mockford, E. J. & Marshall, R. C. (2009) 'Effects of urban noise on song and response behaviour in great tits', *Proceedings of the Royal Society* B, 276.
Mullarney, K., Svensson, L., Zetterström, D. & Grant, P. J. (1999) *Collins Bird Guide*, HarperCollins.
Mynott, J. (2009) *Birdscapes – birds in our imagination and experience*, Princeton University Press.
Rebbeck, M. (1998) 'Nightjars Exposed', *WSRS Journal* (Spring).
Roché, J. C. & Chevereau, J. (2002) *Bird Sounds of Europe and North-west Africa* (10 CD set), Wildsounds.
Rothenberg, D. (2005) *Why Birds Sing*, Penguin.
Scott, J. (1973) *Palaeontology: An Introduction*, Kahn & Averill.
Simms, E. (1985) *British Warblers*, Collins.
Shirihai, H., Gargallo, G. & Helbig, A. J. (2001) 'Sylvia Warblers. Identification, taxonomy and phylogeny of the genus *Sylvia*', Christopher Helm.
Summers, R. W., Jardine, D. C., Marquis, M. & Rae, R. (2002) 'The distribution and habitats of crossbills *Loxia* spp. in Britain, with special reference to the Scottish Crossbill *Loxia scotica*', *Ibis*, 144 (3): 393–410.
Thorpe, W. H. (1961) *Bird-Song: the biology of vocal communication and expression in birds*, Cambridge University Press.
Weary, D. M. & Krebs, J. R. (1992) 'Great tits classify songs by individual voice characteristics', *Animal Behaviour* 43, 283–287.
White, G. (1788) *The Natural History of Selborne*, Penguin, 1941.
Witherby, H. F., Jourdain, F. C. R., Ticehurst, N. F., and Tucker, B. W. (1938–1941) *The Handbook of British Birds*, London.

INDEX

Species